UNDER A
FLAMING SKY

UNDER A FLAMING SKY

THE GREAT HINCKLEY FIRESTORM OF 1894

DANIEL JAMES BROWN

Guilford, Connecticut

An imprint of Rowman & Littlefield

Distributed by NATIONAL BOOK NETWORK

Copyright © 2009, 2016 by Daniel J. Brown

British Library Cataloguing in Publication Information Available

The Library of Congress has cataloged an earlier hardcover edition under the LCCN 2006297560.

ISBN 978-1-4930-2200-7 (paperback)
ISBN 978-1-4930-2201-4 (e-book)

∞™ The paper used in this publication meets the minimum requirements of American National Standard for Information Sciences–Permanence of Paper for Printed Library Materials, ANSI/NISO Z39.48-1992.

FOR THOSE WHO WERE THERE
AND THOSE WHO LOVED THEM

A fact is not a truth until you love it.

—John Keats

CONTENTS

PREFACE

The experience of one who has passed through the Hinckley fire . . .
the truth . . . would seem like the wildest fancies of crazy
imagination; no pen can portray its terrible reality;
no tongue can even tell the bare truth of the awful ordeal.

—*Angus Hay*

FORTY YEARS AFTER THE HINCKLEY FIRESTORM, MY GRANDFATHER
still sometimes awoke in the night, screaming. My mother, who was
then a student at UCLA, was sharing an apartment in Hollywood
with him. The Great Depression had the country in its cold, hard
grip, but my grandfather was fortunate enough to have a job with the
Crown-Zellerbach Company. He was away from the apartment all
day on weekdays, which gave my mother a quiet place to study in
the daytime. The nights, though, were another matter. Once or twice
a week, as my mother bent over her books late at night, my grandfather would begin to thrash back and forth in his bed moaning, whim-
pering, and making the sounds of a frightened animal. Then,
suddenly, he would sit bolt upright in bed with his eyes wide open,
and scream.

Perhaps he was remembering, over and over again, how one
day when he was nine, his father had simply disappeared into a maelstrom of fire. Perhaps he was seeing again the charred bodies scattered up and down the ashen streets of what had been his
hometown. Or perhaps he was hearing again the terrible, low rumbling sound that had preceded any signs of flames, the sound of
something large and unknown rolling toward him like a tidal wave.

Whatever it was, it must have rocked him to his core. This book is the result of my efforts to understand what happened to him that day and, by extension, to understand what happened to the more than 1,200 other people who had the misfortune to find themselves in Hinckley, Minnesota, on the morning of September 1, 1894.

When I began my research for this book, what came to light quickly astonished me. I discovered that what my grandfather had experienced was far from an ordinary forest fire. Ordinary forest fires move in fits and starts. They give people a chance to get out of their way. This fire afforded no such opportunity. It came on faster than a man could flee—even on horseback or even, as it turned out, on a train. As the onrushing wave of fire broke over Hinckley, the winds that propelled it reached hurricane strength and flames towered 200 feet over the surrounding forest. Enormous bubbles of glowing gas drifted in over the town and then suddenly ignited over the heads of the town's terrified citizens, raining fire down on their heads. Fire whirls—tornadoes of fire—danced out ahead of the main fire, knocking down buildings and carrying flaming debris thousands of feet into the red-and-black sky. Temperatures at the core of the fire soared above 1,600 degrees Fahrenheit, the melting point of steel, quickly cremating people who had been alive only minutes before.

As horrific as the fire itself was, though, it was the human story that emerged from my research that surprised me the most. It's a story of overwhelming tragedy but also of extraordinary courage. It both saddens and swells the heart. It tells us of people much like ourselves who were suddenly, unexpectedly, and very unfairly confronted with unimaginable circumstances. It reminds us, in the starkest possible terms, how closely death always shadows us, and how terrible it can be in achieving its ends. It tells us of men, women, and even children, lost, alone in the heat and the smoke, terrified and pleading with God for mercy, who in the end found no mercy and had no choice but to crumple to their knees and lay their heads down unwillingly on pillows of flame.

But it also reminds us that—at least sometimes—we do have the capacity to look death in the face, to take its measure, to spit at it and deny it its will. In this age of terror, it reminds us that we have it in us to endure calamity, to rise above even the most trying circumstances, to replace fear with hope, to throw love and light back in the face of violence and darkness.

DANIEL JAMES BROWN
REDMOND, WASHINGTON
NOVEMBER 29, 2005

UNDER A
FLAMING SKY

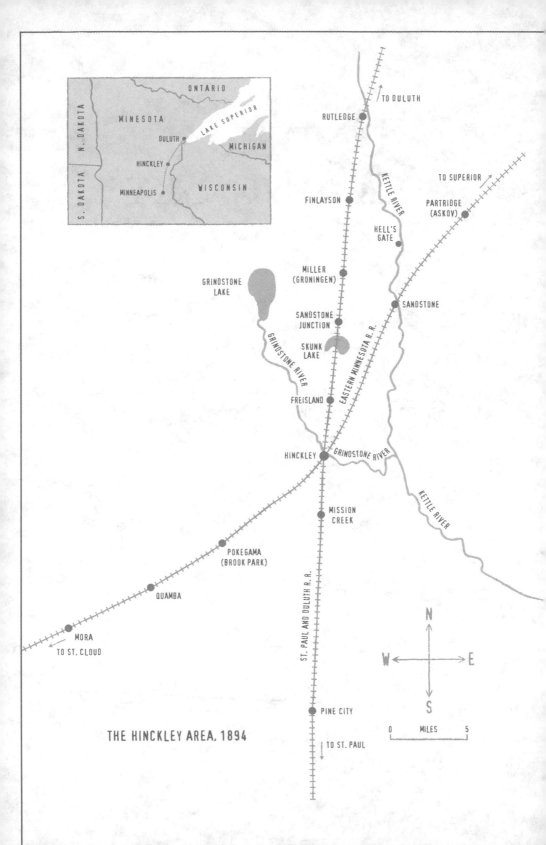

THE HINCKLEY AREA, 1894

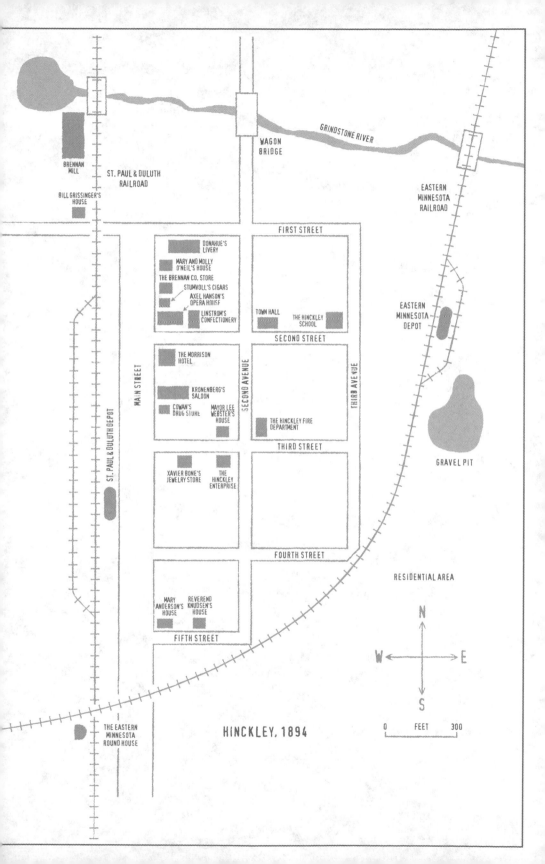

HINCKLEY, 1894

PROLOGUE

If a man look sharply and attentively, he shall see Fortune;
for though she is blind, she is not invisible.

—*Francis Bacon*,
"Of Nature in Men"

SOMETHING WAS AFOOT THAT SUMMER—SOMETHING CONCEALED, not yet revealed. All across the Upper Midwest, a yellow-gray murk obscured the finer details of terrain and landscape, softening and blurring the outlines of everything one could see, and hiding much that one could not see. Silos in Wisconsin, tall pine trees in northern Minnesota, office buildings in Saint Paul and Minneapolis all seemed to be slightly out of focus and forever fading into a vague gray background. Men piloting steamboats on Lake Superior put binoculars to their eyes and struggled to make out familiar landmarks along the shore. Railroad engineers peered through shrouds of haze that hung over the tracks before them, trying to see what they were about to encounter down the line. Even the fierce, unrelenting sun of that summer seemed to strain to make its full force apparent through the milky overcast.

Country women rising early in the morning and stepping out of doors to fetch water from their wells could not see the haze in the predawn darkness, but they noted the sweet smell of wood smoke. Later in the day, even when their kitchens were full of the warm smell of baking bread, they still noted it. People sitting in posh hotel lobbies and ornate railroad stations noted it, even through the ever-present smell of stale cigar smoke. Timber brokers and bankers and clerks working in stuffy city offices in Duluth and Green Bay slid open their office windows and looked out into their gray cities and noted it.

Nobody was surprised by it; nobody expected anything other than smoke and ash in the air at this time of year. It was no shock to anyone that hundreds of small fires burned in the north woods of Minnesota and Wisconsin that summer, as they did every summer. If asked about it, anyone would have said pretty much the same thing: "There's always smoke and fire at this time of year." Nobody was surprised, but everyone remarked on it, and many wondered idly why it seemed so much worse than usual this year, and what if anything it portended. Then, in late July, some of them caught a glimpse of what it portended in a lumbering town called Phillips in northwestern Wisconsin.

Phillips, a town of 1,500, was the economic hub of its region, due mostly to the presence there of the John R. Davis Lumber Company and its sawmill, lumberyards, and box mill. It was a prosperous, successful outfit, and by midsummer, something in the neighborhood of twelve million board feet of white pine lumber lay in three lumberyards on the outskirts of town. Hundreds of uncut logs were stacked along the shores of the chain of lakes on which Phillips was built. To the north of town, acres of hemlock had been cut and the bark peeled off the logs and heaped in large piles awaiting transfer to a tannery in town. The tops and branches of the hemlocks—long since baked to a crisp by the hot summer sun—lay in a tangle on the ground. In some places, they were stacked twelve to fifteen feet high.

On July 26 an early-morning north wind stirred a smoldering fire in the bark piles to life, and by early afternoon the nearby hemlock slash was ablaze and a full-fledged fire was bearing down on the town from the north. The town's volunteer firefighters and mill hands turned out to fight the fire. By early evening, the winds died down. The crews turned back the flames, and the people of Phillips went to bed believing the battle was over.

By the middle of the next day, however, the wind rose again, and all hands turned out again to resume the fight. This time, the fire came from the south. And this time it was no contest. The fire roared out of the surrounding swamps, leapt the town's firebreaks, and entered one of the lumberyards, setting it ablaze. Then a row of houses went up. Then the business district. Then, by early evening, almost the whole town.

Fortunately, a freight train on the Wisconsin Central line had been kept waiting, and Sheriff C. C. Kelleher calmly loaded most of the town's citizenry into its boxcars and dispatched it to the nearby town of Prentice. Many of those who couldn't get to the train made it on foot to a clearing atop nearby Eaton's Hill and rode out the fire there. Hundreds more sought and found safety in the wide-open expanses of the county fairgrounds.

Another four hundred had a harder time. They fled north through the streets to the tannery district along the lakeshore, but there the fire closed in quickly and surrounded them on three sides. With no other choice, they waded into the lake and began splashing water on one another. All of them survived.

The worst of it was what happened on a lake to the west of town. Frank Kliss had taken precautions the day before. When fire had first threatened the town, he'd stocked his large houseboat on Lower Lake with provisions. Now, as the town went up in flames he loaded his wife and daughter and eleven of his neighbors aboard, planning to pole his way to the north shore of the lake and out of danger. But as he set out, the flames made it into one of the big lumberyards along the nearby shore. A newspaperman, Moose Kenyon, witnessed and described what happened next:

> Flames shot a full thousand feet into the air and the whole burning mass took on a rotary motion. Whole piles of burning lumber were carried high into the air, and the suction of the whirling mass seemed to draw everything loose toward it from hundreds of yards outside its periphery. The floating boat house

was caught in this suction and drawn to the burning yard, whirling as it went like a great spinning top.

Frank Kliss died gripping a pike pole, trying to hold the houseboat in place against the awful suction of the fire, when a tongue of flame reached out from the burning lumberyard and enshrouded him in fire. The others crawled and leapt into boats, but the boats were promptly swamped by six- to eight-foot waves stirred up by the draft of air rushing into the base of the lumberyard fire. All of them drowned—nine children and four adults—with the exception of Mrs. Kliss, who was badly burned, lost her eyesight, and when she recovered had to endure for the rest of her life the loss of her husband and all her children.

It was a stark warning—a brief illuminating flash in the night—but it had little effect. The enveloping murk of that summer closed back in on the people of Minnesota and Wisconsin, and the routines and habits of everyday life again obscured the near inevitability of what was coming. As summer crept toward autumn, people went about their daily business. They marveled at the extraordinarily orange harvest moons that rose over the eastern horizon in August. They calmed fidgety livestock. They watched in idle curiosity as odd curlicues of black ash drifted down from the yellow sky. They grumbled when they put white sheets out to dry on the clothesline in the morning and fetched gray ones in at the end of the day. But still they did not see it coming.

On the last evening of August, people in a remote corner of northern Minnesota—people who were about to die or watch their children die—sat around dining-room tables and chatted about their hopes for the future. They gathered around pianos and sang. They read newspapers, they went to their kitchens to get snacks, they kissed their children good-night and tucked them into bed. They crawled into warm beds themselves, by ones or by twos, and put out the lights. When the lights were out, the lovers among them brushed warm lips and pulled each other close and felt each other's hearts beating. Boys lay staring into the dark, thinking about fishing, or about girls. Old men lay remembering. Mothers and fathers lay planning. And one by one they drifted off to sleep, dreaming of things past or things yet to come.

But none of them could have dreamed of what was really coming. None of them could have imagined that within thirty-six hours, people in places as far away as New York, San Francisco, and even London would be reading about the cruel hand that fate was about to deal them.

Chapter One

NIGHT MUSIC

On a starred night Prince Lucifer uprose.
Tired of his dark dominion, swung the fiend
Above the rolling ball in cloud part screened,
Where sinners hugged their spectre of repose.
Poor prey to his hot fit of pride were those.

—George Meredith,
"Lucifer in Starlight"

SEPTEMBER 1, 1894 | 12:30 A.M.

Lying alone on his cot in the darkness, nine-year-old Bill Grissinger wondered what it was that woke him. Then it happened again—the house shuddered, the windows rattled, and the hall door creaked open. This time he heard his mother, Kate, getting up to close the door, and he went out into the hall to meet her. Together, they stood silently by the west-facing window of their small frame house, peering out into the dark streets of Hinckley.

On the northwest side of town, recently installed electric carbon lights illuminated the sprawling yards of the Brennan Lumber Company. The mill was quiet. The night shift was taking its midnight lunch break. But what Bill Grissinger would remember nearly seven decades later was the odd color of the mill's lights that night. Usually intensely white, they had a strange reddish tinge he had not seen before.

The house shuddered again as another gust of wind slammed into it and his mother led him back to his room. He crawled back into bed and waited. Finally he heard the familiar sounds of the mill coming back to life—the rumbling of the carriages carrying huge pine logs into the teeth of the blades, the chomping of the gang saws biting into the wood, the whining of the edgers trimming the boards. He felt comforted by the sounds, but he could not get back to sleep easily. His father was away on a two-day trip, picking cranberries out across the Kettle River, and the house seemed forlorn without him. From time to time, another gust of wind struck the house. Down the hall he could hear his mother singing softly to his younger sister, Callie, trying to lull her back to sleep.

Across town, at about the same time, Clara Anderson was saying good-night to her school friends at Belle Barden's house. The girls whispered in the darkness on the front porch, talking about the school year that would begin on Monday. A cluster of boys stood in the front yard talking softly and jostling one another. It had been a long, boisterous evening of games and dancing and flirting. Earlier, they had rolled up the dining-room carpet to provide a dance floor. Someone had taken out a fiddle, someone else a harmonica, and they'd reeled off song after song as the young people had formed into two squares and flung themselves from partner to partner, clapping and shouting, promenading and do-si-do'ing, stomping wildly on the bare wood floors. Finally, worn out, they had turned down the oil lamps and, sitting on the floor in a circle, Belle and her guests had played Postman, a kissing game. Later, Belle's mother had laid out a late dinner on the sideboard: cold fried chicken, fresh-baked bread, raisin pie, and cold milk.

Now, well past midnight, each girl with a boy to show her home, Belle's guests began disappearing down the dark, dusty street, the boys singing school songs and whooping to one another, the girls shushing them. Clara Anderson told Belle she'd see her at school on Monday. Then she watched as Belle ran back into the house, where Belle's father, Jake, was already putting out the last of the lamps.

At a little before 3:00 A.M., Emil Anderson sat on a bench at Hinckley's Saint Paul and Duluth railway depot, waiting for a train north. A strikingly handsome young man with a boyish face and dark, penetrating eyes, he wore a neatly trimmed, somewhat sparse mustache. He also wore the white, upturned shirt collar of a clergyman. Sitting in a yellow pool of light cast by an oil lamp above him, he pondered why he was waiting there on a railroad platform in the middle of the night. The guest sermon he had delivered that day in Hinckley had gone well enough, but he was nervous about the farewell address that he planned to deliver tomorrow afternoon to his own congregation up in Sandstone. He'd worked intermittently on the address for two weeks now, but he was distinctly unhappy with the results so far. Within a week he planned to be back in Chicago starting his final year at a theological seminary, and he knew that after graduation, he might never again see any of his parishioners. But for now he felt strangely and urgently compelled to be back near them as soon as possible, and so, unable to sleep, he'd decided to start for home now rather than wait for morning. He figured one sleepless night wouldn't do him any harm, and he'd work more on the address as soon as he got home.

At 3:00 A.M., the train pulled into the station and Anderson climbed aboard one of the chair cars. Settling into one of the upholstered seats, he watched the lights of the lumber mill slip by on his left as the train pulled out of town. About four minutes later, the train slowed as it passed through a small brush fire burning on both sides of the track, but it was nothing more than one of many nuisance fires that had been smoldering in the wooded swamps and peat bogs around Hinckley for weeks now. Since early July, fires like these—set by homesteaders clearing land or touched off by sparks from passing trains—had been flaring up and dying down all over Pine County. The train picked up speed, and Anderson sat back in his seat humming Swedish hymns, trying them out for tomorrow. Within another fifteen minutes he was climbing down from the chair car at an unlit crossing called Sandstone Junction. From here it was a three-mile walk to the town of Sandstone and home. Slinging his rucksack over his shoulder, he set off into the dark woods alone.

* * *

9

By 6:30 A.M., the stars were dying quietly, one by one, in the gray dawn sky over Hinckley. Evan Hansen stepped out onto his front porch and let the screen door slam shut behind him. A tall, square-jawed man with blue eyes and black hair parted in the middle, he sat down on the edge of the porch and pulled his work boots on over heavy woolen socks. Out on the wagon road beyond his split-rail fence, men were shuffling by in the dust on their way down the hill to the mill. Murmured bits of Swedish and German and Norwegian floated through the dark.

Behind him in the house, Marie, his wife of twenty-two years, banged pots and pans around on the woodstove, singing something in Norwegian. The house was full of warm morning smells—coffee and bacon and *lefse*, the potato cakes she was frying for the children's breakfast. Hansen laced his boots, stood up, stepped back into the front room, and called out, in English: "Ed, Helen, Josephine—Papa's going to work. Help your mother with the shopping today. And make her speak American!" Then he gave Marie a squeeze from behind and kissed her on the cheek, picked his lunch pail up off the table, and stepped back out through the door before she could turn around to say good-bye.

Hansen walked out past the split-rail fence and joined the procession moving quietly south on the wagon road, down Hinckley Big Hill toward the mill. The sun was up now. Ahead of him, a mile down the hill, spread out beyond the Grindstone River, was the flat expanse of the lumberyard where he would spend the day sorting and stacking freshly cut lumber. As he walked, the sun began to climb into the sky on his left. The sky was yellow with smoke, as it had been for weeks, but this morning it was oddly metallic too—vaguely reflective, like unpolished brass. There was a light breeze blowing from the southwest, though, and it was refreshing after so many hot, still days.

The road ran gently downhill through a tortured landscape of stumps and logging slash—piles of pine limbs and cut brush left behind by lumberjacks and scorched brown now by the unrelenting summer sun. A dense growth of young jack pines and tamaracks was pushing its way up through the slash. Here and there Hansen passed a homestead like his own squatting among the stumps behind a split-rail fence, white wood smoke curling up from its chimney as someone inside hurried to finish the morning's baking before the heat of the day set in. Each homestead had a head-high pile of pine firewood stacked neatly against the house under a lean-to shed, ready for winter. Most had a cow or two, a few chickens, maybe a dog lounging in the dusty yard.

Then the road leveled out and took Hansen straight across a half-mile-wide stretch of marshy bottomland covered with willows taller than a man. The road was corduroyed here: sapling logs had been laid side by side to provide a firm if bumpy roadbed above the usually soggy terrain. But the terrain was anything but soggy now. Among the willows, the marsh grasses were dry and withered.

Emerging from the willows, the road crossed the Grindstone River on a wagon bridge. The Grindstone wasn't much of a river. Even in wet years it was little more than a large creek, and this year it was essentially a string of small, shallow pools strung together in the bottom of a ravine. To the west of the bridge, a wooden dam held back enough water to create a sizable millpond where logs were stored for sawing in the Brennan mill. But below the dam, and under the bridge, what little water the river contained was covered with sawdust and trimmings from the mill, so no one would know, looking at it casually, that it contained any water at all.

When he crossed the river, Hansen entered Hinckley itself, with the mill to his right, a two-story brick schoolhouse to his left, and the center of town a quarter of a mile dead ahead. He left the wagon road and made his way west across the Saint Paul and Duluth tracks and into the lumberyard for the beginning of his ten-hour shift.

Covering thirty-six acres, surrounded by mountains of sawdust, the mill and its lumberyard dominated the north end of Hinckley. The long saw shed was made of unpainted planks cut by the mill's own saws. A tall smokestack rose from one end, and a lower, open-sided shed protruded from the other end. Gray wood smoke drifted briskly off to the northeast from the top of the smokestack. White steam from the boilers that powered the saws billowed out from beneath the building. On a catwalk running along the top of the roof, ten large hogsheads full of water were arranged in a row as a precaution against fire, an ever-present threat to sawmills everywhere. If fire threatened, one man with an ax could run along the catwalk, stave in the barrels, and send several thousand gallons of water cascading over the roof within a minute or two.

Moving through the yard as the 7:00 A.M. whistle sounded, Hansen headed toward an incline where mule-drawn carts full of newly cut lumber were already rattling from the saw shed down to the sorting area. By the end of their shift, he and the rest of his crew expected to sort and stack several thousand more board feet of fresh-cut white pine, adding the boards to the roughly twenty-eight million board feet already stacked out in the open lumberyard, baking under the hot morning sun.

Chapter Two

MORNING

Oh that a man might know
the end of this day's business ere it come.

—*Shakespeare,*
Julius Caesar

BY 7:30 A.M., HINCKLEY WAS LARGELY OPEN FOR BUSINESS. It was the first Saturday in September, a workday. Already the streets were full of wagons, hay carts, drays, buggies, and buckboards, all of them raising clouds of dust as they rattled by, dust that drifted through the hot morning air and settled everywhere—on the broad, sweaty backs of horses, on the green-and-white awnings in front of shops, on the felt hats of men lounging on street corners. The town smelled of wood smoke and horse manure and dust, as it did every summer morning. Men shouted at horses, bridles jingled, hobnailed boots clattered along the wide wooden sidewalks that lined the streets. From behind houses came the *chunk, chunk, chunk* of people splitting kindling for their kitchen stoves. The circular, steam-powered saw at the mill screamed each time it bit into a new pine log. Merchants in white aprons pulled up their window shades, opened front doors, fetched brooms from back rooms, and swept the dust, temporarily, from their bits of sidewalk. Occasionally a boy on a bicycle darted by among the horses and wagons, stirring up his own small cloud of dust before disappearing, rabbit-like, around a corner. In upstairs rooms, people raised their windows, shook still more dust from their bedclothes and their linens, and paused to look out across their town.

A jumble of clapboard wooden buildings jammed into a wedge between two intersecting railroads, Hinckley looked hastily put together, as indeed it was. Running due north and south, the old Lake Superior and Mississippi tracks, now owned by the Saint Paul and Duluth Railroad, defined the western border of town. At the southern end of town the tracks of the Eastern Minnesota Railway, a division of James J. Hill's Great Northern, crossed those of the Saint Paul and Duluth and slanted off to the northeast, defining the eastern border. An ugly gash in the landscape lay just east of the Eastern Minnesota tracks where the railroad's work crews had dug a shallow quarry to supply gravel for the railroad beds on the marshy stretches north of town. The bottom of the resulting three-acre pit was covered with two or three feet of springwater, the water green and stagnant now in the late summer heat. North of town, the Grindstone River, running west to east, defined the northern boundary of the roughly triangular town. A wide road ran south from the mill along the west side of Hinckley, where it served as Main Street.

Both to the east and the west of the triangle, new residential areas were springing up as the town began to escape from the boundaries imposed by the railroad tracks. On the east side, new, neatly painted frame houses like the one belonging to John Craig, the town's twenty-three-year-old fire chief, sat behind picket or wrought-iron fences. Spindly, newly planted trees lined many of the wooden sidewalks; within a few years they would provide much-needed shade for loungers and passersby on hot mornings like this one.

In many ways Hinckley was the archetypal Western town. It was raw, rough, full of energy and optimism, populated almost entirely by adventurous newcomers. Some of them had come from as near as New York, Maine, or Quebec, but most had come from northern Europe—from Ireland, Scotland, Germany, Sweden, Norway, and half a dozen other countries. All of them had come in the last twenty-five years, since the Lake Superior and Mississippi Railroad had opened up this country to settlers in 1869. They had taken a chance on this rough new place, hoping for better jobs and cheaper land, and almost without exception they had found both, right off.

This bonanza had been made possible by a tree called *Pinus strobus*—the white pine. From the time Captain George Weymouth of the British Royal Navy had first sailed up the rivers of Maine in 1605 and seen vast stands of the tree—straight, towering specimens, ideal for making the long masts and spars of English sailing ships— men with a commercial bent had coveted the wood of the white pine. Exceptionally soft and easily worked, lightweight but strong, white pine quickly proved superior for making everything from bob-sleds to banisters. England's appetite for the wood soon grew so great that by the 1760s the American colonists had become deeply resentful of the arrow-shaped ownership blaze that the Surveyor General of His Majesty's Woods in America cut into the bark of every white pine he could find in New England. So it was not sur-prising that the first flag under which the revolutionary forces fought against the king bore the image of a single white pine.

By the time independence was won and another hundred years had passed, the white pine forests of New England were all but gone, and lumbermen from Nova Scotia to New York began looking west, first to Michigan, then to Wisconsin, and finally to northeastern Min-nesota, where large stands still stood untouched. Timber barons like the Lairds, the Nortons, and Frederick Weyerhaeuser already knew the enormous economic potential of these Minnesota forests. All they needed was to be able to get to the trees, and in this they were quickly obliged by enterprising railroad men like James J. Hill. Men like Hill not only built the railroads into the wilderness but also imported hun-dreds of thousands of settlers from the East Coast and from Europe to help cut the timber, man the mills, and finally, buy the land from them—at two to five dollars an acre—once it had been cleared.

By the summer of 1894, Hinckley had grown from a tiny log-ging camp known as Camp Comfort in 1869 to a bustling North-western town, the financial epicenter of Pine County. By now, with a population of over 1,200 people, two railroads, a thriving lumber mill, three churches, five hotels, a new, two-story brick schoolhouse, and a new firehouse, Hinckley could boast of its accomplishments and look forward to a bright future. As Angus Hay, editor of the *Hinckley Enterprise*, had crowed just the previous Wednesday in a four-inch, front-page banner, HINCKLEY IS A CITY THAT IS *RICH* IN GOOD SCHOOLS AND CHURCHES. ITS PEOPLE ARE BOLD IN ENTERPRISE, FIRM IN PURPOSE, LIBERAL IN SUPPORTING PUBLIC MEASURES, MORAL IN THEIR LIVES, WARM IN THEIR HOSPITALITY, AND EVER GLAD TO HELP YOU CLIMB THE LADDER OF SUCCESS.

Hinckley could even provide its citizens a modest selection of luxuries and pleasant diversions. Andrew Stumvoll offered fine, hand-rolled cigars like the popular "Belle of Hinckley" at his shop on the north end of Main Street, which featured a wide front porch where customers could sit in the shade in the company of Stumvoll's wooden Indian, savoring both their cigars and conversation with their neighbors. Not far away, at the Hinckley Laundry, Henry Coffin was always available to wash and starch their Sunday clothes while they enjoyed their cigars. If they were prosperous enough, Stumvoll's customers could stop in at Xavier Bone's jewelry shop on Third Street and select a gold-plated watch from the collection that Bone kept displayed on a green felt-covered shelf in his window. Wine, beer, liquor, billiards tables, and more cigars were always available at Joseph Kronenberg's establishment, and at half a dozen other saloons around town, where barkeeps in white aprons and black bowties stood before elaborately carved back bars and dispensed cool beer from wooden kegs with white porcelain spigots. At the baseball diamond on the south side of town, the Hinckley Crescents played most Sundays during the summer, the cheers of their fans often drowning out the sermons at nearby churches. Ice cream socials and dances were held regularly at the town hall at Second Street and Second Avenue.

Occasionally, the entertainment was more exotic. As recently as the Fourth of July, forty gypsies had been camped on the outside of town, the women telling fortunes in the streets, the men performing with a dancing bear for handouts. A few brothels on the eastern outskirts of town were a mere annoyance as far as most people were concerned, a vital necessity as far as many of the lumberjacks working in Pine County's woods were concerned. More wholesome—if not always entirely innocent—fun could be had at Axel Hanson's Opera Hall. Offering special rates to traveling companies, Hanson's was the scene of many of the town's public gatherings, ranging from the Republican Party's county convention to frequent burlesque shows.

Despite the building heat and the prospect of another long, sweltering day of work, most people in Hinckley were looking forward to the next several days. Tomorrow would be devoted to church services, social events, and rest; Monday would bring the excitement of the first day of school; and on Tuesday the whole country would celebrate Labor Day as a national holiday for the first time. Many of the villagers planned to take the train down to Saint Paul on Tuesday to take in the Barnum & Bailey Circus under the big top. Others would celebrate the holiday by going fishing out at Grindstone Lake, northwest of town. Most people expected to stay in Hinckley for the parades, barbecues, picnics, and dances that were planned all over town. First, though, they had to get through another day's work.

By 8:00 A.M. the Saint Paul and Duluth depot on Main Street and the Eastern Minnesota depot across town on Third Avenue were both bustling with activity. The depots were always the two busiest places in Hinckley. With trains arriving throughout the day and night, something worth watching was almost always happening at the depots—friends and relations coming and going; vendors selling newspapers from Saint Paul, Duluth, Chicago, and even New York; long-anticipated items ordered months ago from catalogs finally arriving.

Many of the town's children had spent much of their summer on one or the other of the depots' platforms, eating freshly made ice cream from Lindstrom's Confectionary and drinking Coca-Colas or Hires root beer, sitting in the shade, propped up against the outside wall of the depot, their heads swiveling as they took in the constantly unfolding spectacle—shrieking train whistles, bellowing blue-coated conductors, screeching metal-on-metal brakes, snorting and hissing steam locomotives. Mountains of baggage, mail, and freight of every imaginable sort were piled on the platform. Steamer trunks and leather valises sporting decals from New York, Hamburg, or Dublin sat side by side with wooden crates full of excited chickens and squealing pigs. Even this early in the morning, everyone seemed to be in a hurry—ladies dressed for the city in wide-brimmed hats and long skirts that swept along the platform as they passed; gentlemen in dark coats, vests, and derbies puffing cigars and checking their pocket watches against their railway schedules; farmers and lumberjacks dressed for work in boots, coveralls, and plaid shirts.

At the Saint Paul and Duluth depot, children were taking turns standing on a crate, peering in through a window to watch the telegrapher, twenty-five-year-old Tommy Dunn, at work inside. Dunn was busy pulling dispatches off the telegraph, sorting them in trays, and tapping the keys that sent messages flying up and down the line, messages that might go as far as New York or San Francisco almost immediately.

By 8:30 A.M., up the street from the Saint Paul and Duluth depot, Dr. Ernest Stephan was seeing his first patients of the morning in an office he kept in a private home with his older partner, Dr. Wellington Cowan. Dr. Stephan, an intense, scholarly young man of twenty-five, was just out of medical school. A bachelor, with round, wire-rimmed glasses and wavy black hair, he had already attracted a great deal of attention from the town's single young women, and he had also gained considerable prestige among the town's men, some of whom had recently elected him chairman of the Pine County Republican Committee. In his day-to-day medical practice, he attended to most of the births in this part of the county, the most recent being that of a particularly robust, twelve-pound baby boy born here in town a week ago today to Mr. and Mrs. John Rodgers. Wellington Cowan, as the senior partner in the office, generally saw the older, more established patients, and as Pine County's coroner he certified every death for miles around, a job that in the days and weeks ahead would stretch his capabilities to the limit.

Morning

The house on Main Street in which doctors Stephan and Cowan kept their office belonged to fifty-three-year-old John Currie, manager of Cowan's Drugstore next door. Currie, a big-boned man, nearly six feet tall and two hundred pounds, with dark hair and almond-shaped, hazel eyes, had only lived in Hinckley for two years. Like Dr. Stephan, though, he was sociable, and he had quickly made a name for himself by managing the drugstore, a job that sooner or later brought him into contact with nearly everyone living in or near Hinckley. From behind his glass-topped counter he dispensed an amazing assortment of curatives, among them: Dr. Pierce's Golden Medical Discovery for those suffering from "impoverished blood" or "deranged organs"; Strong's Headache Killer, which, reassuringly, contained "no poisons"; Piso's Cure for Consumption, which promised to rid one of tuberculosis for a mere twenty-five cents; and, under the counter, Wilson's Electric Belt for Women, which, in addition to curing "female weakness," had the added benefit of banishing "general debility, heart disease, malaria, liver disease, kidney disease, and constipation." The belt—a considerable deal at $3.00, considering its capabilities—also came in an "Extra Fine Quality" version with double the electrical power, for only another $2.00.

Currie's wife Amy, a thin woman with a long, handsome face, was less than half his age at twenty-four. This morning John was out running some errands around town, and Amy was struggling to cope as she tried to wait on a relentless stream of customers in the drugstore while also tending to her three young children.

Around the corner, in his office at Third Street and Second Avenue, Angus Hay was at work on next Wednesday's edition of the *Hinckley Enterprise*. Hay, whose close-set eyes, overhanging brows, and tightly compressed lips gave him a slightly pugnacious look, was a close friend of Dr. Stephan, another bachelor, and another of the town's leading citizens. Like most small-town newspaper editors of his time, Hay served up an eclectic mix of local, national, and international news, spiced liberally with human interest stories, gossip, advertisements disguised as news stories, and healthy doses of the editor's political philosophy, also often disguised as news. As secretary of the county Republican Committee, secretary of the Hinckley Literary Society, and one of the town's most vocal promoters, Hay used his stewardship of the *Enterprise* relentlessly to proclaim both his party's and his town's virtues.

Throughout the summer, much of the national news he chose to report had centered on issues of tariffs and free trade, particularly what he saw as the capitulation of President Grover Cleveland and the Democratic Congress to the dictates of the large trusts and combinations, especially the sugar trust. In this connection, Hay had been having a great deal of fun referring to the 250-pound president's enormous girth. His local news had focused on the comings and goings of the town's citizens, on births, deaths, marriages, and social events. And under the heading "Unfortunate Events," Hay offered a wide array of human interest stories—often of a strikingly morbid nature—from around the country. In last Wednesday's edition alone he had recounted the story of a child dropped accidentally into a kettle of boiling water in Whatcheer, Iowa; a gentleman named Lee Walker in nearby Sherburne killed after he seized the trailing rope of an ascending balloon and then let go; an aged farmer from Ten Mile Run, New Jersey, who had died, according to his physician, from the bite of a cat inflicted two years prior; and another child, this one in Vandalia, Indiana, accidentally given ammonia instead of a stomach remedy, the fourth death in the family within a week (three of them accidental, and one, perhaps understandably, a suicide).

As he worked on next Wednesday's edition of the *Enterprise* this morning, though, Hay was likely focused not on local politics or odd deaths, but on the two things he'd been fretting about in print to his readers all summer long: the hot dry weather and—most urgently—the rash of fires that seemed to be breaking out everywhere.

All summer, he had been using the front page of the *Enterprise* to sound a drumbeat of what would later read like warnings. First, he had reported that a sawmill had burned to the ground in Kerrick, twenty-five miles to the northeast, in the first week of July. Then on July 18 he had written of another sawmill that had burned down and of numerous fires that were burning just a half-mile south of Hinckley, as well as still others near Sandstone, nine miles to the north. On July 25, new fires were burning near Hinckley, west of town this time. On August 1, he had reported the disaster in Phillips across the state line in northern Wisconsin; that twenty-five people had died in Ashland; and that five hundred men, women, and children were said to be living in the Wisconsin woods without shelter. On August 22, fires were again burning near Sandstone. Finally, just last Wednesday, August 29, in what would turn out to be the last issue of the *Enterprise* for a long while, Hay had noted that fires were again burning in the woods outside of Hinckley, destroying a good deal of standing timber and many tons of hay. Then, he had grown cross on the subject, scolding his readers: "If people, generally, would take as much interest in their own fire protection as is shown by the Hinckley Fire Department, it would be more harmonious work for all concerned."

Hay had good reason to fret, both about the fires and the weather that spawned them. It's hard for those of us living in the age of satellite imagery, Doppler radar, and televised weather forecasts to comprehend the uncertainty and anxiety with which people in the nineteenth century gazed skyward and tried to judge what the weather held in store for them. In a time when black clouds on the horizon might, on the one hand, mean that the corn crop would not fail again this year or, on the other hand, that a tornado was about to dance across the cornfield and lift the house and its occupants heavenward, weather always seemed a matter of chance—and often a matter of terror.

Meteorology, as a serious science, was not much beyond its infancy, and those who practiced and preached it were often ridiculed as if they claimed to be alchemists. At the behest of the Congress, the United States Army Signal Corps had created the first National Weather Service on November 1, 1870. At 7:35 A.M. that day, observers had simultaneously recorded meteorological observations at twenty-four stations around the country. Within three years the service was issuing as many as seventy weather-related bulletins and maps a day. For the most part, though, these were simply records of weather that had already happened rather than predictions of future weather events.

Without a great deal of science to rely on in those early days, the National Weather Service encouraged its observers to keep in mind a list of proverbs drawn from folk wisdom when making their forecasts, among them these:

1. A red sun has water in his eye.
2. When the walls are more than unusually damp, rain is expected.
3. Hark! I hear the asses bray. We shall have some rain today.
4. The further the sight, the nearer the rain.
5. Clear moon, frost soon.
6. When deer are in gray coat in October, expect a severe winter.
7. Anvil-shaped clouds are very likely to be followed by a gale of wind.
8. If rain falls during an east wind, it will continue a full day.
9. A light yellow sky at sunset presages wind. A pale yellow sky at sunset presages rain.
10. Much noise made by rats and mice indicates rain.

In July of 1891 the Weather Service was transferred from the War Department to the Department of Agriculture. By now the science of meteorology had improved to some extent and forecasters were attempting to make predictions as much as forty-eight hours in advance, telegraphing these to thousands of post offices across the country. At several hundred of those post offices, large flags were flown over the buildings to let the public know of the expected conditions. A white field with a black square, for instance, indicated that a cold front was coming.

By the summer of 1894, while forecasters could predict short-term trends with considerable accuracy, they were still notoriously unable to predict either longer-term trends or specific weather events that were outside the expected norms, those kind of events that were most likely to prove catastrophic—floods, hurricanes, tornadoes, blizzards, and the unique combination of conditions that might produce major fires.

The facts were there, though, staring everyone in the face that summer. Had anyone been paying strict attention and, even more importantly, known how to read the code, this is what he or she would have noted: Climatic conditions in Minnesota in the late summer of 1894 were extreme by any historical standard, and they had set the stage for a catastrophe. Since June 1 there had been thirty days when thermometers around town had climbed past 90 degrees Fahrenheit. In a normal year there were only six. In recent weeks, the heat had grown worse. For the past ten days, the daily high temperature had averaged ten degrees above normal, sinking temporarily into the mid-seventies on Wednesday but quickly building back up to the high nineties on Thursday and Friday. Now, even before 9:00 A.M. on Saturday morning, the thermometer was already rising rapidly again, already back above where it had been at this time the day before.

The weather had been extraordinarily dry as well. In the parched country around Hinckley, creeks and wells had been petering out for weeks, and one crop after another had failed. At the co-operative weather station in Sandy Lake, fifty miles northwest of Hinckley, only 3.28 inches of rain had fallen since May 1, a record low, more than 12 inches short of the normal 15.72 inches. In Saint Paul, 90 miles to the south, only 2.00 inches of rain had fallen since June, the lowest level in a record that would eventually extend over more than 128 years.

Another set of figures—a by-product of the rainfall and temperature numbers—was even more telling. For weeks now the relative humidity—the ratio of the amount of water in the air compared to the amount of water the air can hold at a given temperature—had been declining steadily throughout eastern Minnesota. Since July the relative humidity had been running—day after day—as much as 13 percent below normal. As a result, what firefighters now call *fine fuels*—twigs, grasses, and pine needles on the ground—had been steadily losing moisture all summer as they came into equilibrium with the air around them. In effect, this meant that the rate at which flames could spread through the white pine needles littering the forest floor around Hinckley had been increasing at a rate of 4.5 percent for every 1 percent that the moisture level in those needles dropped. The soil itself was drying out, and the organic material in it was also becoming potential fuel. And now, with the rapidly rising heat of the last few days, the relative humidity had plummeted to even lower levels. Today's reading at the weather station in Collegeville, sixty miles southeast of Hinckley, showed a relative humidity of only 28 percent. At these levels the air was so dry that it was quickly sucking the remaining moisture out of even larger combustible objects—downed pine logs, stumps, piles of slash, and wooden buildings—turning them all into nearly explosive sources of fuel. And in Hinckley, there was no shortage of such items.

The moneyed lumbermen who came to Minnesota to harvest its white pine set in motion a process that quickly transformed the region and left behind a devastated landscape. When the first commercial lumber mill in Minnesota began operation on August 24, 1839, 70 percent of the land area of Minnesota—thirty-eight million acres—was forested. Within the next seventy years, this forest was almost entirely destroyed, converted into sixty-seven billion board feet of cut lumber, most of it produced during a period of just twenty years, beginning in the 1870s and ending in the 1890s. The lumber barons approached the "pineries," as they called the Minnesota forests, the same way that they had approached the vast virgin forests of the eastern seaboard earlier in the century. Their goal was to extract the maximum profit from the forest as quickly as possible, and anything that got in their way was merely an impediment to be, quite literally, pushed aside.

In practical terms, this meant that the logging crews that worked the woods cut their way willy-nilly through the undergrowth, dropped the giant, straight-grained pines they were after, lopped the branches from the logs, leaving them where they fell, and then used teams of horses or oxen to drag the logs through the brush to the nearest river, where they could be floated to a sawmill. When they finished with one section of land, the crews moved on quickly to another, leaving behind a vast and tangled mass of pine branches, broken saplings, and trampled brush to dry in the sun. No effort was made to clean up the site unless the land happened to be suitable for farming, in which case it was sold off to immigrant settlers for a few dollars per acre. The settlers, confronted with the heaps of slash and brush, often simply set fire to them and went home to wait for the fire to finish the job of clearing the land.

If weather science was struggling to be born in the 1890s, fire science had hardly been conceived. To be sure, it was obvious enough to all that strong winds dramatically increased the likelihood that a given fire would grow rapidly and that the fire would move most rapidly in the direction that the wind blew it. And there was an equally clear general understanding that dry weather also fostered fires. The degree of dryness could even be measured scientifically by whirling an instrument called a *sling psychrometer* over one's head to find the dew point and then using tables to calculate the relative humidity of the air. But beyond that, there was little understanding of why most fires— like the dozens that routinely burned in the woods around Hinckley every summer—could be controlled with shovels and buckets of water, while a very few others—like the inferno at Peshtigo, Wisconsin, twenty-three years before—evolved into monsters that could kill hundreds, or even thousands, in a matter of a few hours.

In addition, little was yet known about the different classes of fuel found in pine forests, or in dry, dusty, Midwestern towns. Even less was known about the complex ways in which fires alter the weather or create their own weather. And nothing at all was known about the internal dynamics of major fires—the physics that in a later age would explain how an ordinary fire, under certain rare circumstances, could grow to become a true firestorm. As a result, to the people of Hinckley in the summer of 1894, and to the great majority of Americans, most fires were mere nuisances, while at the same time, every fire was to some extent a deadly mystery.

One man knew what was at stake, however, and what was likely coming. On August 24, just nine days earlier, General Christopher Columbus Andrews, a Civil War veteran, former ambassador to Sweden, and a longtime advocate of scientific forest management, had addressed the recently created American Forestry Association in Brooklyn. In his paper he called attention to the millions of dollars and scores of lives that were needlessly lost to forest fires annually in the United States. He contrasted the Swedish practice of conserving and actively managing forestlands—cutting them selectively and then replanting the cut areas—with the American practice of laying waste to entire landscapes and littering them with combustible waste. The inevitable conflagrations that regularly resulted were a national disgrace as far as he was concerned: "For the American people thus to allow such calamities habitually to occur, without adopting any adequate means for their prevention, causes our country to be regarded in some respects as only semi-civilized." While this would turn out to be a prescient remark within days, it largely fell on deaf ears. His was a lone voice in the wilderness of greed and ruthless exploitation that was American forestry in the 1890s.

What neither Christopher Columbus Andrews, nor Angus Hay, nor anyone reading the *Enterprise* in Hinckley's dusty streets on this hot Saturday morning could have known was that the time for policy shifts and public warnings had run out. Not far to the south of Hinckley, and unbeknownst to its citizens, at least two new fires were now suddenly on the move. One was most likely the result of a spark that had fallen from a locomotive during the night alongside the Saint Paul and Duluth tracks in the switching yard at Beroun. It had grown now to a patch of fire perhaps an acre in size rippling through the woods south of Mission Creek. The second had probably been set by a farmer clearing a field near the hamlet of Quamba sometime in the last few days and then forgotten about. It was burning now several miles southwest of the hamlet of Pokegama, whose citizens were this morning joyfully gathering to celebrate the completion of a new schoolhouse. Pushed north and northeast by a stiffening breeze, both fires were starting to gain headway. On their current trajectories they were set to meet somewhere near Hinckley before the end of the day.

As Hay fretted and worked on next Wednesday's issue of the *Enterprise* in Hinckley, Hans Nelson was getting ready for work and watching his children with delight eight miles to the south, in the Eastern Minnesota Railroad's section house just outside of Pokegama. Like children all over Pine County this morning, they were trying on and showing off their new, back-to-school clothes. Minnie, his nine-year-old, was particularly proud of a pair of brand-new shoes, and she was strutting around the house, showing them to anyone who would stop to look. Her older sisters, Mabel, fourteen, and Alice, eighteen, were gathering together pails and baskets for the cranberries they planned to pick in the woods later that morning.

At a little after 9:00 A.M., with their containers gathered and their new school clothes put away, Mabel and Alice climbed onto a handcar with their father, and Hans Nelson began to pump the car down the tracks to the southwest.

Chapter Three

HOME

Home is a notion that only the nations of the homeless fully
appreciate and only the uprooted comprehend. What else would one
plant in a wilderness or on a frontier? What loss would hurt more?

—*Wallace Stegner,*
Angle of Repose

MOST OF THE TWO HUNDRED MEN WHO MADE UP THE DAY SHIFT
at the Brennan mill were glad to be working in the shade inside the
saw shed by late morning. A few, not so lucky, were still stacking
lumber out in the yard. The wind was beginning to pick up, but it was
hot and dry and afforded little relief from the fierce sun. Silver heat
waves shimmered among the stacks of lumber. Sweet-smelling pine
pitch oozed from the ends of freshly cut boards.

The rising wind and an unusually heavy pall of smoke to the
south were beginning to make the mill managers nervous. Sometime
before noon, they set Evan Hansen and a dozen or so other men to
hauling barrels of water out the Snake River road to protect the west
side of the mill, just in case any of the small fires that had been burning
for weeks in the peat bogs on that side of town began to creep too near.

In stores, offices, and homes all over town, the heat began to
force both men and women to work in their shirtsleeves. Dr. Stephan
was still seeing patients in his office at the Currie house. At the Saint
Paul and Duluth depot, Tommy Dunn was still sending and receiving
telegrams in his small, stuffy office looking out onto the platform.

Clara Anderson was relaxing at home with her mother, her
eighteen-year-old sister Emily, and her brothers, Charlie and Antone.

At the Dunn home, Clara's seventeen-year-old cousin, Mary Anderson, was taking care of Tommy Dunn's aging mother, known affectionately all over town as Grandma Dunn. At the north end of town, Bill Grissinger, dressed in a blue-and-white sailor suit, was in his front yard tinkering with one of the wheels on his wagon. His younger sisters, Mabel and Callie, were playing in an oilcloth tent that their father had set up as a playhouse before leaving on his cranberry-picking expedition. From time to time, hot gusts of wind filled the tent and snapped taut the lines that held it to the ground.

Down the Eastern Minnesota tracks, Hans Nelson had dropped Alice and Mabel off from his handcar so that they could pick cranberries in the boggy woods south of Pokegama while he and his crew worked a mile or so up the line. With seven or eight hungry railroad workers to feed each night at their section house, the girls and their mother could make good use of the berries for pies, jellies, and assorted treats. The girls were in high spirits, and they had already picked several baskets of berries when at about 11:30 they decided to stop picking and enjoy an early picnic lunch.

At Evan Hansen's homestead just north of Hinckley, his son Ed's hands were buried deep in dry, sandy soil, feeling for potatoes that he might have missed with his digging fork. The tops of the potato plants had browned and withered away a month ago, a month earlier than they usually did, but the potatoes themselves were surprisingly fat and abundant. It was work that Ed liked. He liked the small element of surprise in it, his fingers probing through the warm soil, tunneling blind through the dark, suddenly encountering the smooth coolness of a potato, and then lifting it to the surface to reveal the shape and color of it. And he liked the satisfaction of the bushel baskets gradually filling with potatoes, the cool root cellar beneath the house gradually filling with the heavy baskets.

At the age of nine, Ed looked much like a miniature version of his father, his black hair parted in the middle like Evan's, the same blue eyes and square jaw. He'd been working all morning, and he hoped to be done in time to go into town with his mother and sisters that afternoon. It was the last chance of the summer to see if any of his friends were at the depots, to buy ice cream or a root beer, to while away an entire afternoon without worrying about either chores or schoolwork. Nearby, some of his mother's fifty chickens were scratching in the dust, cackling and squabbling as his older sister Helen scattered cracked corn for them and picked up eggs as she found them, hidden here and there under bushes or in the hollowed-out tops of rotting pine stumps. Up in the linden trees that Ed's father had planted when he had finished building the house, katydids were trilling loudly.

Behind the lindens stood the eight-room house that they had lived in for six years now. Unpainted and simply constructed of pine timbers and boards that Evan brought directly from the mill, wagonload by wagonload, in exchange for some of his salary, the house was typical of, though slightly larger than, most of the houses in the neighborhood. Evan had built it in a little more than two months, with a great deal of help from his neighbors—Louis Wold, Will Costigan, and John Westlund. Each of them had a similar house on a similar forty-acre homestead among the stumps here at the top of what had come to be called, somewhat jokingly, Hinckley Big Hill. In point of fact, Hinckley Big Hill was so slight a deviation from the flatness of the surrounding country that only Midwesterners could—with straight faces or otherwise—call it a hill at all, let alone a big hill. But the name helped to distinguish it from another almost imperceptible rise in the terrain four miles further north called Hinckley Little Hill.

Building this house was the culmination of a dream that Evan Hansen had cultivated for more than two decades. Born in 1849 in Drammen, Norway, the son of a fisherman, and a seaman himself by trade, he had spent much of his adult life yearning for something better, something more secure and profitable than the harsh life of a seaman on the heaving back of the cold, dark North Sea. From the time the American Civil War had ended in 1865, he had watched as one after another of his friends and neighbors climbed aboard tall-masted sailing schooners or steam schooners and departed for America look-ing for a new chance. He had read their enthusiastic letters from places with strange, exotic names, like "Koochiching" and "Min-netonka," telling of land that was practically free and of jobs in the woods that paid a man in a month what he might make in a year on a boat in Norway. He had eagerly devoured books, brochures, and newspaper articles printed in Norwegian but financed by the lumber and railroad companies of the American Midwest, extolling the virtues of life in the north woods. And finally, he too had taken the chance and gone. Promising her he'd send for them when he had a house they could live in comfortably, he'd left Marie with a six-month-old baby boy and two young daughters and boarded a steam schooner. He'd sailed from Oslo to Hull, England, and then from Liv-erpool to New York. Within three weeks he had reached his destina-tion, Chippewa Falls, Wisconsin, where he'd stayed only long enough to hear about a newer place, a better place for an ambitious man, across the state line in Minnesota. Two days later he'd stepped off the train onto the recently completed platform of the Eastern Minnesota Railway in Hinckley.

When the 7:00 A.M. whistle blew at the Brennan mill the next morning, Hansen was at work for the first time in America. Seldom comprehending the orders barked at him in unfamiliar English by foremen with Irish and German accents, he struggled through that first summer working at a series of lowly jobs at the mill and living in a boardinghouse. By fall he had learned a bit of English and made a few friends, mostly other Norwegians and Swedes. From them, he learned that the dollar a day that he was making in the mill was less than half the money he could make working in the woods in the win-ter, where experienced men sometimes put together large enough stakes in a single season to buy forty acres from one of the railway companies. When the lumber companies began to recruit lumber-jacks for the winter cutting season, he eagerly signed up.

Riding a tote wagon filled with supplies to his first lumber camp in October of that year, Hansen entered a world that was more exotic than anything he could have imagined reading brochures back home in Drammen. The shanty boys—or lumberjacks, as they were just now coming to be called—were a rough-and-tumble lot, of all ages and nationalities. There were new immigrants like himself—mostly Swedes and Norwegians and Irishmen and Germans—but there were also men who had worked all their lives in the woods, as had their fathers and grandfathers. These men were mostly French-Canadians or the descendants of New England woodsmen who had moved west as the white pine forests of Maine had given out. Whether their accents were French, Norse, or Yankee, though, everyone in camp spoke a common language, a language of the woods. In their sleep shanties, bed blankets were *shrouds*, lamps were *glims*, the moon was the *jobbers-sun*. In the woods, the men who cut roads through the underbrush were *swampers*, those who kept the roads clean were *road monkeys*, and lazy fellows were *jill-pokes*. In the cook shanty, biscuits were *sinkers*, tea was *swamp water*, beans were *loggin' berries*, donuts were *cold shuts*, and a bad cook was a *stomach robber*. For a man just learning English, almost every conversation was bewildering. But the lumberjacks were almost all good-willed men, and life among them was, from the outset, exhilarating.

From the moment the bull cook awakened them a little before dawn by banging open the door to their sleeping shanty and bellowing "Daylight in the swamp!", Hansen and the other men were in continual motion, either eating or working, both of which they did on a scale Hansen had never known before. Dressed in wool—wool underwear, wool socks, wool shirts, and wool trousers—and sitting at the long eating tables in the cook shanty, the men were served flapjacks, hash made with salt pork and potatoes, beans with blackstrap molasses, donuts, and tea or coffee sweetened with brown sugar. Then, pulling on wool mackinaws and wool hats, they went into the woods, the snow and ice crunching under their caulked boots.

Although he was older than most of the men, Hansen's first job, as a road monkey, was the lowest in the camp. He spent his days running up and down the ice roads along which four-horse teams pulled huge sleds piled high with logs, scooping horse manure out of the ruts, piling snow on bare spots, chipping away at ice accumulations that might upset a sled. It was unglamorous work, and it was hard, but it was important—a badly maintained road might cause a load to spill and kill someone. Hansen liked the responsibility it gave him. When lunchtime came and the bull cook and the *cookee*, his assistant, brought their lunch to them in the woods, the men sat around a large open fire and ate beans, salt pork, and pie off of cold tin plates and talked about the day's work. Sometimes the beans froze on the plates before the men could eat them, and they had to hold the plates up to the fire to thaw them out.

Then it was back to work until sunset, the sawyers pulling on their two-man saws, the trimmers running along the new fallen trees lopping off branches with broad axes, the sawyers back at it again, bucking the logs into manageable lengths, the loaders using long poles called *peaveys* to maneuver the logs delicately up to the tops of huge piles sitting precariously on the sleds, the teamsters driving huge, gray Percheron draft horses that pulled the loaded sleds up and down hills on the roads made of ice. There were shouts, curses, and exultations in Swedish and German and Norwegian and English laced with Irish, Welsh, and Scottish accents; there was the swishing sound of saws slicing through the soft sapwood of the pine and the ringing of ax blades striking cold bark; there was the smell of pinesap and wood smoke and tobacco smoke; there was iron-cold air that slapped you in the face and froze your breath in your whiskers—and Evan Hansen loved it all.

By the time the men returned to the cook shanty, they were famished again, and they sat down at the long tables covered with oilcloth and set with tin plates to find more of what they had eaten at breakfast and lunch, but with the addition of more desserts—dried apple pie, raisin pie, pumpkin pie, cookies, rice pudding or plum pudding, and gingerbread. Then, back in their sleeping shanties, they hung up their wool socks to dry by the box stove, chatted a bit, crawled—two to a bed—into the bunks filled with hay that were stacked four high along each wall of the shanty, turned out the oil lamps, and went to sleep.

By the end of his first winter, Evan Hansen was no longer a *buckwheater*, a greenhorn. He had quickly moved from road monkey to swamper and then again to sawyer, and by the time the ice melted and the logs were afloat in Grindstone Lake, ready to float down to the mill, he was back in Hinckley with a new and better job in the lumberyard and a wad of cash in his pocket. Within another month, he had picked out forty acres he liked near the top of Hinckley Big Hill and made his first payment on it. By now he was nearly fluent in English and confident in his ability to make his way in this strange new place, but it would take another summer at the mill and another winter in the woods before he could send for Marie and the children.

Throughout the morning, the fires that began near Quamba and Beroun continued to move slowly north and northeast, meandering through the woods, feeding lazily on pine needles and brush, lapping at the trunks of the trees but sliding on past them, not yet strong enough to scale them. From time to time, they entered dusty meadows that had been trampled and grazed over by milk cows and were nearly devoid now of grass. Here they slowed almost to a stop, flickering from one sparse tuft to the next, guttering down to mere glowing patches among the weeds, struggling simply to survive. But then the wind touched them, and they moved on. Eventually they entered cutover land and came across piles of dry pine slash. These they burrowed beneath, smoldering for a while, building up heat until, with a *whoosh*, the piles exploded, the flames leaping as if in jubilation fifty feet or more into the air, then dying back down again and resuming their snakelike progress among the trunks and stumps.

As the winds continued to pick up in the late morning, both fires started gradually to change their characters. First, they began to race rather than crawl through the woods and clearings, still running on the ground for the most part, but beginning to leap from one pile of slash to another now, igniting them as quickly as they found them.

Then, just after noon, with the wind still rising, both fires made another change. They reared up on their haunches and roared. They started to leap from the piles of slash up into the lower branches of the pines around them, clawing their way up into the sap-rich twigs and needles above, then racing suddenly to the tops in loud, ripping explosions of flame and smoke.

The fires changed and began to move as they did because they were impelled to do so by enormous but invisible forces that were at work far from Hinckley. For the last twenty-four hours, a high-pressure system had been sitting over the Upper Midwest drying out the air throughout the region, raising temperatures, and generating light northerly winds in eastern Minnesota. That set of conditions was beginning to break down, though. A large low-pressure system had been creeping eastward from the Pacific across British Columbia, Alberta, Saskatchewan, and Manitoba for several days, and by Friday evening it had begun to generate what the National Weather Service reported as "a storm of considerable energy north of North Dakota and Montana." Now, by late morning on Saturday, the low-pressure system had moved farther east, riding generally to the north of but beginning to displace the high-pressure system that had been squatting over upper Mississippi Valley.

This meant double trouble for Hinckley and, indeed, for all of eastern Minnesota and western Wisconsin. In the northern hemisphere, air flows in a counterclockwise direction around a center of low pressure. The deeper the low pressure, the more rapidly the air circulating around it flows. As this particular Canadian low—a deep one judging by the Weather Service's description of the storms it spawned—moved to the east, it was in effect an enormous cartwheel of air, the leading edge of which was flowing rapidly from south to north. As the leading edge of this cartwheel worked its way into northern Minnesota, the north winds of the preceding night gave way to light southeast winds, and then, rapidly, these gave way to strong southwest winds. And the trouble was compounded by another meteorological fact: Air flows from areas of high pressure to areas of low pressure. As the center of low pressure moved to the north of central Minnesota, it began to draw the higher-pressure air to the south in a northerly direction, accelerating the velocity of the winds and quite literally fanning any flames that might lie in the path of the moving air mass. By that evening, storm-warning flags would be flying on Lake Superior and the National Weather Service would be reporting "south gales" in Minnesota.

It was only after the house on Hinckley Big Hill was completed in the spring of 1888 that Evan Hansen went to Duluth to buy steamship tickets and send them to Marie back home in Drammen. Then she, like hundreds of thousands of Scandinavian immigrants before her, sold their furniture and packed into a single steamer trunk all that they had in the world—their clothes, a few pieces of china from her mother, Evan's father's Bible—and set out alone, but for her three children, to a place she could not even begin to imagine, where people spoke a language she would never master.

She followed the same route that Evan had followed two years before, climbing aboard a steamer in Oslo bound for Hull. In her arms she carried two-year-old Eivin, who would become Ed when he disembarked in America. Following behind her was Josefine, eleven, who would become Josephine, and Helga, four, who would become Helen. Together, they clambered up the gangway to the second deck, and then immediately down a stairwell, plunging into the dark, reeking hold belowdecks where they joined almost two hundred other steerage passengers.

Almost immediately, they were overwhelmed by the stench of vomit, urine, and excrement. By the time they arrived in Hull on Monday morning, all four of them had been vomiting intermittently for three days. Two days later, in Liverpool, they climbed up another gangway and down into another dark hold. This time they would be ten days in the dark and the stench, and again they were all sick within an hour of departing, when the heavy Atlantic swells began to roll the boat from side to side.

Finally, on a Friday morning two and a half weeks after they had left Oslo, Marie stepped off the train in Duluth and into the arms of a beaming Evan Hansen, resplendent in a derby hat and a new suit, his coat thrown open to reveal a vest and a gold pocket watch. When they arrived in Hinckley that afternoon on the Saint Paul and Duluth, and Evan rented a buckboard at Dan Donoghue's Livery and drove them up the hill to the house, she saw that he had kept his promise.

It was a house such as no one in her family had ever lived in, with a wide front porch, a spacious front room with a brick fireplace, a separate dining room, and four bedrooms upstairs, one for each of the children and one for her and Evan to share. There was a large, airy kitchen with a white, enameled, wood-burning range, a matching white icebox, and a sunny, south-facing window looking out into what would soon become her flower garden. Best of all, behind the kitchen there was a small sewing room. And when she opened its door for the first time, she found, to her utter amazement, a new sewing machine sitting dead center in the middle of the room. It perched atop its wrought-iron and rosewood stand as if a trophy on a pedestal, the body black and sleek, the word SINGER and elaborate floral designs embossed in gold across the sides, the bobbins gleaming silver in the sunlight that streamed in through the window.

Now, six years later, as Helen clattered into the house with an apron full of eggs, looking for lunch, Marie was comfortably at work in her kitchen, cleaning up after the morning's baking and planning the shopping she would do in town that afternoon. At forty-three, she was a short, somewhat plump, and pleasant-looking woman, her posture habitually stooped slightly forward, her face flushed pink and damp with perspiration from the heat of the woodstove and the heat of the day building outside. Josephine, standing beside her, was a head higher at seventeen, but perhaps twenty pounds lighter than her mother.

After more than half a decade of living in the house, Marie had made it her own. The pine-plank floors were clean, scrubbed almost white with vinegar and water every Monday morning. The windows were brightly dressed with blue-and-yellow curtains she had sewn from material bought on one of the family's occasional trips to Saint Paul or Duluth. There were crocheted doilies on the armchairs, and on the kitchen table a white tablecloth that Marie had embroidered with scenes from the Norwegian countryside—flowers and barns and milk cows. In the front room, before the fireplace, was an oval, blue-and-white cotton rug on which Ed liked to curl up and watch the fire lapping at pine logs on long, dozy winter evenings when his father was away working in the woods. In one corner, Evan's family Bible sat open on an oak stand he had made himself. A white satin bookmark embroidered with a verse from the 23rd Psalm in Norwegian lay between the pages.

Just before 1:00 P.M., when Marie wandered out into the front yard to bring Ed in for lunch, she found him in the potato patch trying to drag a basket of potatoes that weighed more than he did toward the root cellar. She stooped to help him, and then, straightening up, she froze, staring incredulously down the wagon road. This morning, when she had let out her two milk cows, there had been a gray pall of smoke to the southwest, a dark smudge in the sky over Hinckley. Now, there were two towers of smoke, great billowing mountains of smoke, looming behind and beyond town, like thunderclouds but much bigger, and darker. They seemed to be rising from the areas of Mission Creek and Pokegama, but she couldn't tell how far away they were. They were bent to the north, though, leaning in the direction of Hinckley.

Marie bent over again, setting down the basket of potatoes, took Ed by the hand, and hurried back into the house, starting to think, hard.

Chapter Four

SOMETHING WICKED

*Nature works out its complexities. God suffers the
world's necessities along with us,
and suffers our turning away, and joins us in exile.*

—*Annie Dillard,*
For the Time Being

FIRE SCIENTISTS DIVIDE WILDLAND FIRES INTO THREE GENERAL
classifications: *ground fires,* which progress slowly by creeping through
the litter on forest floors or underground by way of smoldering roots;
surface fires, which move more rapidly through brush and undergrowth
and produce flames of moderate height; and *crown fires,* which erupt
into the forest canopy and move through the tops of the trees very rapidly and violently. Once they have crowned, fires often behave errati-
cally, surging ahead and destroying everything in their paths in some
areas but leaping over other areas leaving them unscathed, or nearly so.

By the time a fire has built up enough strength to reach into the
crowns of trees, it is likely to have enough energy to create a *convection column.* Convection is simply the process by which heated gases
or fluids rise until they cool enough to begin to sink, only to be heated
again and rise again, setting up a circular flow. This happens in a pot
on your stove when you boil an egg, and it happens in the atmosphere
when a forest fire gets hot enough to punch a hole in an overlying
layer of cooler air. The heated air that surges up through such a hole
builds a convection column, a tower of gas and smoke that may rise
30,000 feet or more above the surface. As the gases and smoke rush
upward in the column, fresh air is sucked violently inwards toward the

base of the column to fill what would otherwise become a vacuum. At the same time, the heated air at the top of the column begins to cool and sink back toward the ground. The result is a complex pattern of winds generated by the fire itself. As they interact with the naturally prevailing winds both on the ground and aloft, these convective winds both lend strength to the fire and also complicate its movement.

When fires reach this degree of intensity, they often develop multiple flaming fronts where before there was only one. Sometimes tornado-like rotations develop in the column, causing *fire whirls*—tornadoes of fire—to spin off from the main fire. Burning combustible gases produced by the main fire, they dance across the countryside igniting new fires wherever they touch down. Other times, horizontal vortices—essentially, tornadoes of fire laid on their sides—may develop, so that the fire literally rolls forward on the ground like an enormous, flaming rolling pin.

Even before Marie Hansen saw the two columns of smoke looming up behind Hinckley, shortly before 1:00 P.M., both fires had probably crowned. Both were advancing on flaming fronts perhaps two to three miles wide with flames ranging from ten to ninety feet high. One was a mile or so southwest of Pokegama; the other equally far south of Mission Creek. Both were moving toward Hinckley, and each other, about as fast as a man can walk.

When the noon lunch break was over at the Brennan mill, none of the men went back to his accustomed job. No one really believed that the fires could enter the mill, protected as it was by firebreaks on the west and south, by the Saint Paul and Duluth tracks on the east, and by the millpond on the north. Even if fire should somehow breach these defenses, the mill was equipped with what Angus Hay had called on July 25, ". . . the most thorough system of waterworks that can be found." In addition to the hogsheads of water spaced along the roof of the saw shed, the mill had water mains and hydrants throughout the yards. The mill's hose had recently been taken out and pressure-tested and appeared to be in excellent condition. As Hay had assured his readers, "The fire king would most surely meet defeat from the Brennan Lumber Company."

But by now, the mill's managers, like everyone else in town, could see the mountains of smoke building in the southern sky, and they were becoming increasingly uneasy about the fact that nearly an entire year's production of cut lumber was sitting vulnerable in the yard. As a consequence, they directed the foremen to have all of the crews set aside their normal tasks and prepare to protect the mill, just in case.

Some of the men had already begun to use shovels and buckets of water to extinguish embers drifting into the yard and settling on the stacks of lumber. Others now began to work with some of the mill's sixty-five horses, plowing more ground around the yard to extend the firebreaks. Still others, Evan Hansen among them, continued what they had already spent much of the morning doing—filling barrels of water in the millpond and toting them in wagons to strategic locations outside the mill.

By a little after 1:30 P.M., the mood in town began to change markedly. The prevailing winds slowly tilted the convection columns forward to the northeast, so that they now leaned over the town and began to radiate heat down into the streets, like the burners in an enormous oven broiler. The sunlight began to take on a milky, yellowish cast. Ashes began to drift lazily down from the sky, covering everything with a light-gray dusting. The smoke streaming northward overhead began to change from white to light brown and then to black, slowly obscuring the sun. People lit lamps in their stores and offices. As it grew darker outside the wind began to pick up, blowing heavy drifts of smoke and dust through the streets.

At Cowan's Drugstore, Amy Currie decided to keep her children inside, though they were clamoring to go out and see what was happening. She set about gathering all their best clothes together in a bundle and placing it by the front door so that she could grab it if they needed to leave suddenly.

Bill Grissinger and his sisters were still playing in the tent in their yard when a violent gust of hot wind suddenly filled the tent, pulled the stakes free, sent it flying bat-like over their heads, and pinned it, flapping, against the side of the house. The startled children gave a shriek that brought Kate Grissinger running outside. A neighbor, Winnie Ginder, and her three children—Jennie, Willie, and little Winnie, a particularly pretty girl with dark curls—also ran out of their house to see what the commotion was all about. Gathered together in the Grissingers' yard, they all stood watching the black clouds of smoke scudding overhead. After a bit, they decided to go upstairs to get a better look at what was happening, but from the upstairs windows of the Grissinger house all they could see through the smoke were the mill hands plowing the ground around the lumberyard to the north. Winnie Ginder began to wonder aloud why her husband, Will, hadn't yet come home.

In their home on the west side of town, one of Hinckley's young schoolteachers, Mollie McNeil, was trying earnestly to convince her older sister Mary and her eighty-two-year-old mother, also Mary, to pack some belongings and come with her to the Saint Paul and Duluth depot so they could catch the 2:00 P.M. Limited out of town. The older women laughed at what they took to be her excessive anxiety. Mollie began to pack a suitcase of her own anyway.

Clara Anderson's fourteen-year-old brother Antone and two of his schoolmates sat on the Saint Paul and Duluth platform discussing where they and their families should go if the fires were to get close, one boy arguing for the Grindstone River, another for the flooded gravel pit across the Eastern Minnesota tracks. When the northbound Limited Express arrived at 2:00 P.M., two hours late, the boys watched a handful of anxious husbands put wives and children aboard—many of them carrying large bundles of possessions. Behind them, in the telegrapher's office, Tommy Dunn was back at work, having just returned from lunch at his mother's house. Over lunch he had told the little blind woman that as a precaution she should get dressed and be prepared to leave on the next train out of town. Now, as the northbound Limited pulled out, he was puzzling over why he wasn't receiving any telegraph traffic from the south. Mary Anderson had just covered the Dunn's haystack with a tarpaulin and was at work getting Grandma Dunn dressed and packed, and wondering where her own family was. Mollie McNeil began to carry her suitcase and two new dresses toward the Saint Paul and Duluth depot.

At the fire station, chief John Craig convened a meeting of his nineteen volunteer firefighters. Many of the town's foremost citizens served as firefighters—men who commanded respect all over town, like John Currie, mayor Lee Webster, and Father Lawler, the town's Catholic priest. All of them were proud of their affiliation with the department. Two years before, in a competition among all the fire departments west of Chicago, they had come in second, and although they weren't wearing them now, each owned a handsome dress uniform with brass buttons and the letters HFD emblazoned across the chest.

They were also proud of their equipment, and confident of its efficacy. The centerpiece was a brand-new fire engine made by the Waterous Engine Works in Saint Paul. It was a new model, with a shiny, brass-plated boiler and a horse-drawn chassis. For weeks now, in light of the weather, firefighter M. J. Duncan had kept a full head of steam in the boiler day and night. Everyone in the room felt confident that it could generate enough pressure to throw a powerful stream of water anywhere that fire might encroach into the village. After some discussion, they decided that if the fires approached Hinckley they would most likely come from the west or up the Saint Paul and Duluth line from the direction of Mission Creek. Accordingly, they hitched up the engine and a hose cart that they had just finished manufacturing that week, laden with 2,000 feet of fire hose. They positioned themselves on the southwestern corner of town, peering through the shimmering air toward the veil of smoke that was rapidly beginning to obscure everything to the south and west.

Then they began to wait.

Confident or not, as they stood there wondering what they faced, more than a few of them must have thought about Peshtigo. Twenty-three years before and 310 miles to the east, in the autumn of 1871, the

45

same conditions had prevailed across eastern Wisconsin. A long summer of high temperatures and low rainfall had left the land parched. The lumber companies had logged off much of the forestland surrounding the city of Peshtigo, leaving vast tracks of cutover land buried under a tangle of dried-out slash. Fires had burned on and off around the city for weeks, leaving a pall of smoke over the landscape.

Then, on the afternoon of Sunday, October 8, a dry southwest wind began to blow. It started as a breeze, but by late afternoon it had stiffened to over 30 miles per hour. In early evening, it began to howl. Although no one in Wisconsin knew it then, a huge cyclonic storm was rotating around a low-pressure system squatting over southern Nebraska, and they were located squarely on the leading edge of that storm.

At about 8:30 P.M., people in Peshtigo began to hear an ominous rumbling sound bearing down on them from the southwest. When they stepped outside to investigate, they saw that the southern sky was black with clouds, but the clouds were unlike any they had ever seen. They were illuminated by a red, throbbing light. Within a few minutes, hot ashes, sparks, embers, and firebrands began to rain down on Peshtigo. Then the muffled rumbling sound became a roar.

People grabbed what they could from their houses. They cut loose their horses and cattle. They dragged their children by their arms and ran into the street. But most had nowhere to go. Some began frantically digging pits in their front yards, hoping to bury their valuables before the town burned. Others retreated into their houses.

Hundreds of people headed east on a bridge across the Peshtigo River, trying to get out of town. Hundreds more headed west across the same bridge, trying to get into town. The bridge collapsed, dropping all of them and everything they had with them—children, adults, buggies, horses, wagons, cattle, dogs—into the river. In the river, floating logs erupted in flames and seared those who tried to cling to them to keep from drowning. People ran through the streets calling out for loved ones, but the wind-driven firebrands set their clothing and hair on fire. They ran on, streaming trails of flames until they dropped to the ground to die.

And then a mountain of fire—flames and columns of burning gas reaching more than 1,000 feet into the dark sky—moved over Peshtigo and simply obliterated it. Everyone in or near Peshtigo who wasn't safely submerged in the river died, then and there.

The fire roared on northward, leaping the 1,000-foot-wide mouth of the Menominee River and racing up the west side of Green Bay. Sailors on ships two miles out in the bay battled flames in their rigging. Ten miles across the bay, more fire raced up the eastern shore, eating up small towns, lumber mills, and lives.

When it was all over, more than 1,200 people were dead in Wisconsin, victims of the deadliest wildfire in American history. But the larger world hardly noticed. Its attention was focused on the city of Chicago, which had also erupted in flames on the same day and at the same hour as Peshtigo, a casualty of the same convergence of weather and fire. About 250 people died that day in the Great Chicago Fire, a relatively modest toll when held up against the horror of Peshtigo. But the spectacle of a major American city consumed by flames riveted the attention of the press and the public, and so, for much of the country, the Peshtigo firestorm passed quietly into history.

On the same day that Chicago and Peshtigo burned, huge wildfires also swept across parts of Minnesota, causing relatively little loss of life, but an enormous loss of property and timber. So while much of the country might have forgotten October 8, 1871, by the summer of 1894, it's unlikely that many in Midwestern cities and towns like Hinckley had forgotten. And it's even less likely that the handful of men standing at the south end of Hinckley with a single steam-powered fire engine—listening to the deep, muffled rumbling that was growing closer by the minute—could have failed to remember.

Eighty miles to the north of Hinckley, a thin layer of high, smoky clouds had been drifting over Duluth all through the morning and early afternoon. At Union Station, with its two conical towers and ornate facade rising cathedral-like over bustling Superior Street, passengers began to board the southbound Saint Paul and Duluth express bound for Carlton, Hinckley, and Saint Paul shortly before 2:00 P.M. Known as the Limited No. 4, or more informally and affectionately as "the Skalley," the train consisted of a baggage car, a smoking car, two coaches, two chair cars, a coal tender, and a steam locomotive, Saint Paul and Duluth locomotive number 69.

The locomotive could not have been more ordinary. It was of a type that has since come to be called the 4-4-0 for the arrangement of four small driving wheels in front, four larger driving wheels further back, and no driving wheels behind. This was the machine that, more than any other in 1894, was rapidly transforming America from a rural, agrarian society to an urban, industrial nation. Its design was so reliable, its engineering so successful, that just twenty years after the first was built in 1850, 85 percent of the locomotives on American rails were 4-4-0s.

Saint Paul and Duluth number 69 had been built in May of 1888 at the New York Locomotive Works in Rome, New York, one of three identical locomotives. It weighed 45½ tons and could carry eight tons of coal and 3,500 gallons of water in its tender. Standing 14' 9" tall from the rails to the top of its smokestack, it stretched 44' 8" from the front of the boiler to the back of the tender. Inside the boiler were 193 two-inch tubes that carried hot gases from the firebox through the water in the boiler, generating the steam that powered the driving wheels. Going full tilt, it operated at 145 pounds of boiler pressure. Pulling an average load of coal, water, and passenger coaches, it could travel at upwards of 60 miles per hour on a level roadbed, though the Saint Paul and Duluth's speed limit of 40 miles per hour for passenger trains kept it well below its maximum speed most of the time.

At 1:55 P.M., the porter, John Wesley Blair, helped the last of 125 passengers aboard, and the train pulled out of Union Station, white clouds of steam puffing from its cylinders. The man at the throttle was James Root. Root was a large and somewhat homely man with a long, open face and a large, droopy mustache. Fifty-one now, he had worked on railroads since he was fourteen and for the Saint Paul and Duluth for twenty-three years. As the Limited pulled out of Duluth, Root noted dark skies to the south and remarked to his twenty-eight-year-old fireman, Jack McGowan, that he believed they might have a storm ahead. Root had seen plenty of storms, and much else too. As a young man, during the Civil War, he had run William Tecumseh Sherman's advance train as the Union general approached the outskirts of Atlanta. Later, he had been among those who picked their way through the fetid remains of the Andersonville prison camp in Georgia, removing both corpses and survivors. Later still, he had run the hospital train that ferried the living skeletons from Andersonville back to their home states in the North.

Back in the coaches, conductor Thomas Sullivan, a burly thirty-four-year-old Irishman with a mustache that rivaled Root's, began punching tickets. Further back, in the more luxurious chair cars, John Blair started making his first-class passengers comfortable in their overstuffed armchairs, chatting with them about the stifling heat, baseball, whatever people felt like talking about. An affable, round-faced young man with a pencil-thin mustache, Blair was probably the only African-American on the train. With the train going south now, he was heading toward his home in Saint Paul, and he expected to be there in time to have dinner with his wife Emma and his two sons. Among the passengers he was tending to in the rear chair car was a minor dignitary, State Senator Frank Daugherty, and his ten-year-old son, Otto. Also in the car was a high-ranking railroad official, Robert M. Bell, the superintendent of the Duluth Union Station, traveling with his fifteen-year-old daughter, Josie.

As the train proceeded south the skies grew darker. The train stopped to take on another twenty-five passengers in Carlton, bringing the total number of souls aboard to slightly more than 150. By the time Root pulled out of Carlton, conditions outside had grown so dark that McGowan needed to light a lamp in the cab in order to read the water gauge. In the coaches, Blair lit the overhead lamps so the passengers could read their newspapers. When they passed through Barnum, thirty-nine miles south of Duluth, visibility was down to a few dozen feet, and Root had to light the locomotive's headlamp and slow down the train considerably.

They passed through a series of villages, and Daugherty and the other passengers began to note that clusters of people were standing alongside the tracks, their anxious faces turned up to the train as it passed. At Miller, sixty-six miles from Duluth and just nine miles north of Hinckley, cinders began falling through the air, looking, as one passenger observed, "like black snowflakes." Then they began to encounter waves of stiflingly hot air.

Root's train wasn't the only one approaching Hinckley from the north. On the Eastern Minnesota tracks five miles to the east, engineer William Bennet Best's locomotive, another 4-4-0, was pulling two coaches, a smoking car, and two parlor cars, one of them featuring a buffet lunch for first-class passengers. All told, there were about a hundred passengers aboard, many of them just off the steamship *Northwest*, which had arrived in Duluth that morning from the East via the Great Lakes. Most of the passengers were bound for the Twin Cities or destinations farther south on the Mississippi.

Best, born in Quebec in 1856, sported a handlebar mustache on his pleasant, slightly pudgy face. He had been working on American railroads throughout the Midwest since the early 1880s, after failing to find his fortune in the gold-mining business in California in the 1870s.

Like Jim Root, Best was encountering heavy smoke and dark conditions north of Hinckley. He'd lit his lamps and reduced his speed, but he still expected to reach Hinckley nearly on time at 3:25 P.M. Back in the coaches, however, Best's passengers were getting decidedly nervous, and conductor Harry Powers was finding it increasingly difficult to convince them that the smoke and heat were not unusual for this time of year.

A third train had also been moving south toward Hinckley all morning and afternoon on the Eastern Minnesota line. A slow, heavy freight, pulled by yet another 4-4-0, it had departed from West Superior Wisconsin on the Eastern Minnesota tracks at 7 A.M., just as Evan

Hansen was walking into the Brennan lumberyard. By 2:20 P.M., its engineer, Edward Barry, was groping his way through the murk just north
of Hinckley, traveling well below the 18-mile-per-hour speed limit for
freights, pulling ten full boxcars and thirty empty ones. As the smoke
grew heavier, Barry grew increasingly anxious and finally decided he'd
better stop at each bridge and wooden culvert before crossing, just to
make sure that the structure wasn't in flames. Back in the caboose, his
brakeman, C. C. Freeman, realizing that he could not see more than half
the length of the train ahead of him, lit side lamps, hoping that Barry
would be able to see, at least, that the caboose was still there.

As Root, Best, and Barry approached cautiously from the north, a
fourth train departed Hinckley, traveling southbound on the Eastern
Minnesota line, beginning its return trip to Saint Cloud after unloading some freight and taking on water. The train was a light one, with
only one passenger coach and a baggage car. In the cab was one of
the youngest engineers in the Eastern Minnesota's employ, William
Vogel. He had a crew of six, headed up by his conductor, Ed Parr, but
there were only two passengers in the coach—D. A. Kingsley, an advance agent for a theatrical company, and a sixty-five-year-old gentleman named Mr. Carver, who was making the eight-mile trip home
to Pokegama.

A mile out of town, Vogel found that small fires were burning
in the brush on both sides of the track. Not much worried about
them, he opened the throttle so that the train would run past the fires
too fast to let the flames catch hold of it. But before he could go another half-mile, and in what seemed to him to be just an instant,
everything around him, even the air, was suddenly ablaze. Sheets of
flame towered eighty or ninety feet above him on both sides of the
tracks, roaring so loudly Vogel could not, at times, even hear the
sound of his locomotive. As far down the tracks as he could see, there
was nothing but more smoke and more flame ahead. It was too late
to stop, though. Even if he could get the train reversed before the
flames overwhelmed him, Best's passenger train, which he believed

to be right behind him, would likely plow into the rear of his train. So Vogel left the throttle full open and plunged on into the inferno, still hoping to punch through it.

Within a minute or two he was approaching the Pokegama Creek Bridge. Slowing the locomotive slightly, and leaning out of the cab into the searing heat, Vogel could see that the underside of the bridge ahead was engulfed in flames. Worse, the tracks on top looked to be sagging slightly in mid-span. They were still straight, though, and he had no choice, so he threw the throttle open again and the train plunged ahead onto the bridge. He could feel the bridge go soft beneath him as he crossed, but the train was so light and moving so fast that they were over before it could give way.

Still with no real alternative, Vogel left the throttle wide open and the train careened on ahead, rolling from side to side as it ran over rails that were beginning to spread and warp in the heat. Burning trees began to fall across the tracks from both sides, but the locomotive bulldozed them aside with its cowcatcher as it lurched and swayed forward for nearly another mile.

Then, as the train entered a small clearing, it finally hit a section of track where the rails were so badly warped that the locomotive executed a sudden right turn and dove off the embankment into a ditch. The locomotive, belching steam and smoke, pulled the baggage car with it and plowed ahead through the gravel and brush, squealing and screeching as it slid to a stop. The locomotive, the tender, and the baggage car came to rest, listing to one side at a 45-degree angle in the burning brush. The coach remained upright, but it had been pulled sideways, across the tracks. Vogel and his fireman, Joe Lacher, crouched on the floor of the cab trying to get away from the searing heat. Then Vogel noticed a spigot over their heads and opened it. Water from the locomotive's reservoir began to spray over them.

Ed Parr leapt out of the baggage car and sprinted toward the coach up on the tracks, but the flames ripped at him as he ran, and by the time he got inside his hands and face were badly burned. Many of the seat cushions in the coach were on fire, and everyone scrambled to throw and kick them out through the doorway before the fire inside could spread. The wind shrieked and growled as the flames outside streamed past the windows. Kingsley, the advance man, begged the others for a gun with which to shoot himself. Parr and the rest of the crew and passengers ignored him and pressed themselves against the floor of the coach, trying to find fresh air. Parr began to think about what he could do in the next few minutes to settle his accounts with God.

Then, one of the brakemen, M. J. Whalen, remembered that there were still hundreds of gallons of water in the locomotive's reservoir. He scrambled up and down the aisles on the floor, trying to find a container. Finally, he found two old pails and fought his way outside through the smoke and heat to a spigot on the outside of the tender, where he filled the pails and ran back to the coach. The undersides of both the coach and the baggage car had caught fire by now, so he flung the water under the train onto the worst of the flames and dove back into the coach. Two more men took the buckets and ran for the tender and repeated the performance, and then two more took their turn, and soon they had a sort of bucket brigade going, two men at a time.

As Barry's freight neared Hinckley, just before 2:30 P.M., the volunteer firefighters on the south end of town were already beginning to engage spot fires that the main fires had thrown ahead of them into the outskirts of town. The first structure to catch fire in Hinckley was a chicken coop. Two of the volunteers handling the nozzle end of the hose—Horace Gorton and Axel Rosdahl—began to extinguish it, but before they could finish the job, the adjoining house was afire and they turned the stream of water on it. Then it was a barn and another chicken coop, and then another house. Gorton and Rosdahl struggled to put out the structure fires one by one, playing out more and more hose to reach further from the Waterous engine and the well that was their source of water.

Within minutes, small spot fires began to erupt all along the southwest side of town. Chief Craig ordered a general alarm sounded on the whistle at the Brennan mill, northwest of town. Reluctantly, the mill managers, apparently realizing that in order to save the mill they might have to save the town, agreed to release the men and leave the mill largely untended for now. Only a skeleton crew stayed behind, along with a fifteen-year-old boy who was told to stay and to sound a long continuous note on the mill whistle to recall the rest of the men if the mill were threatened. More than two hundred mill workers trotted to the southern and western edges of town carrying shovels, axes, and buckets of water.

Buckets of water were of little avail now, though. Even the nozzle men were struggling to put water on the fires as the wind increased to a gale and beyond, the hot wind blowing the water back into their faces. Many of the burning structures were out of their range; there just wasn't enough hose to reach them. Then Chief Craig received a report of a fire moving up from Mission Creek, toward the east side of town, and hurried off on horseback to investigate, stopping on the way to send a telegram to Rush City, twenty miles to the south, pleading for 1,000 feet of hose to be sent to Hinckley immediately on the northbound Saint Paul and Duluth Express.

Even now, at 3:00 P.M., many of Hinckley's citizens did not believe the fire could make it past the firebreaks and the railroad embankments and enter the heart of town. Will Ginder, a huge bear of a man with a full black beard, formerly the mayor of Hinckley and now a member of the board of supervisors, stood on the corner of Main and Second Street in front of the Morrison Hotel, surveying the scene and chatting with Douglas Greeley, the hotel's manager. Ginder's son, Willie, sent by his mother at the Grissingers' house, ran up asking, "Father, do you want Mother to leave home and seek a place of safety? She wants to know." Ginder told the boy, "Willie, run home and tell Mama the danger is passed."

At the Saint Paul and Duluth depot, in the stifling heat of the small telegraph office overlooking the platform, Tommy Dunn was trying to reach the dispatcher in Duluth, trying to find out when Root's train would arrive. By now, a crowd had gathered outside his window. Mary Anderson was there with her mother, father, three little sisters, two little brothers, and Grandma Dunn. Mollie McNeil was also there with her suitcase and her new dresses, but her sister and mother had not yet shown up. The platform was piled high with steamer trunks and baggage, and more people were arriving with still more baggage every minute. Anxious passengers kept poking their heads in through Dunn's office door, asking about Root's train. Then, finally, Dunn received a telegram, but it wasn't from Duluth. It was from the south. Pokegama, just seven miles to the southwest, was gone. People were dead.

Fire had washed over tiny Pokegama just after 2:00 P.M. Founded the year before, Pokegama, or Brook Park as it was already coming to be called, wasn't much of a place—perhaps 130 people living in about twenty-five homes along the Eastern Minnesota tracks. There was a small sawmill, a general store, a post office, a brand-new schoolhouse, and little else, but it was a town that expected to grow, as the new schoolhouse demonstrated.

The fire that hit Pokegama was more than a mile wide. Almost everyone in town heard it before they saw it—a long, low rumbling sound, as of a gigantic waterfall, coming closer and growing louder all the time. They stopped what they were doing and looked to the southwest, wondering what the sound meant. Some were sure at first that it was a tornado, but then they felt it—a wave of superheated air that rolled along the ground in advance of the fire. When the heat hit, they scattered. Some ran into their houses to escape the heat or to retrieve possessions; some found small creeks and began to splash water on each other; some simply took off running into the woods, trying to outpace the flames that had suddenly become all too visible behind them.

Alice and Mabel Nelson, picking cranberries in the swampy woods just south of town, must have been among the first to hear and feel it. They ran frantically through the woods, tripping on the underbrush, scattering cranberries from the pails they were clutching, trying to make it to their father and his crew on the railroad tracks.

But when they reached the tracks, they saw not their father but an avalanche of fire rolling up the line toward them at the speed of a train. Alice scooped half a pail of brackish water from a ditch by the tracks, and the girls crawled into a niche in the railroad embankment under the roots of an old stump. Mabel ripped her apron in half and the girls dipped the rags in the water and held them over their mouths to breathe. Then they squeezed themselves as far back into the niche as they could and watched in horror as the world outside exploded in flames.

Their father heard it too and ran in the only direction he could go—north, through the woods to his home, where he threw a few prized possessions into a trunk and dragged the trunk out into the heat and smoke of his front yard, hollering for his wife and Minnie to follow him. As her father barked orders to get out of the house, Minnie took off her new school shoes, placed them carefully in a box on a shelf, and put on an old pair of shoes that she didn't mind getting dirty. Then she ran out to join her family. Her father carried the trunk for perhaps a hundred yards before the heat began to sear the back of his neck. He dropped the trunk, grabbed Minnie instead, and ran with his child and wife through the burning woods toward the center of the settlement.

W. W. Braman, a German Jew, and his twenty-seven-year-old son Jay had just finished loading a cart with hay and were driving it south toward town when they heard and felt it. Braman shouted to his son to abandon the wagon and run, but the younger man told his father, ". . . [Y]ou go; I can make a place of safety; you look out for yourself," and turned the wagon to the north, determined to save the horses and the hay. The elder Braman sprinted toward town, where he found the Nelsons and a crowd of other settlers gathered around the sawmill. Taking command, he directed everyone to wade into the small millpond that lay between the mill and an Eastern Minnesota trestle.

Others struggled to reach the pond. An elderly woman hobbled through the driving smoke, trying to catch up with her son, his wife, and her grandchildren, who beckoned to her and shouted encouragement from the pond. But a tongue of flame pulled her down, a few yards short of the water, licking the clothes from her body as she shrieked and writhed on the ground in front of her helpless family. Two men with their clothes and hair afire bolted out of the woods and plunged into the water.

The pond was almost circular, perhaps 150 feet across and fifteen feet deep in the middle. As the fire closed in and began to consume the sawmill, most of the settlers, because they were non-swimmers, had to huddle in the shallows under the Eastern Minnesota trestle. They sat with only their faces out of the water as piles of logs on the opposite side erupted in flames. Then the railroad trestle above them, its timbers soaked in creosote, burst into flames, and they had to shrink away from it, scuttling back around the edge of the pond toward the burning mill, trying to stay in their depth, hoping the flaming trestle wouldn't fall into the pond, praying that Bill Best's train wouldn't.

On his farm outside of town, C. W. Kelsey, one of the town's founders, grabbed a blanket, put a ladder down his well, and with his wife, Lucy, and their three children crawled down to the water level. There, wetting the blanket and holding it over their heads, they clung to the ladder, singing hymns loudly over the roar of the fire above. On another farm, a young man named Fred Molander, with no time to find a ladder, simply jumped into his well. His twenty-five-year-old wife, unwilling to follow him, pulled their three-year-old daughter and one-year-old son into their house, closed the door against the flames, sat down, and held them tight. Not far away, also on Molander's farm, Jay Braman, realizing the fire was gaining on his heavily loaded hay wagon, cut the traces to free his horses. Then he began to run.

About thirty minutes after the Quamba fire overran Pokegama, the Beroun fire edged into Mission Creek, six miles to the east of Pokegama and just three miles south of Hinckley on the Saint Paul and Duluth line. Like Pokegama, Mission Creek was small, hardly even a village, with seventy-three inhabitants living in twenty-six houses scattered through the woods and the clearings that surrounded the town. The town itself consisted of little more than a small sawmill, a hotel, a blacksmith shop, and a general store, all owned by the Laird and Boyle Company. A few modest homes were clustered around these establishments. The company had shut down the mill temporarily to upgrade some of the equipment, and many of the town's men had taken the opportunity to go into the Dakotas to work the fall wheat harvest for a little extra cash. The few men who had stayed behind had spent the morning fighting back small local fires south of town, trying to protect their individual homesteads and their hay fields, but by 2:30 P.M. the wind had risen to the point that all their efforts were proving futile, and everyone had fallen back into the hamlet, trying to decide what to do next. Dragging along suitcases and trunks and furniture from their homes, they converged on the general store and asked the proprietor, Ed Boyle, to telegraph for a train to evacuate them. Before Boyle could even get the message keyed in, however, flames fifty to eighty feet tall rolled out of the woods to the south of them, perhaps forty yards away.

Slightly less intense than the fire that had just swept through Pokegama, this fire was nevertheless far too big and far too fast to outrun. Boyle directed the crowd to the center of a two-acre potato patch immediately behind the general store and told his employees to take a couple of barrels of water on a wagon to the same location. As the flaming front roared toward them, people flung themselves into the furrows, burying their faces in the hot soil, trying to scoop out pockets of cooler air to breathe. Some covered themselves with wet blankets and shawls. In the middle of the crowd, a girl named Jenny Johnson sat in a rocking chair covered with blankets and clutching a doll.

Black smoke and broiling heat rolled over them; cinders, blazing branches, and smoldering pinecones rained down on them. Children screamed as embers burned their backs and mothers beat at smoldering patches on their children's clothes with their bare hands. The heat and the ashes nearly blinded them all, but a few people managed to raise their heads enough to see that all around the potato patch, buildings were beginning to smolder and char before the flames even reached them. Their windows popped out and shattered; their foundations cracked and crumbled simply from the intensity of the heat.

For thirty or maybe forty minutes, the fire roared and snarled around and above them, and then it was over. One by one they raised their heads and looked around at the utterly transformed landscape. Every one of them was alive; none was badly hurt; and together they watched with disbelief as the rolling sea of fire moved off to the north toward Hinckley.

As he finally pulled his freight into Hinckley a few minutes before 3:00 P.M., Ed Barry knew immediately that he had a problem. He needed to take on coal and water and turn his locomotive around for the return trip to Duluth, but he could see at a glance that several small fires were already burning in the Eastern Minnesota yards at the south end of town. Unsure whether he could get to the round-house to turn around, he uncoupled the forty boxcars he'd been pulling, left them on a sidetrack, and proceeded cautiously down the line with the locomotive and tender, trying to get into the yards. Through the smoke and shimmering heat waves, he could see that many of the creosote-soaked ties on the mainline south of town were blazing between the rails. Shielding his face against the heat with one arm, he managed to get to the water tank and fill his reservoir, but he couldn't get to the turntable, so he backed up, sidetracked the loco-motive in front of the depot, and waited for Bill Best's passenger train, due at 3:25 P.M. Because he was scheduled to return to Duluth, and Best was scheduled to continue south, Barry knew his train had the right-of-way on the tracks going north. But he couldn't take advantage of it until Best arrived and got out of his way.

By now Chief Craig had surveyed the scene on the east side of town. Although fire was nibbling its way through brush at the outskirts of the village there, it did not yet seem as bad as on the west side, so he began to make his way back across town on horseback. He was still reasonably confident that the fire could be deflected around the center of town, especially if the men could make a stand and save

Mary Anderson's house, the southernmost house on Main Street. As he drew closer to the west side, however, he saw that more villagers were toting possessions out of their houses and making their way toward the two railroad depots. As he approached the fire line itself, he began to encounter men moving in the other direction, away from the fire line, filtering back into town, starting to look for their families.

Out in front of the fire line, Gorton and Rosdahl were still manning the hose. By now, so much of the water was blowing back in their faces and cooling them that they were largely unaware of the tremendous heat building up around them. They were also unaware that many of the men behind them had been giving up and drifting away for some time. When the water pressure suddenly gave out and the nozzle ran dry, they turned around and saw that the hose had been burned through between them and the Waterous engine. In an instant, they felt the overwhelming heat on their faces and hands and heard a deep rumbling coming from somewhere ahead of them, somewhere beyond the veil of smoke. Something unfathomable was out there, something far greater than any forest fire they had ever seen. Mary Anderson's house erupted in flames. Gorton and Rosdahl dropped the hose and ran. Everyone ran. Ahead of them all, Father Lawler, the Catholic priest, sprinted through town, pounding on doors, shouting, "Leave all you have—save your lives!" John Craig galloped up Main Street, crying out, "We can't save the town; don't lose a moment, but fly!" Angus Hay would later record his impressions of the scene:

> Teams hauling water were dashing along the street; women were afraid, and children were crying; men's faces were a study— bleached with smoke and driven sand and blanched with fear for the safety of their homes and their families.

At the town hall, someone began to toll the large bronze bell wildly. The erratic clanging sound swept across Hinckley on stiffening gusts of wind.

* * *

At 3:25 P.M., just as the fire line collapsed at the far south end of town, Bill Best eased his passenger train to a stop in front of the Eastern Minnesota depot on the northeast side of town, precisely on time. The sky above him had seemed to lighten the last few miles into Hinckley, and he had started to think that he'd left the worst of the smoke and fires behind him. But it had been an illusion, a result of the strong updraft caused by the fires ahead lifting the blanket of smoke, sucking it back up into the sky. Pulling into town, he had seen that the freight office and a number of boxcars were in flames a half-mile ahead of him in the freight yards. Looking farther down the line now, he was appalled to see that everything beyond the yards was a roiling mass of black and red, reaching hundreds of feet into the sky. Flames were dancing through the black clouds without any apparent connection to the ground.

Best glanced at the water-level glass in his cab and saw that his reservoir was critically low. He couldn't go anywhere without taking on more water. And even if he could get water, he didn't dare to back the train out of town without orders from Duluth, lest he run into a southbound train. There wasn't much chance, he thought, of getting a telegram through to Duluth and receiving a reply in time. He noticed that Ed Barry was standing on the siding, staring intently up at him, and he realized that Barry probably had the right-of-way on the northbound tracks.

Best moved his locomotive slowly down the line to the water tank, but the heat and driving smoke made it almost impossible for his fireman, George Ford, to pull down the spout. Finally, on his fourth try, Ford got the spout down, and water flowed into the reservoir; two minutes later, Best backed his train up to the depot.

Scores of people were running out of town now, streaming toward him, dragging children and trunks and all manner of things, shouting and stumbling and gesturing to him. Best's conductor, Harry Powers, swung himself up into the cab.

He'd been talking to Barry, and they had a plan.

Chapter Five

THE CAULDRON

From here on, then, in the blinding smoke, it is no longer a "seeing world," but a "feeling world"—the pain of others and our compassion for them.

—*Norman Maclean,*
Young Men and Fire

ON THE FIRST OF SEPTEMBER 1967, SEVENTY-THREE YEARS TO the day after the Hinckley fire, an uncontrolled wildland fire ripped through an area of dense timber just east of Priest Lake, Idaho. Dubbed the Sundance Fire after a mountain near its point of origin, it started its major run at about 2:00 P.M., and by 11:00 P.M. that evening it had run over nine miles on a front four miles wide, consuming more than 50,000 acres of forest. It reached its peak intensity at about 8:00 P.M. when it temporarily stalled in the area of the Pack River. At that point, its convection column towered 35,000 feet above the surrounding landscape. Within the column, vertical wind speeds—that is, the speed of the winds moving upward in the column—were about 45 miles per hour. Surface winds, mostly generated by the flow of air inward toward the base of the convection column, approached 120 miles per hour. Before the fire ever reached them, thousands of trees were knocked down by these winds. Many hundreds more had their tops snapped off sixty to seventy-five feet above the ground. Those that were knocked down were later found to be pointing in different directions in different areas, indicating that the winds preceding the fire were erratic and cyclonic. When the fire stalled at the Pack River and merged with the spot fires it had thrown out ahead of itself, its energy output surged rapidly as it concentrated its fury on a single area. The fire was now releasing nearly 500 million British thermal units (BTUs) of energy per second, roughly the equivalent of a Hiroshima-sized nuclear bomb going off every five to fifteen minutes.

When a fire achieves the intensity of the Sundance Fire, it no longer fits into any of the three traditional wildfire classifications: ground, surface, or crown fire. It has likely been all of these in the course of its maturation, but it now becomes capable of growing into something quite different, and quite unusual: a *mass fire*, to use the term applied by Stephen J. Pyne in his landmark study, *Fire in America*. In Pyne's terminology, a mass fire that remains stationary is a *firestorm*; one that moves is a *conflagration*. Regardless of this finer distinction, though, all mass fires have certain characteristics that set them apart from ordinary wildfires. They are typically born when two or more smaller fires—often a main fire and the spot fires that it has spawned around its periphery—suddenly merge into a single eruption of flame. Their flaming fronts may tower as high as one hundred feet over the tops of the trees, or two hundred feet above the ground. They may advance as fast as 15 miles per hour on level ground—much faster on a slope—and release energy at rates as high as 30,000 BTUs per foot of fire line per second. They create huge convection columns that loom over the surrounding countryside, radiating heat downward and thus drying out the fuel in their paths.

At one point, toward the peak of the Sundance Fire's intensity, observers saw the entire side of a mountain, the west slope of Apache Ridge, erupt into flames in a single instant. The angle of the ridge had exposed the mountainside to an enormous amount of radiant heat from the convection column, quickly drying out the forest and raising its temperature to the kindling point. The first ember that landed on the mountainside had then ignited the whole thing as if it were soaked in gasoline. In 1929, in a similar incident, Harry Gisborne, one of the fathers of modern fire science, watched two square miles of Glacier National Park's forest ignite in something just less than two minutes at the Half Moon Fire.

Mass fires also generate enormous winds, often of hurricane velocity. Sometimes these winds begin to rotate and become cyclonic, creating fire vortices—tornadoes of fire that may advance well ahead of the main flaming front. Because of the tremendous updraft in their convection columns, mass fires typically pick up thousands of flaming or glowing firebrands—some as large as burning logs. They may carry these as much as 18,000 feet into the air before throwing them miles ahead of their fronts, spawning spot fires wherever the firebrands land in fuel. And because mass fires consume their fuel so rapidly, they often exhaust all the available oxygen in the air before they have finished burning all the carbon and volatile gases that they have released from their fuels. As a result, they produce vast clouds of black smoke, black because it's carrying a heavy load of unburned carbon. As this superheated black smoke rises, it eventually encounters enough oxygen to allow combustion to resume, and flames arc in sheets across the sky. To people on the ground it appears that the sky itself is on fire. Most spectacularly of all, glowing bubbles of the gases released by fire—bubbles that may be as big as a car or even a house—may float some distance ahead of the fire like gigantic balloons dancing in the sky before igniting suddenly over the heads of horrified onlookers.

As two already large fires approach one another, they often begin a kind of tug-of-war, competing over the available fuel and oxygen in the space between them. During this time, which may last only for a few minutes, their pent-up energies build toward a kind of climax. Both generate tremendous winds, but the area between them may be relatively still as the countervailing winds tend to neutralize each other. This area between them also grows extremely hot as both fires radiate heat down onto the surface. Then, suddenly and violently, this state of equilibrium collapses as one of the fires pulls the other into itself, and at that moment the fires will erupt, or *blow up*, to use the firefighter's term. The area between the two fires—heated and dried by both—is likely to be incinerated in a matter of moments, and the mass fire that results is likely to be far larger and more dangerous than the two separate fires that spawned it.

That was what was happening at the south end of Hinckley by the time Bill Best backed his locomotive up to the Eastern Minnesota depot. The fire that started at Quamba and the fire that started at Beroun had arrived almost simultaneously on the west and south sides of Hinckley. Each was now burning on a front about as wide as the Sundance Fire at its peak. Both had spawned numerous spot fires in and around Hinckley. Neither of the main fires nor any of the spot fires yet qualified as a mass fire, but together they were about to become one. The roiling black-and-red monster that Best had seen looming down the tracks was consolidating its enormous strength and preparing to pounce. It was about to become, in effect, the perfect fire.

When it began to move, it would consume more than 300,000 acres and more than 400 lives in a little less time than the Sundance Fire took to burn a mere 50,000 acres.

By 3:45 P.M., things were happening fast in Hinckley. Everyone, indoors and out, could hear the deep rumbling of what was approaching now. A searing wind was blowing dense black smoke, cinders, and firebrands through the dusty streets. When Nels Anderson's house went up in flames and Chief Craig thundered by on his horse shouting, "We can't save the town!", Angus Hay was four blocks from his office. He took off running in that direction, and by the time he got there large cinders were falling all around him. He and his typographer, James Willard, tried to gather together some of the *Enterprise*'s equipment and files, but through the back door he could see that fist-sized coals were already raining down in the yard. Through the front window, he could see people running past outside on Third Street, yelling and looking for their spouses and children. Judging it to be the most valuable thing in the office, Hay grabbed his subscription book and ran outside to help.

A woman with three children stumbled down the street, blinded by the smoke. Hay took her baby from her arms and carried it to a man who was heading toward the Eastern Minnesota depot in a buggy. Then he led the woman and the rest of her children, running northward and eastward through the streets to the flooded gravel pit behind the Eastern depot where he urged them to get in the shallow, green water.

Hay ran back across town to help more people, but rounding the corner in front of the Morrison Hotel, trying to head south on Main Street, he quickly found that he couldn't endure the heat blowing up the street, and he began running east, back toward the gravel pit. Running at full tilt now, he looked to the south to see how far away the fire was. A block down he saw a woman he knew only as Mrs. Blanchard with her eleven-year-old son. As Hay watched, Blanchard tripped on a rail on the Eastern Minnesota tracks and didn't get up. Her boy crumpled to the ground next to her. The heat was too withering in that direction to allow Hay to go to their aid.

A man plunged by with a child in one arm, dragging another by the arm, shouting, "My God, we'll die! My God, we'll die!"

On the west side of town, Dr. Stephan bolted into the Currie house and shouted to Amy Currie to grab her children and come with him. Clutching the children, the two of them ran out the front door, past the bundle of clothing Amy had gathered together, and out into the street. As they ran toward the gravel pit, Dr. Stephan pulled up abruptly, saying he'd forgotten something back at the office. He sprinted back to the drugstore, where John Currie was now running frantically through the building, looking for Amy and the children. Grabbing a few items from his desk, Stephan told Currie where his family was and together they ran back down the street to Amy and the children. Seeing Best's train pulled up at the Eastern Minnesota depot, the Curries joined the crowd pushing its way onto the train.

Dr. Stephan headed back into town and began rounding up some of the dozens of lost children who were running aimlessly through the streets. He snatched them up two at a time in his arms, ran to the Eastern Minnesota platform, thrust them into the arms of strangers boarding the train, and ran back into town for more.

At Bill Grissinger's house on the northwest side of town, still somewhat removed from the worst of it, Kate Grissinger and Winnie Ginder, with their children, were still nervously watching events unfold from an upstairs window. Finally, Kate turned to Winnie and said, as calmly as she could manage, "It seems to be getting worse right along, Mrs. Ginder. Perhaps we should take the train." Winnie agreed but, saying she wanted to go home and change her dress first, she disappeared downstairs into the smoke with her children. A few moments later, Bill, his mother, and his sisters trooped downstairs and out into the yard together, heading for the Saint Paul and Duluth depot. Before they got out of their yard, though, flames roared over their heads. Everyone screamed and scattered, leaving Bill alone in the yard. Through the smoke, he could just make out people running north along the Saint Paul and Duluth tracks. He scrambled up the embankment, hoping his mother and sisters might be among them. They weren't.

Nobody up on the tracks seemed to have a plan; everyone was just running north. Dozens of suitcases and bundles were strewn along the track. Bill Grissinger began to run with the rest of the crowd, up the track, away from the flames and the roaring sound approaching rapidly from the south. He didn't hear his mother calling for him as she ran through the dust and smoke behind their house, dragging Mabel and Callie along with her. She was heading in the wrong direction, away from the tracks.

A quarter of a mile to the south, people were packed into the Saint Paul and Duluth depot, trying to get out of the heat and smoke, waiting for Root's 4:05 P.M. Limited to arrive. Among those waiting were one of the Saint Paul and Duluth's section foremen, John McNamara, his wife, Annie, and their five sons. Annie was clutching a black leather purse. Inside was $3,500, a small fortune that she had saved, unbeknownst to her husband, for her sons' educations. The oldest of her sons, fourteen-year-old John Jr., was due to start school Monday at the Saint Thomas Academy in Saint Paul.

Mary Anderson and her family were in the depot as well, Mary still tending to Grandma Dunn. Tommy Dunn was still at the telegraph, still trying to get word about Root's train, when someone slid open the freight-room doors and yelled, "The depot roof is on fire!" Screaming and pushing, people streamed out onto the platform. Some began to run north on the tracks; others ran around the burning building and headed across town toward the Eastern Minnesota depot. In the blowing smoke in front of the depot, Mary Anderson lost track of her family and began to run up Main Street toward the Brennan Lumber Company Store. She stumbled up the steps and pulled at the doorknob, trying to get out of the smoke and the heat, but the door was locked. Glancing back down the street, she could see that flames were already boiling out of the windows of the Saint Paul and Duluth depot. A friend, Mrs. Kronenberg, ran by with all six of her children heading toward the Eastern Minnesota depot. She shouted at Mary to follow her to the train. "But I haven't any money," Mary shouted back. "Oh, to dickens with the money," the older woman said, and Mary began running with her.

Mollie McNeil was back in the streets too, still lugging her suitcase and carrying her dresses. Someone yelled at her to forget the suitcase and save herself. She dropped her possessions and began to run north, joining with Annie and John McNamara and their sons. Somewhere in the smoke and confusion her mother and sister were also running north, heading for the river.

At Clara Anderson's house, Hans Mattison burst suddenly through the front door, yelling that the town was on fire and looking for his fiancée, Clara's eighteen-year-old sister, Emily. Startled, the Andersons ran from their house toward the Saint Paul and Duluth depot, but when they reached the Morrison Hotel, they could see that the depot down the street was already engulfed in flames. They also realized that Clara wasn't with them. Antone and his father, John, dashed back to the house, but they couldn't find her, so they returned to where the others were waiting in front of the hotel. By now the smoke and heat from the burning depot were blinding them to the point that they could barely keep track of one another.

They started to run north on the wagon road. A hundred yards up the road, Antone discovered he'd outrun his family and started back, finding that they'd crawled onto a wagon driven by a neighbor, Al Fraser, with his wife and three children. Belle Barden's father, Jake, was on the wagon too. A few minutes before, he had put Belle and the rest of his family on the Eastern Minnesota train and then headed north on the wagon road, trying to save his wagon and his team. Antone crawled aboard with the rest and they started north again. But the road was jammed with wagons, buggies, drays, cattle, horses, dogs, and people afoot, all of them trying to cross the narrow bridge over the Grindstone.

Somewhere among the three hundred or so people trying to go north on the wagon road, Evan Hansen was looking for Marie and the children. He knew that they had planned to be in town to shop, so it's likely that he looked there first, bulling his way through the crowd in the Saint Paul and Duluth depot; running through the streets, back and forth, block after block; standing on the platform at the Eastern Minnesota depot, bellowing their names into the smoke and wind and clamor. At some point, he realized that he wasn't going to find them in town, and he started heading north again, toward Hinckley Big Hill and his homestead. Now, this tangle of vehicles, horses, cattle, and people stood between him and his home.

At his back, over the shouting and cursing around him, the rumbling was growing louder and closer. Teams that had bolted away from their drivers were careening up the road dragging empty buggies and wagons, whinnying frantically. In the middle of the crowd his friend, Axel Hanson, crouched in front of his buggy, trying to repair something, cursing loudly in Norwegian. In the buggy, his wife was holding her two crying children, rocking them, trying to comfort them. From the darkness of the buggy, she stared back at the people streaming around them, running north on the road. Among them were Will and Winnie Ginder and their children.

To the south, sheets of flames were rippling across the sky above the village, illuminating the dark underbellies of the smoke clouds in flashes like lightning. Glowing balls of gas were detaching themselves from the main fire and undulating over the town like enormous, red-and-orange jellyfish, then sinking onto buildings, draping them with fire. Fire whirls were dancing out ahead of the main fire, knocking down trees and small buildings, sucking up dust and boards and branches, mixing them all with fire, and carrying them up into the black clouds.

Evan Hansen and the rest of the crowd plunged on across the wagon bridge. In the river below the bridge, Martin Martinson's wife, Ida, and their four daughters were trying to take cover in less than a foot of sawdust-covered water. Others climbed down the bank to join her in the river, among them Mary McNeil and her mother. Mollie McNeil, never seeing them, ran on over the bridge and kept on running north. Al Fraser stopped his wagon at the bridge. He, his family, the Andersons, and Jake Barden scrambled and slid down into the ravine. Almost immediately, though, they decided that the water was too shallow to save them, and they climbed back up to the wagon, clambered into it, and made their way across the bridge.

Axel Rosdahl pounded past them, clattering over the bridge, mounted bareback on a pony that he'd caught after abandoning the fire hose, determined to get home and help his family to safety.

By now, at the Eastern Minnesota depot, Bill Best, Harry Powers, and Ed Barry had almost completed a plan that Powers had hatched almost as soon as they had arrived in town at 3:25 P.M. Seeing Barry's freight train on the siding, Powers had proposed that they put Barry's locomotive on the back end of the passenger train. That way they'd have a locomotive on each end of the train, both locomotives pointed the wrong way but both able to back up with the passenger coaches and boxcars sandwiched between them. Barry had quickly assented. He'd picked up three empty boxcars and a caboose that were sitting idle on the siding. Pushing these in front of his locomotive, he'd coupled them and his locomotive to the back of Best's train.

Now it was just a question of when to leave.

Best knew that the trestle over the Grindstone was probably already burning, or soon would be, and unless he could clear it before it collapsed they would all die here on the tracks in Hinckley. Still, he held the train where it was. From the cab, he could see through the shimmering heat and smoke that people were still streaming out of the burning village and climbing aboard the train. Mothers were trying to shelter their children from the falling cinders with shawls and cloaks. A boy was carrying a dog that was bigger than he was. A middle-aged man was pushing another man in a wheelchair. Women were dragging furniture. A girl carried a parrot in a cage, the bird squawking and beating frantically at the bars of the cage with its wings.

Mary Anderson ran through the crowds alongside the train but could not find her family. She finally climbed into the caboose. Her cousin Clara was looking for her family as well. John Craig had found her a few minutes before in front of the Morrison Hotel, trying to help a sick neighbor make her way to the depot. He'd put both of them in the back of a dray with all the stragglers he could find and raced to the depot with them. Now, climbing into one of the passenger coaches, Clara found that they were packed with people. She began to work her way through the crowd, searching. She found Belle Barden and Belle's mother, but she couldn't find her own parents, or her sister, or her brothers anywhere.

Crouching in the doorway of his cab, trying to keep out of the worst of the heat, and calculating the odds, Bill Best watched the people streaming toward him from the village. He hopped down from the cab and started to jog down the length of the train to talk to Powers about how long they should stay, but Barry, in his cab at the far end, suddenly gave two sharp whistles—the signal to pull out. The train slowly began to back up. Best raced back to his cab, climbed in, and set the air brakes so that the train could go nowhere. Again Barry sounded two whistles, but Best continued to stare out across the town.

Barry's conductor, W. D. Campbell, ran the length of the train and bellowed up to Best in his cab, "Barry will cut off his engine and pull out!" Best looked at him and said, "I guess not." Again two whistles. Men he did not know jumped up onto the locomotive and shouted at Best, "Back up! Back up, or we will all be burned!" Best leaned out of the cab and said, "Boys, don't get excited. We're all right yet." But even as he spoke, he could see people in the village dropping in the streets, crumpling like rag dolls as waves of superheated air caught up with them. A few were already engulfed in flames, staggering, falling, rising again, taking a few more steps and falling again, flailing their flame-enshrouded limbs on the ground. Best's brakeman, O. L. Beach, climbed into the cab and shouted, "Barry says to let the brakes loose!" But looking down the line Best could see that both Powers and Campbell were still helping people up into the boxcars. Again two whistles. Best turned to George Ford, his fireman, and said, as if astonished by his own courage, "Good God, George! Will I sacrifice the train at last?" Finally, Best climbed down to the bottom step of the locomotive one more time and peered down the length of the train. Then he resumed his seat in the cab and released the air brakes, and the train started to back out of town slowly, lumbering toward the Grindstone Bridge.

The passengers in the boxcars closed the sliding doors to keep the flames and smoke out. The air in the cars was stiflingly hot, almost suffocating, but with the doors closed at least they were spared the sight of people running alongside the train, screaming for it to stop. In the coaches, passengers turned away from the windows, sickened, afraid they would recognize someone among those chasing the train. Leaning from the caboose, Mary Anderson watched in horror as people with hair and clothing in flames ran up the tracks behind the receding train. As the train approached the bridge over the Grindstone, a fancily dressed young man on horseback galloped up alongside the train. Passengers on the vestibule of one of the coaches reached out toward him, hoping to catch him when he jumped. But as they shouted and held out their arms, the horse shied away from the train, and horse and rider careened off into a mass of flames.

Just after 4:00 P.M., Best cleared the bridge with almost five hundred souls aboard. As he watched, houses in the northern end of town exploded in flame, one after the other, the walls seeming to melt away in an instant, revealing bedsteads and kitchen tables inside. The roof of the saw shed in the Brennan mill yard collapsed a quarter of a mile to the southwest, the hogsheads full of water that had been set along the roof tumbling into the inferno that the mill had become. Ahead of him, more people, mostly settlers from the surrounding homesteads, were running out of the woods toward the tracks. He whistled to Barry up front to stop, eased back on his throttle, and applied the air brakes again. The train slid to a stop in a clearing alongside a dry marsh, and more people began to climb aboard. Four minutes later, Best whistled to Barry again and released the air brakes, and the train resumed backing through the smoke-filled woods, toward Sandstone, picking up speed. Already, Best was starting to worry about the Kettle River High Bridge at Sandstone.

Behind him almost all of Hinckley was now in flames.

People were still alive in the town, though. Peter Knudsen, Hinckley's Presbyterian minister, and his wife were crouched under a wagon that had just caught fire. The two of them had spent the last half-hour leading people toward Best's train. Encouraged to board the train themselves, while they still had a chance, they had refused, the Reverend Knudsen saying, "No, others are left in the village. We must go back." There was no going back now, though, and with the Best-Barry train gone there was only one chance for survival. Even before the train had pulled out, some villagers had run past the tracks, disregarding the shouts of those on the train, preferring to take shelter in the shallow, fetid water at the bottom of the gravel pit.

Now, crawling on hands and knees from under the wagon, the Knudsens made their way across the blistering hot gravel railway embankment and down into the pit, where more than seventy people were huddled together, sitting in the foul-smelling water with blankets and clothing draped over their heads. Many of them were men who a few minutes before had put their wives and children aboard the train and then turned back to see what, if anything, they could do for their town. A few were community leaders who believed that their standing in the village prohibited them from leaving the scene of a disaster. Angus Hay was here in that capacity. So was fire chief John Craig. And mayor Lee Webster was here as well, wondering about his wife. She must somehow have gotten on the train before he could find her, Webster thought.

Axel Rosdahl rode into the pit still mounted on the exhausted and now terrified stray pony he had found after abandoning the fire hose. He'd ridden the pony across the Grindstone to his family's empty house and back into town, riding hard, pushing the pony to advance into the face of the fire. Now he found his father, Ole, and brother Theodore sitting in the water in the pit. They shouted questions to each other over the roar of the wind and fire, but none of them knew where the rest of the family was.

The banks of the pit were lined with trunks dragged over the railroad embankment from the depot. Buggies and wagons, driven into the water before the horses were cut loose, were scattered around the edge. The horses, along with a few cows that had instinctively sought water, plunged through the water among the villagers, whinnying and bellowing, wild-eyed with fear. Dogs leapt in and out of the water, yelping and baying.

Across the tracks, some people had stayed in their homes too long. John Rodgers and his wife finally ran out of their house, dragging two-year-old Minnie and four-year-old Mary and carrying the still unnamed baby boy that Dr. Stephan had delivered a week ago today. But with no idea where to go, they simply started to run up the street. They made it only a few dozen feet before the flames pulled all five of them to the ground. Kate Grissinger and her daughters, groping for the wrought-iron fence in front of their home, finally gave up trying to find Bill and started running north.

In the Eastern Minnesota rail yards at the south end of town, temperatures now soared past 1,600 degrees Fahrenheit. More than one hundred boxcars full of wheat and manufactured goods erupted in flames. Steel rails and boxcar wheels began to melt, the streams of molten steel running together, gathering in glowing red puddles on the gravel railroad bed.

Twenty miles to the south, the northbound Saint Paul and Duluth Limited, with the 1,000 feet of extra hose Chief Craig had requested, was just pulling out of Rush City.

Out on the wagon road, those who had continued to flee north across the Grindstone made an astonishing and demoralizing discovery just after 4:00 P.M. The fire had leapfrogged them, and a quarter-mile ahead the woods on both sides of the road were engulfed in flames. Worse, the convection winds from the larger fire behind them were drawing the trailing edge of this new fire southward, back toward them. People now had to make split-second decisions. Some started back for the river, but they quickly found even more flames behind them than ahead. Some started running west through the woods toward the Saint Paul and Duluth tracks, remembering that Root's Limited was due in Hinckley at 4:05 P.M. Far more people, though, heard the whistle of Best's train screaming on the Eastern Minnesota tracks to the east and headed for it, running through tall marsh grass and taller willows.

By now Evan Hansen was quickly running out of choices, and chances. Between him and his home there was suddenly a wall of fire. Behind him there was an even greater wall of fire. Everywhere there was suffocating heat and blinding smoke. It was becoming difficult to breathe, to see, or to think. There was a thunderous roar coming from all sides, as if from an enormous waterfall or an avalanche of logs.

At some point, he made a choice and began to run through the dry marshlands heading east with 126 others toward the sound of Best's whistle. Somewhere near him in the smoke and confusion were his neighbor Louis Wold and his family—his wife and three children and his seventy-two-year-old father. The Wolds were all together in a cluster, running through the tall grass and the willows. Louis's wife, Olava, was pushing a baby carriage, and it bounced and lurched over the uneven ground.

By the time he got it over the wagon bridge, Al Fraser's wagon had caught fire. Leaping from it, Antone, Emily, and Charlie Anderson followed their father and mother, running east with the crowd toward the Eastern Minnesota tracks. As Antone ran, his derby hat flew off his head. He glanced up and saw it burning in the air, only the brim remaining, a small circle of fire floating above him against the black sky. Antone's father, John, and his brother Charlie raced ahead of them and reached a swampy clearing by the tracks only to find that the Best-Barry train was already moving again, fast. They waved and shouted as it went by, but the train had already picked up steam and quickly disappeared down the track. They didn't know that Clara was aboard nor, mercifully, did she see them from the coach. Charlie began running up the track after the train. John Anderson stumbled back to where the others were following and told Antone to follow his brother. He would stay here with his mother and sister.

Antone took off running and caught up with Charlie. The hot wind was blowing at his back so hard now that it nearly pushed him off his feet as he ran. It was almost as dark as night; only the flames behind and above him provided any light at all. Sparks and firebrands blew past him, traveling twice the speed at which he was running. The air smelled hot, ashy, and resinous. Out of the darkness a man appeared ahead of him, stumbling alongside the tracks, almost entirely engulfed in flames. Charlie shouted at Antone to cover his face with his hands, and he did. He was running blind now, into the utter blackness behind his hands. Behind him, from the direction of the clearing, Antone thought he heard men and women shouting. Suddenly, he tripped on a rail and fell by the tracks, sprawling in the gravel and then rolling down the embankment. He pressed his hands against a burn on his chest, then passed out.

Back on the wagon road Al Fraser, his family, and Jake Barden were still trying to figure out which way to go. Fraser had just cut the traces to turn the horses loose from his burning wagon when, in an extraordinary piece of luck, another team, pulling an abandoned wagon, loomed up out of the smoke. Fraser grabbed the traces, and all of them climbed aboard this new wagon and started to the east, cross-country. And then, still more luck. They found to their astonishment that there were four full barrels of water and a trunk full of clothes in the back. Pulling up short, and cutting this new team of horses loose, Fraser clambered into the back of the wagon and lifted each of his children into a barrel. Then he, his wife, and Jake Barden began soaking items of clothing from the trunk in the water and wrapping themselves in the wet garments.

A few dozen yards to the east, in the clearing, 127 people were standing in knee-high grass in what, in an ordinary year, would be a swamp. Even now, the soil was slightly damp, and the grass was green and cool-looking. People were huddled together in small groups among abandoned buckboards and overturned baby buggies. Clara Anderson's parents and sister were there. Whole families were there, including most of Evan Hansen's neighbors—all seven of the Wolds, all eight of the Costigans. Fractured families were there, too. Axel Hanson, after abandoning his broken-down buggy on the road, had somehow lost track of his wife and children, and he was there, searching for them. Ellen Donahue was there with her daughters Esther, Katie, and Mary, but she couldn't find her husband, Dan, the proprietor of the town's livery, nor her other two children. Worse, there were children who had been picked up along the road, thrown into the backs of wagons, and who could not find their parents nor anyone they knew. Almost everyone was crying or calling out for someone.

But there was fire on all sides of them now, and the heat was withering, searing their faces and forcing their eyes shut. With every minute that passed, the heat was becoming more unbearable. Instinctively, people got down on their hands and knees and pressed their mouths close to the ground, sucking in the cooler air. People prayed and cried and wailed. They gagged and retched on the smoke. Some simply sat in the grass, staring at the approaching flames as if they could see something through them.

Soon flames dropped down from the trees and danced along the edges of the clearing all around them, rippling through the grass that had looked so cool and green. They made a sharp crackling sound in the grass. Billows of sweet-smelling white smoke drifted up toward the black sky. Moaning, people rose and pulled away from the advancing flames, crowding each other, jostling each other as they pulled back, packing themselves together into the very center of the clearing.

But within moments, there was no more room to pull back and the flames were upon them, lapping at their feet, blistering their ankles and shins, racing up their clothing, slapping at their faces. One by one, the women's long dresses erupted—large, tangerine-orange blossoms of fire wavering in the smoky gloom. Everyone screamed, but the screams came out thin and unnaturally high-pitched. The withering heat had desiccated their vocal cords, pulling them taut like overstretched rubber bands. Grown men suddenly sounded like young girls. When the screams were over they had to breathe in, and when they did they inhaled flames and superheated air, sucking the flames into their very mouths. Then, clawing at the air, black silhouettes dancing among the orange flames, they began to die.

Fifty yards away, Al Fraser—crouched among the water barrels on his wagon—heard them. Years later he would still hear them, never able to forget the sound—the long wailing that rose to a crescendo of dry, brittle shrieks and then died out in less than a minute. Then, nothing but the roar of the wind and the fire again as he desperately splashed more water onto his children.

Chapter Six

RAGNAROK*

Swift as a shadow, short as any dream,
Brief as the lightning in the collied night,
That in a spleen unfolds both heaven and earth,
And ere a man hath power to say "Behold!"
The jaws of darkness do devour it up.
So quick bright things come to confusion.

—Shakespeare,
A Midsummer
Night's Dream

BY 3:45 P.M., MARIE HANSEN HAD BEEN WAITING TWO HOURS FOR
the moment when Evan would arrive with a wagon from Donahue's
livery. She'd packed the steamer trunk—the one she and Evan had
bought in Oslo years ago before he'd left for America. She'd carefully
wrapped her mother's china in her best linen. She'd packed all the
children's clothes, a few of her best dresses, Evan's Sunday suit, his
father's Bible, and his pocket watch. She'd put all their cash, a bit
more than $80, in her handbag, along with photographs of the chil-
dren just made in July by a professional photographer in Duluth.

With help from Helen and Josephine, she had dragged the
trunk and her sewing machine out to the wagon road and stationed
Ed there to watch them while she made a last sweep through the
house, to see if she'd left anything essential behind. Perched on top
of the trunk, Ed watched and waited for his father, but neither Evan
nor any of the other mill hands had come up the road out of the

_____
* Ragnarok, in Norse mythology, is the end of the world.

smoke for half an hour now. All afternoon a hot, withering wind had been blowing black smoke through the woods on both sides of the road, and now the wind was howling through the tops of the trees, tipping their tops over toward the northeast.

At about 3:50 P.M., when she came outside with the girls to look for Evan herself, Marie found that she couldn't see more than twenty yards down the road. Hinckley was obscured behind a black curtain of smoke. Facing into the wind, their long hair blowing back away from their faces, her girls were pale with fright. She shouted over the sound of the wind, telling the girls to fetch the milk cows. They ran off into the deepening gloom, moving toward the barn, their long dresses flapping against their thighs.

Peering into the stinging smoke, Marie finally made out a figure coming up the road, running, and she started down the road to meet him. But it wasn't Evan, not a man, not anyone she knew. It was a woman, and she was running barefoot, holding her shoes in her hands. Her face was black with soot, and her eyes were fixed on the road ahead of her. In her heavily accented English, Marie shouted at the woman, "Vat's happened? Vere are da men?" but the woman never broke stride, never glanced at Marie and Ed. She just plunged past, panting hard, eyes still fixed on the road before her. As the woman passed and disappeared into the smoke up the road, Marie saw that large patches of her dress had been burned from her back, and the flesh showing through was red and blistered.

Over the roar of the wind Marie could hear a low rumbling coming toward them from up the road. The girls appeared out of the smoke, each leading a cow. The cows lowed loudly, their pink, fleshy nostrils flaring wide into the smoke. Their mouths were slobbering, their enormous white eyes rolling from side to side as they pulled at their leads. Marie peered down the road again toward the rumbling. She could see flashes of orange behind the black curtain now, pillars of flame erupting out of the darkness. She looked at her children, who were looking back at her, questioningly. She looked down the road again. Then she turned to the children and shouted, "*Komme her!*"

For a few mad moments, Marie and Josephine tugged at the sewing machine, dragging its wrought-iron legs through the dust, trying to pull it up the road, but they got only a few yards before Josephine lost hold of her end and it toppled over. It hit the ground and exploded noiselessly, whatever sound it made carried away by the wind or covered up by the roar at their backs. Splinters of rosewood scattered in the dust. Wooden spools of bright-colored thread danced and jittered haphazardly up the road, borne along by the wind. Marie stared dumbly at them for a moment; then she turned and faced the fire again, squinting her eyes nearly shut against the driving smoke. Ed and Helen were ten feet back down the road, pulling at the steamer trunk, moving it two or three feet with each tug. Josephine was chasing after one of the cows as it lumbered down the road the wrong way, toward Hinckley.

The black curtain further south was parting now, and Marie could now see clearly for the first time what had lurked behind it. It was a wall of flame, a swirling monstrosity of fire, boiling and seething along the ground, rising up, crackling through the tops of the trees, and vaulting another hundred feet into the sky above them. Spirals of flame were detaching themselves from the main body of the fire and lurching forward, ahead of the mass, toward them.

Marie screamed out Josephine's name and ran back toward Ed. She grabbed his hand and dragged him off the road, plunging into the dark tangle of raspberry vines and tamarack growing alongside the road, leaving the steamer trunk behind in the dusty road. Helen and Josephine, holding hands, followed them into the brush.

Fire kills in several ways, depending on the circumstances. Some are much worse than others. The luckiest of fire's victims die in their sleep, something that is surprisingly easy to do. All fires consume large amounts of oxygen and emit large amounts of carbon monoxide. They may emit a number of other gases as well, depending on the fuel that feeds them, and many of these gases, like carbon dioxide and cyanide, can also kill. But carbon monoxide kills the overwhelming majority of fire victims. Because it is tasteless and odorless, sleeping victims often never awaken to see, hear, or smell the fire that kills them. The brain will scream out for more oxygen if carbon dioxide builds up in the lungs, but carbon monoxide is subtler. A stealth killer, it sets off no alarms. It silently fills the lungs and then—bonding to the hemoglobin in the blood 250 times more readily than oxygen to form a compound called *carboxyhemoglobin* (COHb)—it rapidly displaces the oxygen in the bloodstream. The brain and other vital organs are caught unawares. Suddenly deprived of oxygen, and having no other choice, vital organs such as the brain simply shut down, rather promptly. By the time the saturation of COHb in the bloodstream reaches 90 percent, death comes in minutes.

Unfortunately, death by fire is not always so easy. Fully conscious victims, if they are surrounded by both flames and adequate oxygen, may remain alert until the flames have reached them and begun to consume their flesh. Oxygen ordinarily represents 21 percent of the air we breathe, but we can generally maintain consciousness until that level falls to about 9 percent. Even if the flames themselves don't make it to conscious victims, it sometimes happens that those victims are forced to breathe superheated air—air that still contains some oxygen but is so hot that it burns away the soft tissues in their mouths, throats, and vocal chords. These people know, at least for a few moments, what it is like to be burned alive, both from without and from within. If victims do lose consciousness and therefore stay in one place and continue to breathe the hot gases for a prolonged period of time, the damage from these hot gases may extend into their lower respiratory systems. Then even their alveoli, the 300 million or so tiny air sacks that line the lungs and transfer oxygen to the bloodstream, may be burned away, a fate that many of the people in the dry marsh north of the Grindstone probably suffered. But fire has even worse to offer.

Fire always emits heat in the form of radiation. Radiant heat travels away from its source at the speed of light, so, for all practical purposes, it is felt instantaneously by anyone in the vicinity of a fire. This is the heat you feel on your face sitting in front of a fireplace on a cold winter's evening. If you raise a hand, or any other shield, between your face and the fire, the heat on your face disappears immediately. Remove your hand, and you feel the heat again, immediately. The radiation emitted by a fire falls away fairly quickly with distance, so if you move your chair across the room it is likely that you won't feel any noticeable heat on your face, though the air in the room may well be heated by convection from the fire. If the fire is big enough—say, a bonfire on a beach—you may have to stand quite a distance from it in order to be comfortable. But if it's as big as a forest fire, you may not be able to get far enough away from it fast enough to avoid being broiled alive. This is the unkindest way fire kills, by the sheer application of heat. It is only likely to happen when the victim has enough oxygen to breathe for a sustained period of time—thus remaining fully conscious—but is still near enough to an overwhelming source of heat to be killed by it. Fortunately, since large fires consume enormous amounts of oxygen, this is relatively rare.

It does happen, though. It happened now, in the mud at the bottom of the Grindstone River ravine, where Ida Martinson and her four daughters, ranging in age from two months to nine years, had taken shelter under the wagon bridge. The water was not much more than a foot deep there, but Ida was rolling her girls back and forth in the mud and what water there was, trying to keep them wet and cool as the fire roared overhead. There were other people down there as well—a young couple with their children, two young boys and a baby. And, a bit farther down the river, away from the bridge, Mary McNeil and her eighty-two-year-old mother. The air was relatively free of smoke in the creek as a current of fresh air was being drawn along the bottom of the ravine from somewhere to the east.

By a little after 4:00 P.M., however, the fire overhead had intensified dramatically as the main flaming front reached the bridge. The entire bridge erupted in flames, and within a minute the sanctuary at the bottom of the ravine became a death trap. As the heavy beams of the bridge blazed, the radiant heat scorched the creek bed and those closest to the bridge. Hearing screams, the older Mrs. McNeil peeked out from under the heavy shawls that her daughter had wetted and wrapped her in. Mother and daughter looked back down the creek in the direction of Ida Martinson and her daughters and the other young family, and they were horrified by what they saw and heard. As Mary McNeil would remember it later, "With heartbreaking screams, more like the cries of beasts than of human beings, these suffering ones writhed like worms in the mud as they endeavored to escape." But there was no escape. They were too far gone to rise and run; they could only scream and roll and flail their limbs under the searing heat.

There was nothing for them now but pain—pain that would not end, that could not be endured, but had to be, until they finally stopped screaming and their limbs slowly and finally came to rest in contorted, awkward poses.

Fighting their way through the dense undergrowth in the woods west of the wagon road, Marie Hansen and her children knew that the roaring presence off to their left was relentlessly closing in on them. They couldn't see it, but they could smell it and hear it snarling at them. Tamaracks and wild raspberry vines tore at their arms and faces. Holding up the hem of her full-length skirt with one hand and clutching her handbag and pushing branches out of the way with the other, Marie ran behind her children, herding them forward, shouting at them in urgent bursts of Norwegian to keep moving, to run faster. Drifts of white smoke stung their eyes and made it impossible to see more than ten feet in any direction, and soon, Marie could no longer be certain in what direction they were moving—could not be sure that they weren't running directly toward the fire.

Ed tripped and tumbled facedown into a raspberry patch. He began to cry as he flailed about, trying to extricate himself. Marie bent over him, tore away his shirt, yanked him to his feet, and pushed him forward, bare-chested now, into the lacerating brush. Josephine and Helen were already out of sight.

Somewhere out there in the murk not far away, three young mothers—Mrs. John Westlund, Mrs. Henry Lind, and Sophie Wacke—were also trying desperately to figure out how to save their young children. Surrounded by fire, blinded by smoke, terrorized by the crying of the children, they finally did what so many others had done and herded all eight of them into the Westlunds' storm cellar. There, they sat in the dark, listening to the terrible unknown come closer and closer.

At 4:05 P.M., Jim Root's passenger express, the Limited, cleared the top of Hinckley Big Hill and began the very gradual mile-and-a-half descent into Hinckley on the Saint Paul and Duluth line. For the last ten miles or so, the smoke, heat, and wind had been intensifying at an alarming rate. A Saint Paul doctor back in the coaches, W. H. Crary, was astonished by what he was seeing through the windows. As they approached Hinckley, he calculated that some of the wind gusts driving the smoke must have been blowing at speeds of up to 80 miles per hour. As Bill Best had noticed half an hour ago, though, Root saw now that the smoke on the ground immediately in front of him had lifted some as they'd approached Hinckley. Like Best, he began to think that the worst fires were behind him. If he took on water in Hinckley without delay, he figured he would still be able to arrive in Saint Paul on time that evening.

Root was about to remark on this to his fireman, Jack Mc-Gowan, when he saw a crowd of people streaming up the track directly toward him. Immediately he eased off the throttle and hit his air brakes, lest he run them down. With the air brakes thumping loudly under the cars and the blast pipe on the locomotive billowing smoke and steam, the train came squealing to a stop in the middle of a clearing northwest of Hinckley's commercial district. Through the smoke and shimmering heat waves, Root saw that more people were running out of the woods to his left, stumbling across the clearing through knee-high grass. All told, there appeared to be more than two hundred people converging on the train. Root, with what seems to have been characteristic understatement, turned to McGowan and said, "Jack, there is something wrong."

As the people drew nearer, Root could see what his passengers back in the coaches could also see. Many of those coming out of the woods were half naked, their clothes torn to shreds. They were wild-eyed with fear. Some of those running up the tracks were black with soot and ashes. As they approached the train, Root realized that many of them were shouting incoherently, some making incomprehensible animal sounds. Root swung himself down from the cab as an older woman and her two daughters staggered up the tracks to him. He asked them what exactly was happening, but pushing past him, heading for the coaches, the woman simply panted out, "For God's sake, will you save us?" More people were surging past him now, climbing onto every car down the length of the train. John Blair was out of the chair cars toward the rear of the train with a step stool on the ground, helping people aboard. Root stopped an acquaintance, Benjamin Bartlett, proprietor of Bartlett's Eating House in Hinckley, as he was climbing into a coach, and Bartlett said, "Jim, everything is burned up. Everything is burning, including the depot."

Turning and looking back down the train again, Root saw that his conductor, Tom Sullivan, was running toward him. To his right, people were still swarming across the clearing, but as they approached the tracks they were piling up behind a barbed-wire fence, uncertain what to do. Some of them began to kick the strands of wire off the posts, creating openings for people to crowd through. Farther down the line, though, women were throwing small children over the fence and then crawling underneath, the barbs ripping open the backs of their dresses.

Marie Hansen and her children were among those crowded up against the fence. Marie threw her handbag over the fence, grabbed the lowest strand of wire, and pulled it up so her children could crawl under. Then she scrambled under herself. But by now her eyes were swollen nearly shut by the smoke, and she was nearly blind. She crawled along the fence line, groping for the handbag. Josephine bent over her, screaming at her to get up, to get on the train. Finally, following Josephine's voice, she crawled on all fours up onto the gravel railway embankment, leaving the handbag behind. Then she, Josephine, Helen, and Ed were all in the rear chair car, standing in the aisle, wedged in among dozens of men, women, and children, many of them screaming or calling out for one another, or for those that weren't there.

Outside, Tom Sullivan reached Root at the head of the train. As he'd run the length of the train he'd seen that there were already flames here and there on the underside of the coaches, wherever spots of grease had made the wood especially flammable. Nearly breathless, he shouted, "Jim, we can't stay here long; we have to go back to a place of safety!"

"Look after the end of the train," Root replied. "I am going back to Skunk Lake."

"We will never get there alive."

"Then we will die together," Root shouted back by way of conclusion, and he climbed up into the cab of the engine.

In the days and weeks following the firestorm, a number of people would sharply question both Jim Root's and Bill Best's judgment and actions in continuing to take their trains south toward Hinckley despite what was, in retrospect, clear evidence of a major fire ahead of them. Each of them, after all, had carried more than one hundred souls from areas of perfect safety into the very jaws of the advancing firestorm and thus placed all of them in extreme peril. Neither Root nor Best, though, seems to have given any thought at all to sidelining or reversing their trains until they were literally surrounded by flames.

Several factors probably caused both of them to act as they did. For one thing, until the last moments neither of them perceived what he considered unambiguous evidence of a significant fire down the line. Neither actually saw any flames until he was almost in Hinckley itself. The soaring heat, heavy smoke, and gusting wind that they both experienced while approaching Hinckley—while more extreme than usual—were far from unheard of in the woods of northeastern Minnesota at this time of year, when numerous fires were almost always burning somewhere along their routes. Both of them, like most of the settlers in the area, simply took this to be another hot, dry, smoky day in the north woods.

Then, too, both were career railroad men, and like most of their tribe they were devoted to the twin imperatives of schedule and orders. Even as Root pulled his train to a stop north of Hinckley with hundreds of settlers streaming toward him in the smoke, one of his first and principal thoughts was whether he would still make Saint Paul on time. Even as Best watched the south end of Hinckley erupt in flames, he wondered first how he was supposed to get his train and his passengers out of there without orders from Duluth. Only desperation would ultimately lead both of them to throw out their schedules, violate their standing orders, and take things into their own hands.

But there's another factor that must also have played into the thinking of both men that day. Like nearly everyone else lucky enough to have steady work following the financial panic and depression that had gripped the nation during the preceding months, they didn't want to do anything that might cost them their jobs. They certainly weren't going to take it upon themselves to sideline a train full of angry passengers because of some smoke, and then have to explain that to their superiors.

That summer had been a desperate time for many American workers, and particularly for railroad workers. Just weeks before, on July 12, the railroad men had finally been defeated in one of the bloodiest and cruelest labor disputes in American history. They had lost the best chance their generation would know of improving their working conditions and advancing their meager fortunes. Now they were at the mercy of the men in white collars who owned and operated the railroads, and they knew it.

The battle had started and ended in Pullman, Illinois. As the depression of 1893–1894 took its toll on his business, George M. Pullman of the Pullman Palace Car Company had slashed the wages of the workers in his company town while hiking the rates he charged them for rent and utilities. Outraged, and organized by the labor activist

Eugene Debs, the Pullman workers walked off their jobs on May 11, 1894. The strike quickly spread nationwide as railroad workers across the country refused to work on trains pulling Pullman cars. In separate incidents in May, both Bill Best and Jim Root had walked away from their locomotives, leaving their passengers temporarily stranded. Root was arrested and fined but, having made his position on the Pullman issue clear, he promptly returned to work, as did Best. The strike continued to spread, however, and it soon involved more than 260,000 railroad workers across the country. By early summer, interstate commerce was largely paralyzed. Battles broke out between workers and state and local troops in twenty-six states. More than forty people were killed. On July 4, strikers burned hundreds of rail coaches in Illinois. Finally, President Cleveland sent federal troops to Illinois protect the Pullman plant, and within days the strikers and their cause were crushed.

Even after the strike officially ended on July 12, George Pullman continued to punish those who had dared to defy him. By late August, almost six thousand people—the men Pullman had blacklisted and refused to hire back, along with their families—were near starvation for lack of any means of support. Outraged, John Altgeld, the governor of Illinois, wrote Pullman a series of letters describing the plight of the families and appealing to him to rehire the workers:

> There are nearly six thousand people suffering for the want of food—they were your employees—four-fifths of them women and children—some of these people have worked for you for more than twelve years. I had assumed that even if they were wrong and had been foolish, you would not be willing to see them perish . . . As you refuse to do anything to relieve suffering in this case, I am compelled to appeal to the humanity of the people of Illinois to do so.
>
> Respectfully yours,
> John P. Altgeld

But Pullman would not budge. Eventually the families, defeated, moved away from Pullman as people of goodwill helped them find jobs elsewhere.

In the end, George Pullman paid a heavy price for his policies and practices. He died a bitter and fearful man just three years later. Concerned that his body might be stolen and desecrated by his former employees, he gave careful instructions for his burial. His lead-lined casket was covered with an inch of asphalt, placed in a deep pit into which was poured eight feet of concrete, topped by eight steel rails, and finally, another layer of concrete. Thus was George Pullman finally and forever buffered from the insolence of his employees.

By the end of August 1894, the lesson of the Pullman strike was clear to working people everywhere, and particularly to railroad men: capital had won, labor had lost, and the latter could expect no quarter from the former. It was a lesson that must have been fresh in the minds of Bill Best and Jim Root as they sat in their locomotive surrounded by flames, trying to figure out how they were going to get out of this with their jobs, and their lives.

From the vantage point of his cab sitting on the Saint Paul and Duluth line north of Hinckley, Root could see that a wall of flames was advancing toward him out of the south, perhaps 150 yards away. People were still running up the tracks toward him, but he could see that many of them didn't have a chance of making it; the flames were closing in on them too fast.

Mollie McNeil appeared out of the smoke by the door of the cab, panting and exhausted, her dress burned through in several places. Then she fainted onto the gravel siding. McGowan pulled her into the cab and revived her with some water, and a male passenger carried her back to the baggage car.

Sullivan climbed aboard the first-class coach and tugged the bell cord three times to signal Root to back up. On the third pull it felt as if the cord had burned through, so Sullivan pushed his way forward into the smoking car and gave one more tug. In the cab, Root threw the Johnson bar into the reverse position and opened the throttle, and the train slowly began to back up, with over three hundred passengers on board now. As they realized that the train was leaving, many of the passengers in the coaches implored Sullivan to stop the train, to hold it until their husbands, wives, fathers, children, and friends could get there and get aboard.

Twenty yards down the tracks, Bill Grissinger was one of those running toward the train. He'd run hundreds of yards now, all the way from his home in Hinckley, along a track strewn with suitcases and bags. He could just make out the headlight at first, then the wavering form of the train's boiler, looming ahead out of the smoke. He had not expected to find a train; he had merely been running away from the thing that was chasing him, hoping to find his mother and sisters.

Almost as soon as he saw it, he realized that the train was already backing up, moving slowly but inexorably away from him. He ran harder, pounding along the gravel right-of-way. As he caught up with the locomotive and gradually passed it, he realized that someone running behind him was clawing at his back. A hand grabbed at his shoulder and got hold of the wide collar of his sailor suit. Grissinger made a lunge for the handrail on the first coach, and the collar ripped loose in the anonymous hand. Pulling himself up onto the first step of the landing, he glanced back and saw that several men were running alongside him, but they were starting to lose ground to the train. One of them made a grab for the handrail, but the effort threw him off his feet. Grissinger watched over his shoulder as the man rolled down the bank into the dry brush alongside, coming to rest on his back, lying there, staring up at the train as it pulled away. Grissinger clambered up the steps, opened a door, and stepped into the coach full of people. He quickly scanned the faces, looking for his mother and his sisters.

Then something hit the train. Something big.

Nobody aboard the train that day knew what it was that struck them, but in account after account witnesses later reported that a sudden and enormous blast of flames rocked the train and blew out many of the windows. In retrospect, it's possible to piece together what must have happened. All summer, lumber had been accumulating in the Brennan lumberyards. With no kiln in which to dry the cut lumber, the mill hands had stacked boards, posts, shingles, and beams in huge piles to air-dry in the yards. By the end of that exceptionally hot August, all twenty-eight million board feet of finished lumber in the yard had been baked drier than would have been possible in the best of kilns, and yet drier still.

With a firestorm boiling through the village just south of the mill, the ambient temperature in the yards must have soared, and the stacked lumber must have rapidly approached its kindling point of nearly 700 degrees Fahrenheit. At about 4:15 P.M., with the saw shed already fully engulfed in flames, the entire twenty-eight million feet of lumber stacked in the yards must have suddenly and immediately ignited, much as Apache Ridge in Idaho would ignite all at once seventy-three years later.

The result seems to have amounted to an enormous explosion. The sudden updraft created by so much heat trying to rise into the atmosphere at once carried whole stacks of flaming lumber hundreds of feet into the air before spewing them out across the surrounding countryside, as survivors later reported. The convection winds pulling air toward the main fire in the village fed oxygen into the base of this new eruption of flame like the air jets that supply oxygen to a blast furnace. Within a few moments, the burning lumber released more energy than could immediately be discharged into the atmosphere above it, and a blast of superheated air rushed laterally away from the center of the fire, much like the thermal pulse from a small nuclear detonation.

Perhaps a quarter of a mile to the north, Root's train was just gaining a full head of steam when the blast wave slammed into the train. It blew out every window on the west side of the train and rocked the coaches nearly off the tracks. It punched out the windshield in Root's cab. Out of the corner of his eye he saw the plate of glass carried over his head to the top of the cab where it shattered. Shards of glass cascaded down onto him, slicing open his face and the left side of his neck.

As the train backed into the cut at the top of Hinckley Big Hill, Root heard shouting and he saw three men down the track, running through the smoke toward the receding train. He began to apply the air brakes, but then he realized that if he stopped now, the flames under the train were sure to burn through his air hose and render the train inoperable. So he released the brakes and shoved the throttle back into the open position. Two of the men managed to throw themselves onto the locomotive's pilot before the train regained its speed. Within a few hundred yards one of the two fell off, and Root watched helplessly as his body tumbled alongside the track before disappearing into the smoke. Then things began to go black for Jim Root. In the stifling heat, and with the floor of the cab already sticky with the blood slowly draining from the wound on his neck, he fainted, slumping over onto the throttle that he had been holding open.

In the coaches, many of the passengers who were already on the verge of hysteria now went over the edge. Some tried to crawl under the seats. Some fainted in the aisles. Most crowded, screaming and pushing, toward the east side of the train, away from the tongues of flame that were suddenly licking in through the broken windows on the west side. In the smoking car, one man raised his leg and kicked out a window on the east side. When he withdrew his leg, another man dove through the opening, disappearing into the flames outside. Yet another man attempted to follow him, but Tom Sullivan grabbed him and pulled him back into the car, nearly severing the would-be jumper's hand from his arm on the broken glass. The man stared dumbly at his bleeding wrist and asked Sullivan, "Can you do anything for my hand?" Sullivan turned away and began to work his way through the cars, bellowing at people to keep quiet, assuring them that everything was going to be all right.

It was a tough sell. People continued to try to press their way toward the doors unthinkingly, simply wanting to be somewhere other than on this train, no matter the consequences.

A few people kept their heads and began to take positive action. Some of the calmer and stouter men posted themselves in front of the doors, guarding against jumpers. A flaming pine knot flew in through a window and landed on the plush seat beside Bill Grissinger. For a few moments, he simply stared at it as it lay there, hissing and popping, but when the seat burst into flames he began beating at it with his bare hands, extinguishing the fire but burning his hands badly. Another seat began blazing a few rows ahead. A large man whom Bill Grissinger didn't recognize somehow wrenched a water cooler from its fastenings on the wall and, muscling his way down the aisle with his arms around the cooler, he upended it on the seat, extinguishing the fire. Women began to wrench cushions off the seats, soaking them in water from the water cooler and then holding the cushions up to the windows to block the entry of flames. Back in the rear chair car, Robert Bell stationed himself in the ladies' washroom, where he began to wet some towels and hand them out to men and women in the aisles.

John Blair moved from passenger to passenger, leaning over them, looking them in the eyes, calming them, helping them move away from the flames. As people began to gag on the smoke pouring in through the windows, Blair joined Bell in the washroom, instructing people to pass the wet towels down the aisle and to hold them over their faces.

It must have been a sudden and unexpected role reversal for Blair, a man who had had to be deferential to his mostly white passengers throughout his lifetime, and who now found himself more or less in command of the situation. And it must have been no less of a reversal for the passengers to find themselves looking now to this quiet, unassuming porter with his sweet, boyish face for strength and reassurance in the midst of the crisis of their lives.

It was even more of a crisis than most of the passengers yet knew. By now, every car in the train was on fire to some extent. The baggage car was fully engulfed, and flames were streaming off the roofs of several other cars. The undercarriages of most of the coaches were also on fire, and the coal in the tender had begun to burn ferociously.

Worse, the train was slowing down dramatically, losing its race with the fire outside. As more flames began to reach in through the shattered windows, Tom Sullivan started to wonder what Root was thinking up there in the cab, why he was slowing down now of all times.

In fact, Root wasn't thinking or doing much of anything. He'd been out to the world for the last mile and a half, slumped forward in his seat, his weight slowly closing the throttle. His fireman, Jack McGowan, had taken refuge in the water reservoir on the tender, poking his head out through the manhole from time to time to see whether the train was still moving. By now, though, the train was slowing nearly to a crawl, and Root was hanging over the controls with his head swinging from side to side.

McGowan realized that he needed to see what he could do to help Root. Crawling out of the water tank and reaching out to steady him, McGowan dripped some water on Root's bloodied face. That awakened Root, who croaked out, "My God! Give me some more of that." McGowan poured more water over Root's head, and the engineer began to revive. Looking at the gauges, he saw that in leaning forward on the throttle, he had cut off much of the steam to the cylinders. The gauge was down to 95 pounds of pressure, far less than the 145 pounds usually exerted to maintain maximum speed. He threw the throttle back open and the train began to pick up speed. Looking now at his hands, he saw that they were red and terribly swollen, and he realized that he had been gripping the blistering hot metal throttle the whole time. He told McGowan to fetch another pail of water, shouting, "My hands are all burnt. I don't dare rub them for fear of rubbing the flesh all off."

As the train regained speed, the resulting rush of air fanned the flames. A torrent of fire from the burning baggage car washed back over the tender and the locomotive, and things began to deteriorate again back in the coaches. The transoms overhead in many of the cars began to crack open, and flames slithered in from above, fluttering along the ceilings and forcing the passengers to crouch on the floors. People's clothing began to smoke and smolder from the heat radiating down from the ceilings and up from under the cars. The air in the coaches was oven-like now, and it smelled of hot metal and burned fabric. The windows on the east side of the train began to implode from the still-greater heat outside, popping inward one by one with a shower of glass, and flames reached into the cars from both sides now. Screams erupted whenever an especially long flame flew into a car, flapping its orange wings over the passengers' heads as if to grasp its prey and pull it back out the window.

There didn't seem to be anywhere to go to get away from the flames. One of those who would survive the day, a Mrs. Lawrence, later remembered the moment. "The wild panic was horrible. There was no humanity in it. Every fear-crazed person was for himself, and they did not care how they got out of the swirling, rushing avalanche of flames."

In their chair car, Marie, Josephine, Helen, and Ed Hansen crouched on the floor between two rows of seats. Marie's stinging eyes were clenched tight. She spread her arms out over the backs of all three of her children, trying to shield them from the pushing crowd as much as from the flames.

In the other chair car, John Blair had found a chemical fire extinguisher. He began to stride up and down the aisles, ordering people to lie down and then sprinkling them as they lay prostrate on the floor between the chairs. In their coach, senator Frank Daugherty's son Otto turned to his father and said, "Have we got to die, Papa?" Daugherty was just beginning to assure him that all would be well when a large man stood up and pushed his way up the aisle, shouting, "We are all going to heaven together!"

Up in the cab, Root started to slow the train considerably, deliberately this time. Leaning out of the locomotive's open doorway, his head and face blasted by heat, he peered back down the length of the train, watching for something. Finally, through the smoke, he made out a glint of water alongside the tracks. He hit the air brakes hard and the train lurched to a stop. This was what he'd been hoping to reach, Skunk Lake. It wasn't really a lake so much as a marshy bog. The railroad embankment bisected it, with perhaps two acres of shallow, muddy water on the east side and another acre or so on the west side. Surrounded by a margin of cattails and knee-deep black muck, the water in the smaller, western portion was deeper than in the eastern portion, though probably not much more than three feet deep at most—scant protection from the inferno that was bearing down on Root and his passengers.

As the train came to a stop at Skunk Lake, it was perhaps ten minutes ahead of the main fire, which was closing in rapidly from the south. In advance of the flaming front, spot fires were already burning here and there in the pinewoods surrounding the lake. More immediately threatening than either the advancing main fire or the spot fires, though, were the fires that had been burning on the undersides and along the roofs of the coaches. With the train stopped, flames now began to billow out from underneath the train, making it nearly impossible to get down the steps from the vestibules. McGowan tried to help Root out of the locomotive, but Root snapped at him, "Leave me alone and go help the passengers into the water."

"You can't live here," replied McGowan.

"Go!"

McGowan grabbed a bucket and leapt out of the locomotive. Dredging muddy water from alongside the track, he raced from one coach to the next, throwing water onto the steps as bewildered passengers began to emerge from the front coaches. Sullivan, running toward the front of the train, took the bucket from him and began to bail water onto the steps of the coaches and chair cars further back while McGowan helped people out of the first two cars. John Blair was out of the train now, too, next to the furthest-back chair car, holding another fire extinguisher. As people clambered down the steps, Blair stopped each of them, spraying their clothes down before letting them pass. Robert Bell stood beside him, flinging buckets of water onto the steps.

Most of the passengers had no idea where they were, nor why they had stopped here. Many assumed that the train had simply run out of steam or that something was obstructing the track and that it could go no further. For the most part, they believed they were about to die. In the cars, they shouted and pushed at each other, trying to get to the doorways. They emerged through flames to an unpromising landscape of driving smoke and withering heat. An enormous rumbling sound was bearing down on them from somewhere out there in the smoke, somewhere down the tracks.

When Mollie McNeil emerged from the train, her already-singed dress caught fire almost immediately, but she found herself on a short section of trestle over one of the marshier portions of Skunk Lake, so she simply dropped into the water and mud below. There, face-to-face with a snake that had taken refuge in an old barrel a few feet from her, she began rolling back and forth in the mud to extinguish the flames.

C. A. Vandaveer, an Iowan, took a nightshirt from his valise, soaked it in water from a cooler, wrapped it around his head, and stepped out into the maelstrom of smoke and fire. He hesitated, unsure of which way to go. Where he stood, flames were rolling up from both sides of the track and arcing over the roof of the train. A woman near him shrieked, "Help me! Help me! I am burning," and streaked by him, her long hair in flames. Vandaveer tackled her. He removed the wet nightshirt from his head, used it to extinguish the flames, and then wrapped it around the woman's head.

Most people began to stagger and stumble toward the sheen of water, but they encountered another barbed-wire fence, and again they began to pile up in front of it. Marie Hansen and her children climbed down from the rear chair car, helped by Blair. Marie could see almost nothing, but she herded her children in the general direction that most other people seemed to be going, down the embankment to the west.

Blair's fire extinguisher ran dry. He cast it aside and ran down the embankment to the barbed-wire fence. He and some of the passengers began kicking the strands of wire off the posts and hollering into the smoke and wind, urging people to come his way.

Bill Grissinger was one of the last off his coach. Hearing Blair's booming voice, he headed toward it, crawled under the barbed-wire fence, and slid down the embankment to the edge of the marsh where he waded out through the black mud to the open water. The adults around him were knee-deep, struggling through the mud; he was nearly up to his waist and it was harder going for him, but he finally made it to the middle of the lake. He settled into the cold water and, turning to face the train, he saw that all the coaches were now fully engulfed in flames. With the cold of the water settling into his bones, he realized for the first time how hot his burned hands were. He tried not to think about it, but he knew that his mother and sisters must be dead somewhere back in Hinckley, and the realization of it washed over him again and again in waves, like nausea.

By now, McGowan had returned for Root in the locomotive. The tender, immediately behind the locomotive, was half full of blazing coal, and the heat was ferocious as he approached, but he could see Root, half conscious again, slumped in the engineer's seat. Shielding himself as best he could, McGowan managed to get a hold of Root's coat and drag him from the cab and down to the lake.

Everyone now appeared to be out of the train. But, in fact, not everyone was. A young man named Albert Speyer, running through the mud toward the water, suddenly pulled up short and said to his badly burned companion, George Sjoqvist, "Did you hear a child crying?" Sjoqvist said no, but Speyer was already running back toward the train when suddenly, everyone within earshot heard screams coming from one of the burning cars. Speyer paused several times, trying to ascertain which car the screams were coming from. Then, without any further hesitation, he approached a car, part of which had already collapsed in flames. He kicked at the flaming splinters on the ground, shielding his face with his arm, and disappeared into the flames. Sjoqvist and the others who were aware of this latest drama stood watching, transfixed in the heat and the wind and the smoke.

A few moments later they saw something white moving through the flames, but it disappeared in a swirl of black smoke. Then it reappeared, and Speyer staggered from the fire in his shirtsleeves, carrying a dark bundle. His hair was singed, his shirt and trousers were largely burned off, and his face, throat, and hands were badly blistered, but he had a young girl wrapped up in his coat. "I got her out alive! I got her out alive!" he exulted over and over again as he carried her down to the water.

North of the train, Tom Sullivan, Robert Bell and his daughter Josie, Annie and John McNamara and their sons, and a handful of others were running up the tracks. Sullivan was determined to get to the next telegraph station, at Miller, two miles up the line, to summon help. The others, apparently unaware of the lake, were just running for their lives. A couple of hundred yards behind them the main fire was following, rolling toward Skunk Lake, towering at times 100 to 150 feet above the ground.

Minutes later, it reached the lake. For the next hour, the wind shrieked as waves of flame and superheated air washed over Skunk Lake. With each new wave, people ducked under the water, or as far underwater as they could. One of the first waves caught Bill Grissinger unawares, and his right ear was scorched. But he hardly noticed. He was simply too scared. Marie clutched Ed in her arms, both of them up to their necks in the water. Josephine and Helen clung to them.

With her eyes now swollen shut, Marie was effectively blind. Hers was a world of startling sensations. There was the cold grip of the water below and the melting heat of the air above. There was the stinging smell of wood smoke and the fetid smell of mud. There were screams and moans and curses, and the relentless roar of the wind in the background.

And, closer, warmer, more intimate, more pressing than anything else, there were the pleadings of her children, whispered desperately into her ears.

Chapter Seven

UNDER THE STONE

Every man's work shall be made manifest:
for the day shall declare it, because it shall be revealed by fire;
and the fire shall try every man's work.

—*Saint Paul,*
I Corinthians 3

BY THE TIME ROOT'S TRAIN REACHED SKUNK LAKE AT ABOUT 4:25 P.M., Bill Best and Ed Barry had backed their two-headed combination train six or seven miles out of Hinckley on the Eastern Minnesota line. In dense, black smoke, they were feeling their way along the tracks toward the town of Sandstone, nine miles northeast of Skunk Lake. The main fire was perhaps fifteen minutes behind them now, but it was pursuing them relentlessly, traveling nearly as fast as they were. The whole way, Best had been chastising himself for having held the train so long at Hinckley. He was sure that at any moment now, the train would come to a burned-out bridge or culvert and be forced to stop—if there was even time to stop. With Barry's engine pulling from the front and Best's pushing from the back, stopping the train was no easy matter. Barry first had to signal Best with his whistle and then wait for Best's answering whistle before either could apply their brakes. Among other things, this meant that if Barry's lead engine plunged into a creek or ravine before he could sound his whistle, Best's engine would most likely keep pushing the passenger coaches and boxcars packed with people over the brink one by one, unaware of what was happening up front.

There was a pretty good chance that something of the sort was about to happen. Barry's eyes were so irritated by the smoke that he was largely blind. He had to rely on four brakemen—O. L. Beach, Peter McLaughlin, George Gilham, and Charles Freeman—who had volunteered to stand watch on his tank and coal tender out in front of the locomotive and holler or signal to him if they saw trouble ahead. But like Barry, all four of the brakemen were nearly blinded by the thick smoke. As they came to each bridge and culvert, they had to signal Barry to slow to a crawl so that they could try to see whether it was safe to proceed. None of them wanted to think about what would happen if it wasn't.

Aside from burned-out bridges, there was plenty of other trouble to watch for as well. Spot fires were erupting in the woods all around them. In places, the ties between the rails were already blazing, threatening to heat the rails to the point that they would spread or warp and derail the train. The wind was howling through the tops of the pines above their heads, knocking down trees—some of them already aflame—on both sides of the track and showering them with firebrands. The brakemen's positions on the tender and the tank were so exposed that they had to take turns dipping water out of the tank and splashing it on one another in order to bear the heat.

Approaching one forty-foot-high bridge just south of Sandstone, they came to what all of them had been dreading. The brakemen could see that its underpinnings were on fire, and they flashed Barry the "brakes on" signal. Barry sounded the whistle. A chill ran up Best's spine. He whistled back and applied his brakes, but was sure now that he was about to die, and, worse, that he would be held accountable by history for the deaths of hundreds. As the train came to a stop, he turned to his fireman, George Ford, and said softly, "George, the jig is up." They looked briefly at each other, but there was nothing more to say. They simply sat and listened as the deep rumbling behind them grew closer and louder.

A long, harrowing half-minute passed. A shuddering, wailing sound arose from the refugees in the coaches, who had no idea why they'd stopped out here in the burning woods but knew that it couldn't be good. The passengers packed into the dark boxcars were even more confused by the stop. Many thought they might be in Sandstone, but they were afraid to open the sliding doors to look—the heat outside was too great, the smoke too dense, the rumbling sound too close. Finally, Barry, recognizing the inevitable—that it was better to take a chance on the burning bridge than to sit waiting for the main fire to catch them—whistled "brakes off." Best gratefully released the brakes again and the train crept safely over the bridge.

Even with the train rolling again, though, panic and sorrow reigned in the coaches and the boxcars. Almost everyone on the train was separated from someone he or she loved. In the coaches, people sobbed in their seats, or prayed, or pushed their way up and down the aisles, calling out names. Dr. Stephan worked his way back and forth among the passenger coaches, still finding children and leading them to their parents, trying to reassure parents whose children he couldn't find. He found Mary Anderson in the caboose and led her forward to the baggage car where her parents and all five of her siblings—sitting dejected on the floor, believing they had left her behind in the burning town—rose to their feet and shouted with joy and astonishment when they saw her. "What a great blessing—we are all saved!" exclaimed her mother. There was little such comfort back in the boxcars, though, where overwhelming heat and smoke were mingled with confusion, grief, and terror in the suffocating darkness.

A few minutes after clearing the burning bridge, the combination train slid backwards into the depot at Sandstone, the whistles of both engines shrieking to attract the attention of the town's people. A short way up the line, the brakemen standing on Barry's boiler and tender could see the Kettle River High Bridge waiting for them, a spiderweb of thin steel and wooden beams stretching 850 feet across the gorge, carrying the tracks 132 feet above the water and the rocks. Beyond it they could see that a spot fire on the far side of the river had already begun to burn down into the gorge around the trestle's footings.

Sandstone was smaller than Hinckley, with only about 350 permanent residents and seventy-five buildings, but it was a prosperous and contented town. Perched on a bluff above the Kettle River, it boasted a large stone schoolhouse, a hotel, two churches, a few dozen homes, a dozen or so businesses strung along South First Street, and two small sawmills on the outskirts of town. The mills, though, were not the source of the town's good fortune. That came from the stone down by the river.

A little more than a billion years ago, a massive geological feature called the Midcontinent Rift ran from the northeast end of Lake Superior southwest into what is now Oklahoma. Essentially a tear in the earth's crust, it formed what geologists call a *graben*, a long valley caused by subsidence of the earth's surface. As ancient rivers poured into this enormous valley, long, narrow lakes laid, and over millions of years, thick deposits of sediment laid upon layer of sandstone beneath these lakes. Eventually the lakes were covered over by gravelly glacial till as ice ages came and went, and glaciers spread south from Canada and retreated. When the last—or at least, most recent—of these ice ages ended 10,000 years ago, the melting ice produced tremendous volumes of water that rushed over the landscape and carved deep channels down through the glacial till and into the hard sandstone bedrock underneath. In one of these old meltwater channels, the beautiful Kettle River now slides quietly and darkly over a cobbled bottom between sheer cliffs of ancient sandstone.

The buff-colored sandstone is exceptionally hard and durable. The sand of which it is composed—worked and reworked by ancient waves washing away softer minerals—is almost entirely quartz. Stone like this is the kind of stuff that is useful for building courthouses, schools, railway stations, and the mansions of tycoons, the kind of imposing buildings that America loved to build in the second half of the nineteenth century. It was also, as James J. Hill soon found out, first-rate for building the foundations of railroad bridges, and he was soon using it for that purpose as far away as Montana and Idaho. And so, on August 22, 1885, the Minneapolis Trust Company opened a stone quarry on the Kettle River and named Peter Peterson as superintendent. Soon dynamite blasts were rocking the hamlet on the bluff up above the quarry, and Sandstone began to flourish.

A steep wagon road, etched into the side of the cliff, led from the quarry down by the river up to the town. A stream of men in boots and overalls had been trudging up the road since 2:00 p.m, when Peter Peterson had told them they could go home if they wanted. By then, dark clouds blowing high overhead had all but blotted out the sun, making it too dark to work safely with heavy stone, block and tackle, and dynamite. Despite the black clouds and the heat, though, throughout the afternoon most people in Sandstone hadn't believed there was much to worry about, or if there was, what exactly they could do about it. Some didn't think there was a fire at all, but instead, that the odd conditions might be the result of an eclipse of the sun or a tornado brewing.

Now, at 4:30 P.M., just as people had done earlier that afternoon in Hinckley, Sandstone's residents were lighting lamps in their homes and businesses. Many of those who ventured outside carried lanterns, as if it were nighttime. At the Sandstone Congregational Church, Emil Anderson's congregation adjourned early. Growing curious and perhaps finally a little nervous about what was happening outside, they'd decided to cut short the farewell festivities for their young minister, saving him from having to deliver the farewell address that he had worked on for two weeks but had never really felt satisfied with. Finally freed from this obligation, Anderson said his good-byes, pumped hands, accepted the best wishes of his parishioners, and set off to pack for his trip to Chicago.

With all his men having left for the day, Peter Peterson finally made the long, hot climb from the quarry up to the town himself and settled into his own home to wait and see what would happen. Like everyone else, he lit the lamps in his house. The only flames he could see looking out his window were those of the small fire that Best's and Barry's brakemen had already noticed burning around the Eastern Minnesota tracks on the far side of the river. A light breeze seemed to be blowing out of the northeast, pushing the flames there back toward the river where they would obviously stop, so they didn't seem to be a threat, except possibly to the High Bridge.

At Mrs. David Lefebre's house, her brother-in-law, Peter Bilado, was helping her light the lamps. Bilado had brought his eight-year-old daughter Emma into town to spend the day with her cousins, leaving his wife, Louise, three other daughters, and their baby boy at home on their homestead four miles to the east. As they lit the oil lamps, Bilado was puzzling about something that he couldn't quite figure out. Earlier in the afternoon, starting at about 3:45 P.M., there had been a long, continuous wailing sound from down in Hinckley. It sounded as if someone had tied the lever to the Brennan mill whistle down and gone off and left it. Then, just before 4:00 P.M., it had stopped abruptly.

Out at their homestead, Louise Bilado was sitting on her doorstep, holding her baby boy in her arms, waiting for her girls to bring the cattle up from the pasture so she could put dinner on the table. She'd noted the dark smoke drifting overhead, and she'd heard from a neighbor that there might be a forest fire burning near Hinckley. And, like Peter, she'd heard the distant, eerie scream of the mill whistle, but none of this was terribly out of the ordinary, and she hadn't given any of it much thought.

Nearby, at John Samuelson's homestead, a wedding party was in full swing. Samuelson was preparing to give his daughter Minnie away to a young man named John Derosier. All afternoon the guests had been eating, playing games, drinking cider, and joking with the groom in Samuelson's front yard. Now, with only about an hour to go before the ceremony and with spirits soaring, people had moved into the small, wood-frame house to get ready for the big moment.

* * *

Aboard Best and Barry's train at the Sandstone depot, Clara Anderson and the other refugees from Hinckley peered out through smoke-darkened windows at the platform. Surprisingly, only a few people were at the depot to see why this strange combination train had backed up from Hinckley with its whistles shrieking. Those few stared back at the refugees, dumbfounded at the sight of the blackened coaches and the sooty, sobbing passengers.

They were even more astonished when the doors of the boxcars began to slide open, revealing more frightened and disheveled passengers packed into the freight cars, some of them coughing and gasping for air, others calling out to the bystanders, asking them for water and urging them to climb aboard. Passengers in the coaches began pulling down their windows and hanging out of the train, screaming at the strangely inert people on the platform, telling them to run, to get their families, to get on the train, to save themselves. Almost without exception, though, the onlookers simply wandered away in stunned disbelief.

The train's firemen worked their way through the coaches with buckets of water, doling it out, trying to revive passengers who had fainted. Best leaned out of his cab and saw Barry and the conductors jogging back down the train toward him. When they reached him, Barry called up to Best, "The conductors are going to stop here." Best was horrified, and he climbed down to argue with them. He knew that it was a matter of minutes before the thing that had been chasing them got here. "We want to get out of here as quickly as possible," he told them. "The fire is coming on us fast." The conductors, pointing to the spot fire beyond the Kettle River, said they were afraid that the supports for the High Bridge might already be on fire and that it would be unsafe to cross. This time, though, Barry was with Best, and the two engineers finally prevailed. Powers turned to Barry, and said, grudgingly, "All right, go ahead. You are running the engine and have the right of the road."

All this had taken five, maybe ten minutes. Barry and Best had expected that hundreds more would be trying to board the train at

Sandstone. But, in fact, almost no one had gotten aboard. Best tried to talk the few people who were still on the platform into boarding the train, but despite the increasingly obvious evidence to the contrary, they said that they didn't believe the fire would reach Sandstone, that they'd be all right, that they could take care of themselves, that they needed to look after their property, at any rate.

The refusal of Sandstone's residents to believe that they were in peril was not as unusual as it might seem. Psychologists in the United States and Great Britain who study the behavior of people in emergencies say that fires and other disasters often reveal the extent to which, without realizing it, we live our lives according to internal scripts. These scripts tend to dictate our expectations of what roles we and those around us should play—who should do what, and how—as well as what can be expected to happen at a particular time, in a particular place. The research also demonstrates that we are surprisingly unwilling to step outside of our expected roles, even when staring certain doom in the face.

When a fire broke out under the stands at a soccer match in Bradford, England, in May 1995, few fans took much notice at first. They were there to enjoy a game, and they weren't about to be distracted by some burning rubbish. A few took snapshots of the fire and then turned their attention back to the game. But the seventy-year-old structure was made of wood, and within a few minutes it was fully ablaze, with most of the fire concentrated toward the back of the stands. As people finally began to turn their attention from the game to the fire, they started to make their way toward the exits at the rear, the way they'd come in, and thus, the way their internal scripts called for them to leave. Almost immediately, all these exits were clogged with people, but more and more fans piled up behind them, trying to push their way through the tunnels. Down at field level, only a four-foot wall stood between them and the absolute safety of the wide-open playing field, but almost nobody took this simple and obvious escape route. When the fire was finally put out, fifty bodies had to be pulled out of the exit tunnels and adjoining areas.

In a 1979 fire at a Woolworths in London, most of the shoppers who were already standing moved out of the building as soon as they became aware of the fire, but people seated at the lunch counter were for the most part unwilling to follow them. They had waited for a seat, they were comfortably off their feet, and they finally had hot food in front of them. Their scripts didn't include leaving a perfectly good meal sitting on a counter and going back out into the rain. Ten of them died on or near their stools.

More recently, when fire broke out behind the stage at the Station nightclub in West Warwick, Rhode Island, in 2003, the band Great White kept playing and dozens of fans kept dancing even as flames climbed the walls in plain sight of all. The script called for a spectacular show, so the fans assumed they were seeing just that. Then, when they finally realized that the flames were not part of the show, virtually all of them tried to go out the way they had come in, even though it was almost immediately obvious that the main door couldn't accommodate everyone.

The fact is that when confronted by an emergency, at the very moment when thinking "outside the box" might pay the richest dividends, most of us, most of the time, think very much inside the box, paralyzed by our own expectations of how things should unfold.

And so it was that the astonished villagers at Sandstone, gaping at the desperate and disheveled refugees on the Best-Barry train, were not ready to throw down whatever they were doing. They had not yet seen what was coming at them. They could not yet comprehend it. It just didn't fit.

When it was clear that nobody else was going to board the train, Barry whistled "brakes off," Best climbed up into his cab to release the brakes, and the train began to creep northeast toward the Kettle River High Bridge. The bridge was extraordinarily long and high by the standards of the day. Even under the best of circumstances, engineers were required to wait for a signal from a watchman before crossing it, and they were required to proceed across at 4 miles per hour or slower.

As they backed toward the bridge now, Best and Barry could see that the fire on the other side had burned down into the gorge. Smoke was boiling up around the bridge, but from their positions in their cabs they couldn't see the underpinnings of the structure itself. As they rolled slowly forward, they both knew that for the third time today they were going to take their train and the hundreds of souls aboard out onto a bridge that might well collapse beneath them. They eased the train toward the brink of the gorge, watching for Wallace Damuth, the old man who served as one of two watchmen for the bridge. When he finally appeared out of the smoke, standing by the tracks just short of the bridge, he shouted up to Barry, "For God's sake, go on—you can cross it now. It will go down in five minutes. The fire has just struck it!"

Once again Best heard the all-clear whistle from Barry's engine up ahead of him. With his gut in his throat, he opened the throttle a bit, and the train rattled out onto the trestle. A dog belonging to the other watchman, M. W. Jesmer, ran out onto the bridge, chasing the train, yapping at it. Back in the coaches, Clara Anderson, Dr. Stephan, and the other refugees could see the dense white smoke billowing up around them from beneath the tracks. It was an eerie, unnerving sensation, and everyone froze, grabbing hold of something, anything solid. Many held their breath or closed their eyes, waiting to feel the floor fall out from under them. It was easier for those in the dark freight cars, who couldn't see the smoke and only knew that they were once again moving away from the thing that had tried to kill them in Hinckley. In less than a minute, Best's engine and tender, bringing up the rear, cleared the bridge, and the train began to pick up speed as both engineers threw their throttles open. Before they'd moved 2,000 yards down the line, the eastern end of the bridge collapsed into the gorge with a roar and a shower of sparks and flame.

The old watchman, Damuth, stood by the tracks, stunned and immobilized, seeming to realize for the first time what was about to happen.

In town, Emil Anderson was seriously alarmed now that the train had left. Within ten minutes of its departure, he and everyone else in town began to hear and see things that were new and entirely unexpected, things they couldn't, at first, quite make sense of. The sound was the same that people in Pokegama and Hinckley had heard earlier in the day—a deep, continuous rumbling, like thunder. Here, though, it was accompanied by a sudden reddening of the dark, smoky sky to the south, as if enormous, red railroad lanterns, shining up from below, were illuminating the heavens. Nobody in town had ever heard or seen anything like this. Many thought it must be a tornado, in addition to a fire, because a tornado was the only thing they knew that could make a sound like that.

Emil Anderson had no doubts about what it was. He began to run from house to house, pounding on doors, urging people to go to the river. At first, almost nobody did so. A few people began to pack cherished possessions into trunks. A few others decided to cover the haystacks that their cattle would need for the winter. But most people simply continued to go about their business, albeit nervously.

Anderson ran down the wagon road to the town's waterworks to warn the man in charge of the pumps there, August Swenson, pleading with him to go home to get his family. But Swenson, afraid, like so many others that day, that he might lose his job if he left, simply sent his eleven-year-old son home to fetch a lantern so that he could see the gauges on the machinery better. Anderson tried again with a family he came across as he ran back into town, but they pointed to a few barrels and washtubs of water, which they said they were confident would get them through anything that was likely to come.

When the firestorm hit Sandstone, a little after 5:15 P.M., it rubbed the town off the sandstone bluff on which it sat in mere minutes. As at

Hinckley, huge flaming bubbles of gas floated in over the town before the main fire arrived, exploding over the heads of terrified onlookers, raining fire down on their heads and setting both people and
buildings on fire. Minutes later, the flaming front rolled through the
streets, traveling on the ground but rising more than a hundred feet
into the sky. Since leaving the remains of Hinckley in its tracks, the
fire had surged unimpeded across nine miles of dense, new-growth
pine forests and tinder-dry slash, traveling over gradually rising
ground. It was more than ten miles wide now. With near hurricane-
force winds propelling it forward, it hit Sandstone even more sav-
agely than it had hit Hinckley.

It was as if a gigantic blowtorch had been suddenly turned on
the town. Along First Street, dozens of people ran out of their homes
and businesses and were simply incinerated before they could run
100 feet. Out at the waterworks, August Swenson and his boy
jumped into the well inside the pump house, but almost immediately
the flaming walls of the building were blown in, collapsing on them.
In the cellar of his house, where he and his wife and two children had
taken shelter, Frank Anderson began to dig frantically at the earthen
walls with his bare hands as the house above exploded in flames. He
was able to excavate only a few inches before the fire sucked the oxygen out of the cellar and he and his family suffocated.

Emil Anderson took off running toward the river ahead of the
fire, but he saw a lamp in a cellar window under a house and realized
that someone had taken shelter there, mistakenly believing, like so
many others, that a tornado was approaching. Anderson burst
through the door into the cellar and found three families huddled
there. He hollered at them that it was a fire, to run for the river.

They rose and rushed through the door—all but one young
mother holding a six-month-old baby. Her husband had bolted from
the cellar without her, and she emerged slowly, bewildered, not knowing where he had gone or what she should do. As she stepped outside,
an enormous blast of hot air slammed into the house, bowling mother
and child over, tumbling them twenty-five or thirty feet into a nearby

cornfield. Anderson ran to them and knelt beside the dazed mother, imploring her to let him take the baby. He'd save its life if he could save his own, he screamed into her face. She resisted at first, but then looked where Anderson was pointing, at the wall of flame advancing toward them, and thrust the baby into Anderson's arms.

Then he was on his feet, clutching the baby to his chest and running, stumbling down the hill, everything around him now on fire, the heat clawing at his back. Ahead of him was the home of his church's deacon, and again he saw a light through a window. He rushed in through the kitchen door and through the already-burning house calling out for the deacon, but no one was home. He rushed down the main hall and headed for the front door. It was locked. Still clutching the baby, he pushed at the door with his shoulders, kicked at it, slammed his whole body into it, again and again, until finally it gave way. Beyond the door, there were flames. But there were flames at his back, too, inside the house, rushing down the halls and up the staircase. He took a breath and plunged out through the door.

Almost immediately he was swept half off his feet and down the hill by the tremendous winds that were now howling through the Kettle River Gorge in advance of the fire. He flew more than ran for the better part of 1,000 feet down the long slant of the wagon road and came stumbling to a halt on the cobbled riverside. The banks were lined with people, hundreds of them, most of them too afraid of the swift flowing water to enter it yet. But Anderson's clothes were smoldering and he didn't hesitate. He staggered into the cold water and sat down, holding the baby's head and his own just above the surface. The cold water gripped his privates, his belly, and his chest like a vise, pressing the breath out of him and making him gasp. But it numbed the pain of the burns on his back. The baby was red-faced, bawling, its small face screwed up with fear and rage and shock.

As Anderson watched, a large boardinghouse set up for quarry workers near the river immediately below town burst into flames. Some burning haystacks nearby were lifted into the air and carried out over the river, smearing streaks of orange across the dark, glowering sky. Moaning as the flames billowed closer overhead, the lines of people along the banks began to move reluctantly into the water. There was no choice now. Over the roar of the fire, they could hear screams from up in the town.

Flames had cut off the wagon road as an escape option for those few who were still alive in town. Jesmer, the younger bridge watchman, had dragged a trunk full of his possessions out of his house into a potato field and abandoned it there. Now, he made for the High Bridge, or what was left of it. The middle span was made of steel, and it was still standing, but the eastern approach had entirely collapsed into the gorge and the western approach wouldn't last long. But Jesmer knew that there was a foot trail leading from near the western end down the bluff to a deep swirling pool on the river, where he had already sent his family. He started down, using his hands to shield his face from the radiant heat thrown off by the burning bridge. Partway down, he looked up and saw Damuth, the old man, looking dazed, walking along the tracks toward the burning bridge. Jesmer called out to him to come down to the river, but the old man just kept walking toward the flaming bridge as if he was in a trance, and Jesmer scrambled on down the path.

Peter Bilado and his daughter Emma were the last ones out of his sister-in-law's house. Taking Emma by the hand, Bilado raced with her across the front yard. They made for a ditch fifty yards away and, reaching it, flung themselves facedown into the grass at the bottom. But the grass began to burn. Bilado's hands were seared as he flailed at the burning grass, and getting to his knees, he shouted out to Emma, "We can't stay here!" Emma rose, looked around her with unseeing eyes, and ran toward the main fire. She looked around again, called out, "Papa, Papa!" and ran again, disappearing this time into the smoke and flames. In the ditch, Bilado covered his eyes with the burned and blistering flesh of his hands and sank back to the ground in the burning grass, the flames ripping at his clothing and his flesh. Cinders fell on his back like hot sand.

* * *

At the Bilados' homestead, Louise came out of the house at about 5:30 P.M., after serving her children dinner, and saw flames licking through the woods a quarter of a mile to the south. The wind was suddenly picking up. The tops of the tall pine trees all around her danced and bobbed wildly. Startled, she ran to their lean-to barn and turned their milk cows and horses loose. Then she hurried to fill some buckets at their well, planning to fight the fire when it reached the house. Almost at once, though, she abandoned that idea as the flames began to roar into the crowns of the pines to the south of her and she realized the magnitude of the thing she was facing.

Sprinting back into the house, Louise told the children they had to run for McKay's Lake, one of several ponds in the woods nearby. She took the baby in one arm and a single bucket of water in the other. Her oldest daughter, Flora, took a sheet and two blankets, and the two younger girls simply grabbed hold of their mother's dress. As they ran across the yard, the main fire was perhaps one hundred yards behind them. They clambered over their split-rail fence, but firebrands were raining down on them now, and Louise realized they'd never make it to McKay's Lake. She herded the girls into a large, freshly plowed rutabaga patch and made them lie down in the furrows. She wet the sheet with the water in the bucket, covered the girls and the baby, and ran back to the well for more water. As she returned, lugging the water, a burned and terrified deer bounded up to her as if looking for protection. It turned and ran a few feet and dropped in its tracks, kicked the air a few times, and then lay still, suddenly dead.

By the time she got back to her children, the wind was screaming through the trees and long tails of flame were streaming over their heads. The girls were clinging to the sheet, trying to keep it from blowing away. Flora shouted to her mother, "Are we going to die?" Louise shouted back, "Trust in God." She wet the two blankets in a bucket and tried to spread one over the girls, but the wind pulled it away and it sailed off into the woods. She managed to spread the second blanket and get underneath it, she and Flora on either side, the baby and the two younger girls wedged between them. But no sooner were they under the blanket than Flora, shouting that she was going to retrieve the first blanket, crawled out and stood up. Her mother called out to her, trying to make herself heard above the roar of the wind and fire, telling her to get back under the blanket, but Flora ran toward the woods. Before she could make it to the blanket her clothes erupted in flames and she crumpled to the ground. Louise, peering out from under the blanket, screamed as she watched her daughter, wreathed in orange, jerking and kicking on the ground, but her own hair and the upper part of her own dress were beginning to catch on fire and she had to beat at the flames with a corner of the blanket. By the time she could look toward Flora again, there was nothing to see but a swirl of smoke and flame dancing around something black and still.

The heat and wind had nearly dried out the blanket by now, and Louise desperately began to rub mud from under the blanket onto smoldering patches. Her baby boy, lying next to her chest, was turning blue and gasping for air. She took his head between her hands and breathed into his mouth, and he seemed to revive, kicking at her and wailing again. The other two girls lay motionless beside her, and Louise did not know if they were alive or dead.

On another homestead outside of town, a French-Canadian farmer, Oliver Dubois, hearing the approaching roar and seeing the black clouds rolling in overhead—and also believing that a tornado was approaching—climbed down into a twelve-foot-deep dry well. Within minutes flames were boiling overhead, and the air at the bottom of the well grew stifling and nearly devoid of oxygen. Gasping for air, he found that he could just barely breathe by excavating a small hole in the damp earth at the bottom of the well and pressing his face into it. As each hole dried out he had to shift position and dig a new one.

Nearby, at John Samuelson's place, everything was just about ready for the wedding ceremony. The guests had come in from the front yard and gathered in the parlor. Minnie Samuelson, the bride, was making final preparations. Her intended, John Derosier, was joking with his friends. There was music, and the house was full of loud conversation, everyone straining to hear and be heard over the music. No one could hear what was approaching outside.

When the fire hit, it hit all at once. It dropped down out of the sky, igniting the house all at once. Flames punched through the windows and reached into the house, sucking the air from the parlor with a huge rushing sound. People who just moments ago had been laughing, chatting, and flirting, screamed and pushed at one another, trying to get through the front door. They tumbled out across the wooden porch into the yard, where there was a patch of bare dirt, clear of flames for the moment. One of the guests spotted steps leading down into a root cellar a short distance away, and, making what for many had already been a fatal decision this afternoon, he shouted, "The root cellar can save us!" They all rushed for it, and they all made it in, slamming the wooden door closed behind themselves and locking it.

Within a few minutes, they began to realize that they might have made a bad choice. They were in utter darkness except for a bit of orange light flickering under the door from the flames outside. The air was stiflingly hot and getting hotter by the moment. In the dark, people were bumping into one another, pulling at each other, falling down. They could hear the roaring thing outside now, all too well. The door began to smoke and to char. Pieces of it began to fall away, and flames reached in through the holes, pushing people back against the far wall.

Then somebody felt something cool and wet in the dark and called out. It was a large can of fresh milk, one of twenty from Samuelson's cows. They dragged one of the cans to the door and began to ladle milk out with their hands, splashing it onto the door where it sizzled and smoked. The cellar filled with the sour stench of scorched milk, but they kept splashing the door, and it held together. Nonetheless, the heat continued to mount as the inferno outside baked the earth covering the root cellar. It quickly grew almost unbearable, and people began to splash and pour milk over each other.

It ran through their hair, under their clothes and over their hot skin, pooling in the dirt at their feet. In the darkness, as the worst of the fire overhead rolled on to the north, some of the wedding guests dropped to their knees in the puddles, and thanked God for this cold, wet, white blessing.

By 5:50 P.M., the ferocity of the fire at Sandstone began to ebb, but there was still tremendous heat in the air, and in the rocks. The roughly two hundred survivors huddled in the cold Kettle River were astonished when they heard sharp cracking sounds from the cliffs across the river. Large slabs of sandstone were breaking away and tumbling into the river. Wave after wave of superheated air slamming into it had fractured the rock face of the eastern cliff, and it was exfoliating, layers of it peeling off like so much dead skin from a badly burned body. Emil Anderson was still holding onto the baby that he had carried down to the river, but the combined effect of the burns he had suffered and the chill of the water he had been sitting in for nearly an hour had left him weak, and he was having trouble keeping his own and the baby's head above water. Seeing the baby start to slip underwater, someone nearby reached out and pulled both man and child into shallower water, and then sat behind them, propping them up.

Everyone in the river was bone cold, many shivering uncontrollably, some starting to slip into hypothermia despite the searing heat radiating down from the rock cliffs. Some were naked, or nearly so, their clothes having been ripped or burned from them as they ran for the river. Now and then someone cried out in pain, or in grief for someone just lost, but for the most part it was beginning to grow quiet on the river as the fire on the bluffs above them rumbled away.

Then, unexpectedly, they all heard a long, eerie wailing sound coming from above, from somewhere atop the steel center span of the High Bridge. No one could see what or who it was through the murk of smoke in the failing late-afternoon light. M. W. Jesmer, clinging to the rocks with his family in the deep pool below the bridge, thought he knew what it was, though. The old watchman, Wallace

Minnesota lumberjacks posing in front of their sleep shanty, 1893.
Reprinted by permission of the Minnesota Historical Society

Skidding white pine logs out of the woods on an ice road,
a hazardous business at best.
Reprinted by permission of the Minnesota Historical Society

Minnesota lumberjacks sharpening axes in their sleep shanty, about 1890.
Reprinted by permission of the Minnesota Historical Society

*The west side of Hinckley before the firestorm. The large two-story building
in the center is Hanson's Saloon and Opera Hall.
The second house from the left is Mary and Mollie McNeil's.*
Reprinted by permission of the Hinckley Fire Museum

The saw shed at the Brennan Lumber Mill, with ten hogsheads
full of water arrayed along the roof in case of fire.
Reprinted by permission of the Hinckley Fire Museum

The men of the Hinckley Fire Department in their dress uniforms,
displaying their new Waterous fire apparatus.
Reprinted by permission of the Hinckley Fire Museum

*Students and teachers posing in front of the Hinckley school
shortly before the firestorm.*
Reprinted by permission of the Hinckley Fire Museum

The Hinckley school after the firestorm.
Reprinted by permission of the Hinckley Fire Museum

From left to right: Doctor Cowan, Doctor Stephan, Angus Hay,
Father Lawler. All four were leading members of the community.
Reprinted by permission of the Hinckley Fire Museum

Angus Hay, editor of the
Hinckley Enterprise.
Reprinted by permission of the
Hinckley Fire Museum

The Reverend Emil
Anderson of Sandstone.
Reprinted by permission of the
Hinckley Fire Museum

Engineer William Best.
Wilkinson: *Memorials of the*
Minnesota Forest Fires

Engineer Edward Barry.
Wilkinson: *Memorials of the
Minnesota Forest Fires*

Superior Street in Duluth, with Union Station to the right, 1889.
Reprinted by permission of the Minnesota Historical Society

Engineer Jim Root.
Wilkinson: *Memorials of the*
Minnesota Forest Fires

John Blair, porter on
Root's train.
Wilkinson: *Memorials of the*
Minnesota Forest Fires

Tom Sullivan, conductor on Root's train.
Wilkinson: *Memorials of the Minnesota Forest Fires*

Root's locomotive, Saint Paul and Duluth Number 69.
Reprinted by permission of the Hinckley Fire Museum

Olive Brown, telegraph operator at Rush City, stayed at her post for more than thirty-six hours relaying information to and from rescue workers.
Wilkinson: *Memorials of the Minnesota Forest Fires*

Dave Williams, station master at Duluth's Union Station, was the first to reach Skunk Lake with relief supplies.
Wilkinson: *Memorials of the Minnesota Forest Fires*

Rails twisted by the searing heat in Hinckley.
Wilkinson: *Memorials of the Minnesota Forest Fires*

Searchers gathering bodies from the ashes of a homestead.
Wilkinson: *Memorials of the Minnesota Forest Fires*

Remains of the entire Lovell family: Tom (38), Louise (35),
Esther (14), and Chester (11).
Wilkinson: *Memorials of the Minnesota Forest Fires*

Bodies piled up at the cemetery near Hinckley.
Wilkinson: *Memorials of the Minnesota Forest Fires*

Searching for someone in a burial trench.
Reprinted by permission of the Hinckley Fire Museum

The bell that tolled Hinckley's fate lies in the ruins of the town hall.
Reprinted by permission of the Hinckley Fire Museum

*The flooded gravel pit in Hinckley, with a partially burned
wagon in the foreground.*
Reprinted by permission of the Hinckley Fire Museum

The millpond at Pokegama.
Wilkinson: *Memorials of the Minnesota Forest Fires*

Tourists came by the trainload to gawk at Skunk Lake.
Reprinted with permission of the Hinckley Fire Museum

Skunk Lake today.
Photo by author

The Hinckley Fire Monument, with four burial trenches in the foreground.
Photo by author

Damuth, must have gotten out onto the mid-span of the bridge, must be stuck out there dying on its searing hot steel frame.

By the time the Best-Barry train, still racing ahead of the flames, backed into the village of Partridge (now Askov), six miles north of Sandstone, a number of the refugees in the boxcars had again passed out from the effects of heat and smoke exposure. As soon as the train stopped, a clamor for water arose from both the coaches and the boxcars, as it had in Sandstone. Up in the lead locomotive, Ed Barry bathed his eyes in water from the locomotive and took stock of things. Partridge was just a hamlet, little more than a glorified logging camp, really. With a couple of lumber companies, a hotel, an Eastern Minnesota section house, several private homes, two stores, and the railway depot and telegraph station, it was home to perhaps fifty people, mostly of Danish extraction. There was no way to know how soon the fire would arrive here, but a quick check of his tender and reservoir made clear to Barry that he could go no further without taking on both coal and water.

When he climbed down from his locomotive, still largely blinded by smoke, twenty-eight-year-old Mary Boyington, the town's telegrapher, handed him a dispatch that had arrived earlier in the day, advising him that the southbound Number 22 freight had been stopped and sidetracked at Dedham to the north. The news must have been a huge relief to both Barry and Best, who since leaving Sandstone hadn't known whether or not they were running against the down-line Number 22 train. Both engineers must have been wondering—and doubting—whether the half-blind spotters riding up front on Barry's tender would see the oncoming freight through the smoke in time to avoid a head-on collision.

While some of his crew worked to take on coal and water, Barry and some male passengers walked to the nearby O'Neil logging camp and rustled up a number of tin pails and cups. Returning to the train, they began passing cups of water to the parched passengers in the coaches and boxcars.

As in Sandstone, both the crew and the refugees on the train called out to the villagers, imploring them to run for their possessions and climb aboard the train before it was too late. But, as in Sandstone, almost nobody took the advice. A Partridge survivor later wrote, "It [the train] stopped briefly and we were urged to get on board but, strangely, we all refused like one man, for what reason I still fail to understand, and the train left."

Twenty or twenty-five minutes after it arrived, the train backed out of town. Shortly thereafter, Mary Boyington and her husband Dan, manager of the hotel, began to have second thoughts, as did all of their fellow villagers. The wall of smoke that had seemed to them to be at least fifteen miles to the south a few minutes earlier now suddenly seemed to be no more than two miles distant, and as it rolled toward them and parted, they could see that it was followed by a wall of fire, the flames rippling high above the tops of the trees. Mary Boyington lingered in the telegraph office in case any helpful news came over the wire. But within a few minutes it was clear that it was too late for helpful news. Boyington grabbed some of the company's records and ran. A few of the villagers commandeered handcars and started pumping their way up the tracks; others simply ran along the rails behind them. The largest group, though, remaining remarkably clear-headed, set out on a road toward a logging camp where a hundred acres had previously been burned over by another fire. It was three miles away—a long haul—and there was no chance to pause or rest, as a survivor later remembered: "All the time the fire was right behind us. The smoke had gathered again and thickened into a grayish-black mass which rolled forward at an incredible speed with a deafening roar, whining and rumbling. We had barely reached our place of refuge when the great wall of smoke behind us split, or rather was flung asunder, and a blood-red flame of fire shot out like a flash of lightning. In a moment, every particle of smoke had disappeared and in its place we saw a sea of fire as far as the eye could scan."

Somewhere in that sea of fire, all of Partridge was already in ashes.

* * *

Forty-five miles to the north, in downtown Duluth, anxiety had been building all afternoon. The sky had been darkening with smoke since about 1:00 P.M., and by 4:00 P.M. the electric lights in the sawmill along the banks of Lake Superior had been lit. Shops had shut down, and people were flocking out onto the streets, gathering in public places, asking one another what was going on. The tension was greatest at Union Station, where railroad employees moving through the crowds were unable to conceal their obvious and growing concern. Southbound trains had been sidetracked along their routes or were being held there in Duluth, and several northbound trains were now late and unaccounted for. Relatives and friends of passengers on the missing trains had formed in anxious knots in the waiting areas. Things were particularly grim in the Saint Paul and Duluth telegrapher's office, where telegraph traffic from much of Pine County—after a flurry of dispatches describing a large fire moving northward—had fallen mostly silent by mid afternoon.

Then, at 5:55 P.M., exactly four hours after Root's train had pulled out of this station earlier that afternoon, the telegraph finally clattered back to life. The message was from Tom Sullivan, Root's conductor. He had run, stumbled, and crawled two miles north from Skunk Lake to a telegrapher's shack next to the Saint Paul and Duluth tracks at a lonely spot called Miller Station, where a spur line running west from the Kettle River met the mainline. Blinded by the smoke and heat, he had had to stay between the rails in order to be sure of the way, sometimes getting down on hands and knees and groping his way along, feeling for the hot rails with his hands. Then, barging into the telegrapher's shack, Sullivan, nearly insane with pain in his eyes, had tried to compose a message for Abraham Lincoln Thompson, the depot agent and telegrapher. But Thompson, apparently unsure whether the sooty, wild-eyed figure before him was alive or an apparition, had keyed in a confused and confusing message: "The country is all burning up. No. 4 [Root's train] burned up—Sullivan dead—For God's sake, send relief." Then, before he could get any more out, the line had gone dead. The Duluth telegrapher, C. M. Phillips, tried now to send a response, but he got only silence in return. He and the crowd gathered around him could only wonder whether the line had burned through or Thompson was running for his life.

The answer was both. Moments after Thompson had sent the message, more exhausted passengers from Root's train had appeared at his door. Among them were Robert Bell; his fifteen-year-old daughter, Josie; and Root's brakeman John Monahan, who had carried another fifteen-year-old girl, May Wellman, nearly all the way from Skunk Lake. They found Sullivan sitting on a bench in the telegraph shack, moaning and bathing his head with water, frantic with the pain in his eyes and with remorse. Recognizing Bell, Sullivan croaked out, "Oh, Mr. Bell, all the passengers are burned." Bell tried to calm Sullivan, to reassure him that the worst was now over, but within minutes hot waves of air began washing over Miller Station and they heard the roaring again, rapidly growing closer outside. Sullivan, Bell and his daughter, John Monahan, May Wellman, Thompson and his wife and children, and more survivors from Root's train—twenty-one people in all—began running north on the tracks again, the thing that had chased them for two hours now still hot on their heels.

Far to the south, in Pokegama, C. W. Kelsey, his hands badly burned, crawled back up the ladder and peered over the rim of his well shortly before 6:00 P.M. For as far as he could see, everything combustible—his house, the woods, the town, the railroad trestle—was gone, simply licked off the face of the earth. Flames were still lapping silently at charred trunks and smoke still drifted across the ashes, but nothing else was moving anywhere. He and his family climbed out of the well and made their way to the millpond, where twenty-three of their fellow villagers were just pulling themselves out onto the ashen banks. Everyone here had survived, though many were badly burned. Dozens of dead fish floated on the surface of the pond, suffocated by the thick, black layer of ash that now blanketed the water. The trestle over the pond and the lumber piles nearby still blazed brightly, the flames crackling and popping loudly.

Hans Nelson, his wife, and Minnie crawled out of the pond just in time to see Alice and Mabel stumbling up the track clutching the damp halves of Mabel's apron, their clothing in tatters, nearly burned off. Their father, seeing them approach, fell to his knees and embraced them, sobbing with relief. But on his farm, Fred Molander was dead of asphyxiation at the bottom of his well, his body not to be found for another six weeks. The charred body of Molander's wife was in the ashes of their house, holding two smaller blackened corpses. In a field on Molander's farm, near a set of iron tires, a bit of burned harness, and the charred remains of two horses, Jay Braman lay dead. Eighteen other bodies lay scattered across the stark, black-and-gray landscape around Pokegama.

The Pokegama survivors were lying exhausted on the banks of the millpond when a small party of men appeared out of the smoke. It was Will Vogel, his crew, and his two passengers. They'd walked down the tracks from the wreck of their train in search of shelter and food, but now, seeing the miserable state of the people huddled by the pond, they realized at once that they would have to be rescuers rather than rescued. Vogel and his conductor, Ed Parr, gathered the shaken survivors and the party trooped off together, back up the line toward the wreck. There they would at least have fresh water from the locomotive's reservoir and shelter from the cold of the night air.

As they set off, Alice Nelson took a one-year-old baby from his mother, who was having trouble walking on her burned feet. Holding the baby in one arm and supporting the mother with the other arm, she shuffled along between the rails in the dim, late-afternoon light, turned eerily yellow now by the smoke, trying not to trip or stumble on the charred ties. Before they'd gone far, she began to see the bodies of animals that had been overtaken by the fire and died on the tracks—deer, rabbits, foxes—their fur singed off and their eyes staring vacantly back at her. Then, abruptly, they came across the body of one of her father's section men sprawled in the ashes, a man she realized that she knew when her father stooped over the body and muttered his name. But it was hard for her to make the connection between this thing sprawled in the gravel beside the tracks—naked and bloated and black—and the man she had known. After a few minutes of staring at the body, not sure what to do about it, the group trudged on up the tracks.

Outside Sandstone, Oliver Dubois climbed out of his well and began to stumble into town to see what had happened. The smoke had begun to lift and it was light enough that he could make out the remains of the streets among the ashes. And he could make out the bodies, dozens of them scattered up and down the streets in front of what had been their homes. He called out, and then called out again and again, but no one answered. The bustling town he had walked through not more than two hours before on his way home to his farm was now absolutely devoid of sound or life. Shaking, he began to make his way down the wagon road toward the river. Along the way he counted what he reckoned to be fifty bodies.

By the time he made it down the wagon road to the quarry, the people there were beginning to crawl out of the river, pulling themselves on all fours out of the relentless, icy pull of the water, sprawling on gravel bars and sandbanks that were still almost too hot to bear, but better now than the cutting cold of the river. All around them in the smoke they could hear the shouts and sobbing of others like themselves who were burned or who could not find loved ones. From time to time, the same weird wailing sound that they had heard earlier floated down to them from up on the middle span of the High Bridge, but weaker and less frequent now.

Pulled up onto the gravel bank by a stranger, still holding the baby he had been clinging to for two hours, Emil Anderson had regained some of his strength. Staggering up and down the beach, wet and shaking with cold, he came across the baby's father. The father gathered his child into his arms and kissed him over and over, astonished to find him alive. A few minutes later he and Anderson found the mother, who had somehow made it down to the river from the cornfield where Anderson had last seen her. Clinging to one another, the couple stood apart on the beach with their baby, stunned and silent, overwhelmed by their good luck.

Anderson waded back into the river, helping others who were too weak to get themselves out of the water onto a huge, flat slab of sandstone in the river. Almost a hundred people had already gathered on the rock, and when they recognized their minister in the smoky gloom, they asked him to climb onto the rock and pray with them. Those who could manage it rose to their knees, and with Anderson leading them, they prayed for those they had just lost. When the prayers ended, they sat in silence, listening to the keening of their fellow sufferers on the riverside.

Then a single voice, singing, rose from the darkness that was quickly closing in around the rock. Then another, and another, and soon everyone on the rock was singing a Swedish hymn, "The Mighty Fortress":

> Rock of Ages, give, oh give me,
> Strength to sing the praise of love,
> With the roaring flames around me,
> Till I rest in peace above.

When they finished and were silent again, the black water all around them passed swiftly and ceaselessly by, sliding irrevocably into the past.

Chapter Eight

INTO THE RING

There is an electric fire in human nature tending to purify—
so that among these human creatures there is continually
some birth of heroism. The pity is that we must wonder at it,
as we should at finding a pearl in the rubbish.

— John Keats,
"Letter to George and
Georgiana Keats"

WHEN TOM SULLIVAN'S ABORTED TELEGRAM ARRIVED IN DULUTH just before 6:00 P.M., it stunned the anxious railroad officials clustered around C. M. Phillips in the Saint Paul and Duluth telegrapher's office. Word of its contents quickly spread through the clamoring depot and out into the city's streets. Hundreds of people in Duluth had friends and relatives in the fire area, and within half an hour scores of them were converging on Union Station. As they walked and ran through the streets, the evening sky to the south was red and glowering. No one was sure that the fire wasn't about to sweep into Duluth itself. One Duluthian later described the scene:

> . . . as the sun went down, the great whirlwinds of flame, though none nearer than fifty miles, lit up the smoky sky with an effect so strange and awful that an oppressive feeling of gruesome apprehension took hold of nearly everyone. . . . in every direction the air seemed a vast mass of molten metal, threatening universal destruction.

Standing beside Phillips in the telegrapher's office was at least one man who wasn't worried about Duluth—Union Station's yard-master, Dave Williams. He was thinking about his friend Jim Root, his boss Robert Bell, and the other passengers on Root's train. Williams was a veteran engineer himself, a man of action, and he wasn't about to sit there in the station and wait for developments to unfold. He ordered Phillips to send a flurry of telegrams to all the stations that could be reached south of Duluth, inquiring about available trains. It took only a few minutes to find what he wanted. Engineer Peter Kelly and his conductor, John Roper, had sidelined their freight train at Willow River, twenty miles north of Hinckley. Williams told Phillips to wire them instructions to take their engine with their caboose and some boxcars as far south as they could go, searching for Root's train. To underscore the seriousness of the situation, Williams concluded the telegram, "Hurry, for God's sake. Miller reports them all burned up."

Then he hurried out into the yard, looking for a locomotive he could commandeer himself.

At about 6:30 P.M. in Hinckley, Axel Rosdahl scrambled up the Eastern Minnesota embankment, out of the gravel pit. The air was still so hot he could only breathe by holding a wet rag to his face, the smoke so thick he was unable to see more than a dozen feet in front of him, but the main fire had burned through town, so he decided to resume searching for his family. He began to work his way north along the Eastern Minnesota tracks toward the Grindstone River, thinking he might find them there. When he reached the river and clambered down into the ravine, he found John Westlund, one of Evan Hansen's neighbors, lying dead in the shallow water. Near him were Mary McNeil and McNeil's eighty-two-year-old mother. Both were burned and exhausted, but they were alive. Neither of them had shoes on and the sawdust floating on the river was still burning, so Rosdahl took them on his back one at a time, and stumbling and weaving his way through the flames, he carried them along the bottom of the ravine to the remains of the Eastern Minnesota trestle. Then came the harder part. It was fifteen feet up the side of the ravine to the tracks, and the bank was all blistering hot gravel, sand, and ash. Grappling for a foothold or a handhold wherever he could find it in the hot gravel, Rosdahl helped each of the injured women up the bank. By the time they were both up to the tracks he could do no more. He pointed the women south, toward the gravel pit, lay down, and fell asleep in the still-warm ashes beside the tracks.

Other people were also beginning to venture out of the pit, gathering on the Eastern Minnesota's gravel embankment. The smoke and searing heat had parched their throats, and most of them, especially the children, were desperately thirsty. There was nothing to drink, though, except for the green, stagnant water in which they had been sitting. The Reverend Peter Knudsen made his way to a burned-over field nearby where he found six small watermelons. They were burned on the outside, but he cut each of them in half, scooping out the juicy pulp and handing it around. Then his wife appeared, carrying a pail she'd found in the ashes of the Eastern Minnesota depot. Wading back into the pit, she led Amy Currie's cow—which had saved itself in the water—up onto the embankment and began to milk her. When the pail was full, she used the twelve hollowed-out watermelon rinds as bowls, distributing the sweet, warm milk to the children among them, as well as to any of the adults who were burned and dehydrated.

The milk must have been a soothing and welcome relief for the parched throats of the dozens who received it, but it could not have begun to address the enormous physical suffering that was beginning to unfold for them and hundreds more across Pine County.

Being badly burned is just about the worst thing that can happen to a body short of immediate dismemberment and death. No other type of injury creates the same kind of long-lasting physiological mayhem, the same potential for pain, the same degree of uncertainty about the outcome, the same kind of disfigurement for those who manage to survive.

Any burn that is second-degree or higher—reaching the dermal layer of skin or deeper—and that covers more than 20 percent of the body's surface area, if left untreated, sets in motion a cascade of highly consequential events within the body. In a process called *fluid shift*, large volumes of plasma, the liquid component of blood, seep through the walls of blood vessels and into surrounding tissues, producing edema, a severe and often grotesque swelling, particularly in the lips, genitals, throat, and mouth. The swelling tissues press on blood vessels and internal organs. The swollen linings of the airway threaten to close off the flow of air to the lungs. Along with its load of plasma, the bloodstream loses the proteins, fats, sugars, and electrolytes that it normally carries, including chemicals like potassium and magnesium that regulate the function of the muscles and various vital organs. The blood, lacking its liquid constituent, gradually thickens into a kind of sludge that the heart struggles ever more desperately to pump around the body. The lungs fill with fluid. Blood pressure drops precipitously. Body temperature drops, threatening hypothermia. Patients shiver uncontrollably, even in a warm environment. Then burn shock sets in.

With the onset of burn shock, the flow of urine slows or stops. The pulse grows weak and erratic. Fingertips and other extremities turn blue. Individual cells begin to die, tissue is damaged, and organs may fail. The victim often becomes lethargic and unresponsive. And very often, that's the end of the story—the victim dies then and there.

But that's just the first twenty-four hours or so. If the victim survives longer, a host of other threats are waiting in the wings. Serious burns are unusual in that they do not generally heal themselves as time goes on, like most other kinds of injuries. Instead, they get worse. As Barbara Ravage points out in her highly informative book, *Burn Unit: Saving Lives After the Flames*, ". . . a burn is an evolving wound; the initial injury is only the beginning of an ongoing disease process that must be stopped or it will end in death." For one thing, the inflammatory response that the body launches in an attempt to heal the burns often spins out of control, overwhelmed by the magnitude of the damage, and the consequences spread far beyond the area of the burned tissue. A flood of hormones, leukocytes, macrophages, and chemical messengers and mediators washes through the body, setting off reactions that alter the body's physiology in unpredictable and often destructive ways—expanding vessels that should be contracting, clotting blood that should be thinning, killing off cells that should be left alone, releasing toxins that damage vital organs.

Meanwhile, deprived of oxygen under dead tissue, burns penetrating the dermis may actually expand over time, working their way deeper into the underlying tissue and spreading outward as macrophages and scavenger cells sent to destroy dead cells attack and destroy adjacent living cells instead.

Then, as more time goes by, the body may begin to cannibalize itself on a larger scale. By the second day after the initial burn injury, the victim is likely to experience a condition called *hypermetabolism*. In order to feed the runaway inflammatory process, the body needs enormous amounts of fuel and oxygen. In response to this need, the metabolic system goes into overdrive, burning calories at a furious rate. And oddly, for biochemical reasons that are not fully understood, the hypermetabolic body doesn't burn fat as it ordinarily would, but rather, it begins to consume protein—the lean meat and sinews our bodies are built of. The victim begins to waste away, consumed by his own metabolic system.

That, unfortunately, sets the stage for even more trouble. As the body's lean-mass diminishes, so does its ability to fight infection, the ultimate cause of death for most burn victims who survive the first twenty-four hours.

From the moment the flames subside, a legion of microbial life begins to attack the burn victim from both inside and outside the body. Many of the invaders are familiar to us and to our bodies. They live on or in us, either doing us good by breaking down the food in our digestive tracks or at least doing us no harm living in small numbers in folds of our skin, under our nails, on our clothes, on things we touch, safely kept at bay by our intact skin, the closed system of our digestive tract, and our immune systems.

But a serious burn injury is a party invitation for microbes. It breaks the protective seal of our skin and, in a process similar to fluid shift, it allows the normally helpful bacteria in our guts to penetrate the lining of the intestines and escape into the bloodstream.

The burns themselves create ideal environments for bacteria— moist pockets of dead flesh often sealed safely away from oxygen by layers of overlying dead skin, perfect havens for the oxygen-phobic anaerobic bacteria in particular. Among those who are likely to come to the party in the first few days are *Streptococcus, E. coli, Clostridium perfringens*, and *Staphylococcus aureus*. A bit later, *Klebsiella pneumoniae, Escherichia*, and *Pseudomonas aeruginosa* may show up. A number of these organisms move downward through the burn itself and enter the bloodstream, giving them access to the victim's entire body and further compromising the immune system. By now, the partygoers have completely overwhelmed the body's defenses, and the door is thrown wide open for yeasts like *Candida albicans* and filamentous fungi like *Aspergillus* to move in and take up residence. Without effective intervention, the inevitable consequence of this feeding frenzy is sepsis, organ failure, and death.

When the burned survivors in Hinckley crawled out of the dirty water of the gravel pit and drank the unpasteurized milk of Amy Currie's cow, many of them already carried on them, and within them, the invisible agents of their impending demise.

At 6:48 P.M., the sun set over Pine County, and the fire's advance began to slow dramatically. The low-pressure system that in the morning had squatted over northern Iowa and Manitoba moved eastward over Ontario and eastern Minnesota, and the rapidly cooling atmosphere began to weigh on the fire, knocking down the convection column and slowly smothering the flaming front like an enormous blanket applied from above. Before it stopped moving completely, though, the fire quickly and efficiently devastated one more small community, as if as a mere afterthought. In Finlayson, on the Saint Paul and Duluth line, the fire swept away a number of houses, but all eighty-five residents survived, most by crowding into a small pond on Mrs. A. G. Crocker's farm. Mrs. Crocker was nine months pregnant and, as it turned out, just hours from delivering a baby boy.

Among the few people in the Finlayson area who didn't head for Crocker's pond were Anna Cheney and her children. Instead, they took shelter in an underground root cellar. As the flaming front arrived, though, the fire quickly sucked almost all of the oxygen out of their hiding place. They were struggling to find their last few breaths of air when an unlikely savior arrived, in an unexpected way. By luck, a donkey fleeing the fire above crashed through the earth-and-wood roof and landed among them, braying loudly in the hot, smoky, but suddenly well-ventilated root cellar.

And with that, the fire finally curled up and lay down. The thing that it had been, it no longer was. It shattered into thousands upon thousands of smaller things, things burning and burned, within an oval ring of flames sprawling across much of Pine County. The ring stretched roughly thirty-four miles from north to south, sixteen miles from east to west. Outside of the ring, the oil lamps of scattered homesteads and villages shimmered here and there in the dark, smoke-filled woods of northern Minnesota. Within it, across almost five hundred square miles of burned-over land, hundreds of thousands of burning trees and stumps sparkled like constellations of stars in a black night sky.

A few constellations shone brighter than the others. In Hinckley, more than a hundred carloads of grain were still blazing furiously in the Eastern Minnesota yards. Across town, the site of the Brennan lumberyard was awash in flames, as it would be for days. To the north, on the tracks that crossed Skunk Lake, flames were still shooting fifty feet into the air from Jim Root's coal tender. On either side of the Kettle River at Sandstone, huge piles of timbers from the collapsed approaches to the High Bridge were still burning brightly, like oversized bonfires.

All across the flame-studded countryside, huddled in lakes and streams or sprawled in potato and rutabaga patches, illuminated only by the burning stumps, hundreds of people were struggling to survive, and hundreds more were dead. Overhead, a thin, waxing crescent moon crept across the darkening sky, dipping toward the western horizon.

At 7:00 P.M., a second telegram arrived in Duluth, this one at the Eastern Minnesota's telegraph office. It had been forwarded up the line in advance of the Best-Barry combination train, which was now out of the ring of fire and backing up toward West Superior and Duluth. The telegram said that the train would arrive in Duluth at 9:00 P.M., with about five hundred survivors from Hinckley aboard. Duluth's mayor, Ray Lewis, immediately ordered his chief of police to begin preparations for crowd control at Union Station, where hundreds had now gathered on the platforms. As word of the second telegram filtered through the crowd, the effect was largely to further terrorize those who were waiting to hear from friends and relatives. At least they knew now that there were some survivors, but 500 from a town of 1,200 was not particularly reassuring, and many were wondering who among them would be lucky and who would not when the refugees began to climb down from the train.

Five minutes later, Dave Williams pulled out of the station on the Saint Paul and Duluth line, heading south. In the hour that had passed since Sullivan's telegram arrived, he'd assembled a crew of volunteer rescuers, among them four doctors and a few journalists eager to get to what was beginning to sound like the story of their careers. In boxcars behind the coaches, Williams had collected cases of food, medicine, surgical supplies, and blankets—everything he could get his hands on in the short amount of time he was willing to delay his departure. He hoped to be at Skunk Lake, where Kelly and Roper should be waiting for him, in another hour.

Kelly and Roper were finding it tough going, though. They were creeping along the tracks just south of Finlayson watching for burned-out culverts. At 7:38 P.M., the sliver of moon slipped below the western horizon and they found themselves in a dark, fantastical landscape, entirely black but for the thousands upon thousands of burning stumps that surrounded them on all sides, flickering and flaring in shades of red and orange everywhere they looked, for as far as they could see. Then, in the smoky cone of light cast by his headlamps on the tracks ahead of him, Kelly saw a group of figures moving up the line, directly toward him.

It was Tom Sullivan, Robert Bell, and nineteen others, most of whom had come all the way from Skunk Lake. Bell was carrying his daughter in his arms again, staggering under her weight. Sullivan had his hands clasped to his eyes, and he was stumbling and tripping along the tracks, wondering what the light ahead of him was, not yet aware that it was the headlamp of a locomotive. When Roper climbed down from the train and approached him, Sullivan recognized his voice, uncovered his eyes, and croaked, "John, is that you? For God's sake, give me some water." Roper told him they were on the way to Root's train, but Sullivan—after guzzling the water Kelly offered him and then pouring it over his face, trying to cool and rinse his eyes—shook his head mournfully and said, "I'm afraid you cannot do it." Bell explained that there were bridges and culverts burned out south of Miller, and that they'd never get a train through. Asked about Root and his passengers, Bell and Sullivan just stared back and shook their heads.

Roper told Sullivan, Bell, and the others to walk another quarter-mile up the line to the Finlayson depot, as yet unburned, and to wait there until they returned. He and Kelly intended to try to go as far south as they could to search for other survivors. They'd pick them up on the way back to Duluth. Then they climbed back into the cab and resumed their slow, creeping progress southward.

Almost immediately, they began to come across small groups of settlers standing by the tracks, many of them blackened with ashes, some of them burned and in pain, others dripping wet from the ponds and ditches where they had ridden out the fire. Kelly stopped, and he and Roper helped each group aboard the boxcars before they proceeded cautiously on down the line. But the farther they went, the hotter the air temperatures got. The paint on the front of the engine began to blister and peel off.

They passed the burned-out station at Miller, from which Sullivan had sent the first telegram to Duluth a little less than two hours ago, reduced now to a heap of glowing coals. Then, slowing down even more as they approached a small stream, Kelly asked Roper to take a look and see if the tracks were passable over the culvert. Roper leaned out of the cab, hesitated a moment, and then turned to Kelly, suddenly hollering at him to stop, to apply the brakes. When the train lurched and jolted to a stop, Roper hopped out of the cab, walked ahead a few paces to the culvert, and held his lantern out over the water. Down in the stream was a face, a woman's face, turned up out of the water, pale and deathly white against the oily black water, staring silently back at him. The woman was holding something out toward him, a baby, and it was alive, squirming and kicking slowly in its wet swaddling. Roper scrambled down the bank and plucked the baby from the woman's arms, laying it beside him in the warm ashes on the bank. Then he reached out and took the woman's cold hands in his own and dragged her slowly up onto the bank on her back. Kelly climbed down into the streambed and together they carried both mother and baby to the caboose and wrapped them in blankets.

They continued down the line, but soon came to a fifteen-foot-long bridge that was completely burned out, as Bell had told them they would. The bridge would have to be rebuilt before the train could get any closer than this to Skunk Lake. But they knew now that the track behind them was sound, so Kelly reversed direction, threw open the throttle, and began to roll back toward Finlayson.

When they got there, they found that Sullivan, Bell, and the others had fled further up the tracks, still not believing that what had been chasing them had stopped. Kelly and Roper found them another two miles on, sitting by the tracks where the railway cut through a hill. They took them aboard quickly, and a few minutes later, at about 8:30 P.M., they pulled into the station at Willow River where Dave Williams had just arrived from Duluth with his hastily made-up relief train and four doctors. Williams rushed to Sullivan and asked what he knew about the fate of Root's train and passengers. But by now Sullivan was in such pain from his eyes and so confused by stress that he was ranting incoherently. The doctors were afraid he was, or was about to become, insane, so they led him away and Williams turned to Bell and asked the same question. Bell's answer was not what he wanted to hear.

"Everything is burned, everyone dead," Bell murmured.

At the wreck of Vogel's train, north of Pokegama, Alice, Mabel, and Minnie Nelson and their parents were trying to find places to rest in the crowded passenger coach. The best spots, on the floor between the now cushion-less seats, were reserved for the burned survivors, some of whom were now delirious with shock and pain. Many of the windows had been broken out either by the derailment or by the fire, and the smoke drifting through the coach was still nearly suffocating. Everyone who was conscious enough to do so was holding some kind of wet cloth to his or her face. Every five minutes or so, conductor Ed Parr and Bill Vogel put freshly wet scraps of cloth over the mouths of those who were most badly burned. Those who had sought shelter in the millpond were still wearing wet clothes, and they were getting cold now. But most of them counted themselves fortunate. Those who had had to run through the fire to get to the pond had almost no clothes at all.

The three Nelson girls finally gave up on trying to find a place to stretch out and perched instead on the stove and the coal box in one corner of the coach. As some of the adults finally managed to fall asleep, the girls began to take turns tending to those who couldn't help themselves, propping their heads up to give them sips of water, laying wet cloths on their faces.

At about 9:00 P.M., four miles to the northeast in Mission Creek, where seventy-three people had survived in the potato patch, a surprisingly bountiful dinner was put on the table in the one remaining structure, a small log house in a wide clearing. In the same patch where the settlers had lain as the fire burned over them, they had dug dozens of potatoes, already roasted, from the soft, still warm ground. A large deer, badly burned and panicked, had bounded by and become entangled in strands of barbed wire while they were digging. The men had fallen on it, killed it, and dragged it to the house. Now, except for a few men they had posted outside to make sure falling embers didn't set the roof afire, they took turns sitting at the long table to eat.

Their meal was interrupted at 9:30 or 10:00 P.M. when a small crew of men drifted in out of the flaming dark. They were from a repair train that had been working its way north from Pine City to repair burned-out culverts and bridges on the Saint Paul and Duluth line south of Mission Creek. They had thought that the damage they were repairing was the result of a small local fire that had been burning for days near Brown's Hill, and they were astonished to find that Mission Creek had all but disappeared.

Then at about 10:30 P.M., more men appeared. This group arrived from the north, on a handcar, and as bad as the Mission Creek people had looked to one another after their trial in the potato patch, they were shocked when they saw these latest arrivals. They looked more dead than alive, and with good reason—they had come from Hinckley.

One of them was Angus Hay.

From the moment he had crawled out of the stagnant water at the bottom of the gravel pit in Hinckley at about 7:00 P.M., Hay had been determined to get help for the devastated villagers huddled there. They were, he would later say, "the worst used-up crowd I have ever seen." At first he had trudged bewildered and aimlessly through the smoking, ashen remains of the town, barely comprehending what he was seeing in the failing light of evening. There was almost nothing left, nothing to show what Hinckley had been just a few hours before. All that remained was the crumbling, black shell of the schoolhouse, the sheet-metal roundhouse in the Eastern Minnesota yards, the Eastern Minnesota's water tank, a bank vault, and the iron fence that had surrounded the town hall. To the northwest, where the Brennan lumberyard had been, flames were still shooting a hundred feet or more into the air, but other than the crackling and popping of the flames, there was no sound at all, only a still and unnerving hush. Here and there, inert, vaguely human black shapes lay sprawled in the gray ashes, but Hay had looked away from these, looked beyond them, trying to find something else, something he could do that might make a difference. When he had come to the roundhouse and looked inside, he had been amazed to find a cluster of people alive there, sitting on the floor between the tracks, their heads hanging abjectly between their legs. They looked up at him quietly, with despairing eyes. At the height of the fire, the heat in the Eastern Minnesota yards surrounding the roundhouse had been ferocious enough to melt steel rails, but the roundhouse's sheet-metal siding had reflected just enough of it to keep the structure intact and this handful of people inside alive.

At first, Hay had slumped on the floor among them. Then other people had come stumbling in from the gravel pit, their faces caked in gray ash like his own, their clothes, like his, dripping green slime. A bit later, three young men had appeared at the door of the roundhouse with coats pulled over their heads and their feet wrapped in torn strips of cloth. They had crawled out of Skunk Lake and walked the seven miles south to Hinckley from the wreck of Root's train. One of them, Jim Lobdell, a traveling salesman from Saint Paul, poured out the story of the harrowing train ride to the lake. The last he'd seen of Root, he said, he was lying on the deck of his engine, surrounded by flames and not moving.

By 8:30 P.M., Hay and Lobdell had found a lantern and knew what they wanted to do. Mission Creek was only three miles to the south, and if they could get there they might find help. They and five other volunteers had found a handcar in the roundhouse and pushed it through drifts of ashes to the tracks adjacent to what had been the Saint Paul and Duluth depot. The heat had warped and twisted the rails all out of shape—like huge, black strands of spaghetti—so Hay and the others had carried the handcar south, past the blistered remains of John Craig's Waterous fire engine, until they found a section of track that was straight. And so it had gone for almost two hours, the exhausted men alternately carrying the handcar through the ashes and running it on the tracks, until they had finally made it to Mission Creek—only to find that Mission Creek, like Hinckley, no longer existed.

If Hay was surprised to find Mission Creek gone, the Mission Creek villagers and the repair crew were stunned to hear what Hay had to say about Hinckley and what Lobdell had to say about Root's train. Within a half an hour they had Hay and Lobdell on the repair train heading south to Pine City, the county seat, to tell the wider world.

At 9:30 P.M., after stopping briefly in West Superior, Wisconsin, to switch engines, the Best-Barry train pulled across Saint Louis Bay and into the long, low shed behind Duluth Union Station with 476 survivors from Hinckley aboard. The police had cordoned off the platform so that doctors could be the first to reach the passengers, but hundreds of people—friends, relatives, reporters, politicians, and the merely curious—were waiting anxiously inside the ornate depot.

As the refugees emerged from the train, blackened and disheveled, pandemonium ensued. Many of them wore only burned shreds of clothing. A few of the men were wrapped only in blankets. Some of the women were wearing men's coats that they'd borrowed to cover themselves. Some of the children in the boxcars were entirely naked. But no one was thinking much about the state of his or her dress. Many of those getting off of the coaches ran back down the train to the boxcars, where the doors were just being slid open. They called out the names of loved ones, peered anxiously into the faces emerging from the cars, tried to find missing children, spouses, parents, friends. Here and there they succeeded, and people threw themselves together, shrieking and sobbing with relief. John and Amy Currie, carrying their children, climbed down from a coach and made their way through the crowd, heading for a hotel. Clara

Anderson pushed her way along the platform calling out for her parents, her brothers, and her sister. Belle Barden, her brothers, and her mother called out for Belle's father Jake, but no one answered.

Doctors worked their way among the refugees, peeling back clothing to look at burns, bathing eyes in cold water. Some people were too badly burned even to walk, and these were laid out on stretchers and borne away through the station to horse-drawn ambulances waiting in front of the depot out on Superior Street.

Slowly, the shrieking and shouting began to subside, as those who could find their loved ones moved happily through a corridor of policemen into the depot. Those who could not followed them in, sobbing or silent. Inside the depot, under the ornate high ceiling, in a haze of tobacco smoke, there was more pandemonium as friends and relatives behind the police cordon saw or failed to see those they were looking for. Reporters pushed through the police lines and gathered around clusters of passengers, peppering them with questions. Mayor Lewis shook the hands of as many refugees as he could, telling them that Duluth was going to take good care of them.

Out in the smoke and the dark, on the Saint Paul and Duluth line, Dave Williams was still trying to get to Skunk Lake. After sending his rescue train back toward Duluth, carrying Tom Sullivan and the other refugees that Kelly and Roper had rescued, he'd decided to take Kelly's heat-blistered engine, along with a boxcar containing building supplies, south to the fifteen-foot burned-out trestle that had blocked Kelly and Roper. Once there, he'd rebuild it and push on to the wreck of Root's train. One of the just-rescued refugees, his boss, Bob Bell, had decided to go with him. So had Peter Kelly and John Roper and two of the doctors Williams had brought down from Duluth, doctors Magie and Codding.

By 10:00 P.M., they'd reached the trestle, and when they'd rebuilt it well enough to bear the weight of the engine and the boxcar, they moved slowly over it. Almost immediately they came to another burned out trestle, this one over a twelve-foot-deep ravine. They loaded a few medical supplies, some water, and some food onto a handcar and pushed it down into the ravine, across the creek, and up the other side. Then they resumed moving southward on the track, the smoke so thick now that they had to tie wet handkerchiefs over their faces in order to breathe.

The stumps burning all around them flickered and glowed eerily through the drifting, dark smoke. The air was acrid, their eyes were stinging, and the effort of pumping the handcar while breathing through the handkerchiefs was quickly exhausting them. Then the first bodies began to appear, looming up out of the smoky darkness ahead of them, sprawled across the tracks, their heads pointed north, their feet south. They were all naked, burned to a crisp, and grotesque in the lantern light. Gingerly, Williams and his men moved them to the side of the tracks and kept moving south.

Again and again, they came to burned-out culverts and had to carry or push the handcar past the obstacles. Still they moved on. It was Williams more than anyone who was driving them onward through the darkness. No one really wanted to turn back, but only Williams really believed there was any urgency to reach the train. The trail of bodies only seemed to confirm what was becoming increasingly obvious to the rest of them.

Near Sandstone Junction, where Emil Anderson had gotten off the train to walk home just nineteen hours before, they came across a cluster of bodies—a woman and three boys, all nude, all burned beyond recognition. When they moved one of the boys off the tracks they found underneath him a woman's black leather handbag, mostly unburned. They tried to pry it open but the heat had fused the clasp closed, so they tossed it on the handcar and continued on their way. When they opened it in the morning they would find the astonishing sum of $3,500. Later still, they would learn that the woman was Annie McNamara; the children, three of her sons, John Jr., James, and Michael; the money, the boys' education fund.

Pine City was Hinckley's nearest surviving neighbor of any size, sitting just thirteen miles to the south on the Saint Paul and Duluth line.

As late as 8:00 or 9:00 P.M., few people in Pine City had seen reason for much alarm, either for themselves or for Hinckley. They knew that a small but stubborn fire had been burning for days at Brown's Hill just to their north, but with the wind blowing all the smoke away from them, to the northeast, they'd had no reason to suspect anything larger. When the telegraph line to Hinckley and points north had gone out at about 4:00 P.M., most people had just assumed the Brown's Hill fire was to blame. Even when the northbound Limited had been sidetracked here just before 5:00 P.M., they had figured it was just a sensible precaution, made necessary because without a telegraph line, there was no way to tell whether southbound trains might be on the track. Nobody, apparently, was aware of the 1,000 feet of extra fire hose that had been requested by Chief Craig earlier in the afternoon and that was still sitting in the Limited's baggage car.

But by late evening, with the Limited still at the depot, full of increasingly frustrated passengers, and with nothing but silence from the north for six hours now, Pine City's concern began to deepen. At 10:30 P.M., John Stone, a hotel proprietor and the Pine City correspondent for the *Saint Paul Pioneer Press*, sent a dispatch south to his paper:

> There is no communication with Hinckley, but it is feared here that the town is in imminent danger . . . At this writing the wind has died away and hope has correspondingly increased. No danger to this town at present.

> Stone

A few minutes later, the repair train returned from Mission Creek, and everything changed at once. Stone was still at the Pine City depot after sending his dispatch when the train pulled in, and he was in the crowd that gathered around Angus Hay and Jim Lobdell on the platform as they began to tell their stories. When they finished, Stone raced back into the telegrapher's office to put a new message on the wire to Saint Paul:

Hinckley burned to ashes; many people lost their lives in the fire, balance are homeless and destitute; send relief if possible . . . Engineer Jim Root probably fatally burned. Situation appalling and heart-rending in the extreme.

Stone

The news brought by Hay and Lobdell galvanized Pine City. Mill whistles and church bells were sounded. A crowd quickly assembled in Robinson Park and held an impromptu meeting by lantern light to decide on a course of action. They elected James Hurley chairman of an emergency relief committee. Boys and girls ran from house to house, where they pounded on doors, waking people up, asking for food, clothing, and blankets. People emptied their larders, dragged blankets and coats out of closets, heaped them in the children's arms, and told them to come back for more. The town's three doctors gathered together boxes of medicines, bandages, cotton batting, and liquor. The railroad men coupled an engine to two coaches, and at 11:30 P.M., just forty-five minutes after Hay and Lobdell had arrived, a special section of Saint Paul and Duluth train No. 3, laden with supplies, pulled out heading north. No one was worried about southbound trains on the track now. When the train had left, Stone sent another telegram to Saint Paul:

Relief party has gone from here with medical aid for the suffering and provisions for the hungry . . . The Limited train from Duluth, Root, engineer, was caught in the fire and Root standing to his post like a hero, ran his train back to Skunk Lake with it all on fire . . . Relief temporary, substantial, and immediate is needed and needed bad . . . Poor Root! He ought to live, such men are always heroes in time of need.

Stone

Another ten miles to the south, in Rush City, a young telegrapher named Olive Brown had already worked all day and now much of the night, refusing to go home at the end of her shift out of concern for what might be happening up the line. Two fully loaded passenger trains were being held there in the yard, unable to proceed north, and the passengers had been besieging her all afternoon and evening, seeking information, sending and receiving telegrams, venting their frustrations on her. As great as her concern was, though, it was dwarfed by that of the other person in the office, Mrs. James Root. Root's train was now more than six hours late arriving in Rush City, where she had expected to meet it at about 5:00 P.M. She had been camped in the telegraph office all evening, peering up the tracks into the darkness, watching for a headlamp, waiting for some kind of explanation. Then, sometime after 11:00 P.M., as the two women were anxiously talking the situation over, a message from Pine City finally came in:

> Hinckley, Mission Creek and No. 4 train are all burned up, except the engine. The passengers on No. 4 train are in Skunk Lake, about six miles north of Hinckley, and about half the people in Hinckley are dead. We want all the assistance possible. Notify both doctors at Rush City, and others that can be got here at once.

Olive Brown rushed out of the office, searching for the doctors. No one remained in the office to record what Mrs. Root said or did.

SUNDAY | SEPTEMBER 2, 1894

At midnight, Dave Williams, along with Robert Bell, Peter Kelly, John Roper, and doctors Magie and Codding, finally approached Skunk Lake on their handcar. Peering over their wetted handkerchiefs with stinging eyes, they'd watched the fountain of flame erupting from Root's coal tender grow steadily brighter as they'd drawn closer, like a beacon on a dark sea. Now, as they rolled quietly to a stop, the blazing coal illuminated a desolate scene. Only the locomotive and the steel frames of the coaches were left standing on the tracks, and they were twisted and contorted, mangled by the heat. Reflections from the flames shimmered on the dark water on either side of the tracks. The water was studded with burned stumps and black hummocks, but there was no sign of life anywhere. Everything was silent.

The men stood, quiet, grimly watching the reflections dance on the lake, even Williams finally starting to wonder if their efforts had been in vain. Bell turned to Magie and said, "Can it be that they are all dead?"

Finally, Bell and Magie called out together, "Hallo!" A long moment of silence passed before voices—first one, then another, and finally a feeble chorus—began to float across the water and out of the darkness. Then some of the stumps and hummocks began to move. Men, women, and children began to rise out of the water, gesturing blindly in different directions, calling out for help. The rescuers ran along the gravel toward the burning wreck and saw now in the glare of the blaze that dozens more people were lying prostrate along the marshy margins of the lake.

John Blair clambered wet and shivering up the embankment toward the knot of men and began to deliver a report to Bell. For seven hours he had been moving ceaselessly from passenger to passenger, trying to tend to their needs, and by now he knew where each survivor was and who needed the most help. For over an hour—at the height of the fire—he had stood with his back to the wind, burning embers and smoke howling past him, splashing water onto children who were too frightened to move. When the fury of the fire had abated somewhat, he had ventured out of the lake, searching for and finding people who had not been able to find the water, and leading any who were still alive back to the lake so he could bathe their eyes and their burns with cool water. Then as the evening had grown colder, he had begun pulling people out of the lake, carrying or dragging them toward the burning coal tender, try-ing to keep them warm and conscious.

Among those Blair had helped out of the lake were Marie Hansen and her children. Marie lay on her back now among the charred rushes on the foul-smelling, muddy bank. Her eyes were still swollen shut, and her body numb, but she could hear the excited voices of the men talking to Blair up on the bank, and she knew they were new voices. Ed and Helen were lying beside her, pressed against her for warmth. Josephine was a few feet away, also on her back, pale and white, shaking convulsively. From time to time Josephine called out for her father, then sobbed quietly to herself for a while. Each time, hearing her, Marie clutched Helen and Ed tighter.

Nearby, Bill Grissinger was lying on a tussock of unburned grass, just out of the water. One of his ears was nearly burned off, and his hands were also badly burned, but both were numb and he was hardly aware of them. He had been in and out of consciousness for the last several hours, trying to remember where he was and why his parents weren't there. Hearing the low murmur of the men's voices up by the track now, though, he felt comforted and fell back asleep. It had been twenty-four hours since the wind had awakened him in his bed at home the night before.

Williams and Bell asked where Root was, and Blair gestured down the tracks toward the head of the train. When they reached the locomotive, they held their lanterns high and peered into the cab. They found Root lying on the iron deck of the cab, blind, blistered, and delirious, but alive.

The locomotive had been separated from the burning coal ten-der and moved ahead of the rest of the train. Earlier, telling Mc-Gowan, "I'm chilling to death," Root had crawled out of the lake, where he had grown numb from his waist down, and staggered back to the locomotive, determined to save it from further damage and to warm himself in the process. Somehow, he had managed to uncou-ple the locomotive from the burning tender and drive it forward per-haps fifty feet before collapsing again onto the deck.

Bell summoned Dr. Magie, who bathed Root's eyes with water and applied salves and bandages to his burned hands and the cut on his neck. At first Root was unable to comprehend where he was or who was tending to him, but gradually, he began to recollect what had happened.

The men clustered around Root discussed what they should do next. Few if any of the survivors were in any shape to hike out of there, and the handcar would only hold a dozen or so. Until a train could be gotten through, most people were going to have to wait things out right there. Williams was anxious to get word back to Duluth about the true situation, and Bell was nearly as exhausted as those in the lake, so they decided to leave the doctors there and to return to Willow River on the handcar with as many of the badly injured as would fit, no more than five on six. They helped Root onto the handcar, but when Root realized that he could not even sit up and that his prostrate body would take the room of three who could sit, he refused to go, insisting that he be helped back to his engine where he could at least lie down and be warm again. Within a few minutes, Williams and Bell were on the car again, pumping it slowly northward.

Nestled in the crook of his mother's arm in the cold mud beside the lake, Ed Hansen watched the lanterns on the handcar receding and disappearing into the night. Then there was only the flaring light of the burning coal tender again, illuminating the stark skeleton of the train, and the doctors' lanterns, moving silently like fireflies across the dark water.

Chapter Nine

OUT OF THE ASHES

Each new morn
New widows howl, new orphans cry, new sorrows
Strike heaven on the face.

—*Shakespeare,*
Macbeth

THE FIRST RELIEF TRAIN FROM PINE CITY CREPT INTO THE south end of Hinckley at 12:30 A.M., as soon as the tracks between Mission Creek and Hinckley had been repaired. Among the seventy-five or so men who climbed down from the train was Angus Hay, there both as a reporter and as a rescuer, though he had been rescued himself only a few hours earlier. Also there was Dr. E. E. Barnum, leading the contingent of doctors who had just been roused from their beds in Pine City. Barnum had a particular reason to be there and to be worried: his thirteen-year-old daughter Kate had been in Hinckley yesterday afternoon, at the time of the fire, and she hadn't been heard from since.

James Hurley, just elected chairman of the relief effort at the torchlight meeting in Robinson Park in Pine City, was here too. Standing in the smoky dark by the locomotive and peering up the line at the eerie landscape, Hurley could see at a glance that it would be impossible to proceed any farther than this with the train. From this point northward, for as far as he could make out by the light of the locomotive's headlamp, the tracks were spread, warped out of shape, or entirely melted. Except for the tracks, the roundhouse, and the water tank nearby, there was nothing to be seen in any direction but ashes, stone foundations, and blackened bodies, both animal and human. The air was cold now. The smell of burned meat—terrible in its implications—lay over the landscape like a blanket. Hurley gathered the men around him and ordered the bulk of them to take lanterns and begin to scour the rubble of Hinckley for possible survivors.

Then Hay led Hurley, Barnum, and the other doctors to the Eastern Minnesota roundhouse, where Hay knew that most of the survivors from the gravel pit had gathered. When they trooped into the sheet-metal building, the sight flickering before them in the lantern light startled Hurley and the doctors. More than a hundred people were stretched out among the rails on the gravel floor now. Many of them were burned in some way or another, some of them horribly. All of them were wet and filthy—black with ashes and soot. The most badly burned among them were moaning; a few of them were ranting. The doctors began to treat the worst of the injured while those who could walk were helped to the train, where they were given milk, sausage, and bread.

Hurley and the other rescuers went back out into the dark and joined the search for other survivors. Mostly, though, they found bodies. They found them in piles amid the foundations of houses, where whole families had died huddled together, clutching one another. They found them in wells and root cellars, asphyxiated but unburned. They found them splayed out facedown in the streets, burned to a crisp. Between the ashes of the Saint Paul and Duluth depot and the Grindstone River, they found the remains of Tommy Dunn. When they worked their way down into the river bottom, they found Ida Martinson and her children half buried in the mud, the clothes burned off their blackened backs. As they got closer to the Brennan lumber mill, where huge piles of logs were still burning furiously, they found the bodies of the skeleton crew that had stayed behind at the mill—bodies that were little more than piles of white ashes and bone fragments scattered with jewelry and pocket watches that glistened and gleamed in the lantern light. As they found them, they piled those bodies that were more or less intact in a heap near the junction of the two railroads.

As the relief party prepared to run the train back down to Pine City with its first load of refugees, Axel Rosdahl appeared out of the darkness, walking wearily down the tracks from the spot where he had passed out earlier after helping three women up out of the Grindstone. He climbed aboard the train and had some milk and sausage, but as the train began to back up toward Pine City he got off and went back to the roundhouse to sleep some more. He intended to start looking for his mother and his brothers at first light.

When the train left Hinckley, sometime after 1:00 A.M., John Powell, a crew foreman for the Saint Paul and Duluth, and J. W. Sargent, a conductor, went back to work. Powell and his crew had been laboring since early evening, rebuilding bridges and laying passing track around the worst sections between Mission Creek and Hinckley. Now that he was in Hinckley, though, he didn't intend to stop so long as Root's passenger train was unaccounted for somewhere to the north.

Powell and Sargent and a volunteer crew carried and pushed five handcars through the ashes to the Saint Paul and Duluth trestle over the Grindstone. The span was iron, the rails still searingly hot. Cautiously, Powell and three other men eased a handcar out onto the bridge. The lumberyard was just to the southwest, and the radiant heat from the towering flames still roaring there threatened to fry the men as they ventured out onto the trestle. But they made it across and signaled the others to follow. Slowly, each of the remaining cars crossed, each carrying another four volunteers, among them both Angus Hay and Dr. Barnum, who was still looking for his daughter. Then they set off through the dark toward Skunk Lake, moving slowly, picking up bodies and laying them carefully by the side of the tracks.

By the time they arrived at Skunk Lake at about 4:30 A.M., they had moved thirty-one bodies. At the lake, they discovered that Dave Williams and his party had already been there from the north and had since left. Most of the survivors were still in the lake or on its margins, though, being attended to by doctors Magie and Codding. The coal in Root's tender was still burning brightly, still illuminating the scene in eerie fits and starts. They found Root alone, propped up, but apparently unconscious in the cab of his locomotive. When Powell called out to him, "Hello, Jim! How do you feel?" Root opened his eyes and said simply, "I am poorly."

Someone called for Dr. Barnum.

Someone else muttered, "A doctor is no good now."

Nevertheless, Barnum and the other doctors began to attend to Root. One of the party—an attorney named Roberts—offered Root a cup of warm milk. Root may well have recognized him. Roberts had been instrumental in having Root arrested and fined when he had walked off his train in Pine City during the Pullman strike.

Powell and a couple of his men took one of the handcars and pressed on north into the smoky, predawn darkness, looking for more survivors. A few miles up the line, they came across Powell's friend and fellow section foreman, John McNamara, wandering along the track, dazed and disoriented, looking for his wife Annie and his sons. He hadn't seen them since they had arrived together at Skunk Lake on Root's train and, piling off of the train into the smoke and confusion, had begun to run north on the tracks. Powell took McNamara onto the handcar and they continued north another mile or two looking for McNamara's family, not knowing that Williams and his men had removed the bodies of Annie McNamara and three of her sons from beside the tracks hours before.

Back at Skunk Lake, a short time after Powell left, Root began to feel better. He climbed down from his locomotive, found a handcar that had just arrived, and told the men aboard it that he wanted to go home. He climbed aboard and lay down. One of his passengers, Mrs. E. W. Saunders, sat down next to Root and cradled his head in her lap.

In New York, someone laying out the Sunday-morning edition of *The New York Times* found a bit of room on the front page to squeeze in a short notice picked up from one of the wire services at 1:00 A.M.:

Pine City, Minn., Sept. 2—1 A.M.—Fire has destroyed Hinckley
utterly. Fifty people were burned to death. Mission Creek is also
destroyed.

At dawn on Sunday, in Sandstone, Emil Anderson and a half-dozen
of his fellow survivors crawled out from under a half-burned boat
where they had spent the night next to the Kettle River. The eerie
howling that everyone had heard on and off all through the night
floated down again from the steel center span of the High Bridge.
Looking up at it now, they could see in the dim, gray light that it
wasn't the old watchman, Wallace Damuth, who was howling, but
rather M. W. Jesmer's badly burned dog. As the light improved, they
could soon also see that Damuth was in fact sprawled out on the hot
stringers near the dog, dead.

Anderson made his way slowly along the riverbank, among the
shivering survivors stretched out on sandbanks and gravel bars. A
hundred yards up the river, one building—the bright-red office of the
quarry's operators, the Minneapolis Trust Company—had survived,
sheltered from the worst of the firestorm in the lee of the cliff. Entering it, Anderson found that foreman Peter Peterson had already
gathered together several dozen of the most badly burned victims,
laying them out carefully on the pine-plank floor.

No one had heard a sound from the town itself, up on the bluff
above, since the screaming they had all heard at the height of the fire
had ended. Peterson moved among the men gathered outside the office, organizing a search party to reconnoiter the town. Emil Anderson joined them as they trudged through the ashes up the long slant
of the wagon road. As they walked, the men talked softly about what
had happened and how they could get help for the town. But when
they reached the top and entered First Street they fell silent. Dozens
of twisted, charred bodies were scattered up and down the street in
front of what had been homes or businesses. Those that were recog-
nizably human wore lipless grimaces and stared back at them

through leathery, black masks. It was impossible to recognize most of them, but as he moved from one pile of bodies to another, Emil Anderson began to weep, realizing that the smaller corpses must represent at least half of his Sunday school class.

As the men made their way quietly back down to the river, with no survivors to bring to the shelter, they began to realize how entirely they were cut off from the outside world. With the High Bridge down and the swift, wide Kettle River on the north side of town, and with dozens of smaller bridges no doubt burned out to the south toward Hinckley, they knew they had no prospect of immediate relief. Gradually it occurred to them that, in fact, no one outside the Sandstone area might even know what had happened here. And no one might get here to find out for days. If they were going to get help any time soon, somebody was going to have to go looking for it. The best hope was a boardinghouse at Hell's Gate, five miles up the river.

One of their number, Chris Heisler, had managed to save his two horses and his wagon in the river, and he volunteered to carry some of those who could not walk but who could stand to ride. Most could neither walk nor ride that far, though, and when Emil Anderson and the others left with Heisler's wagon, almost three hundred people had to remain behind, some of them badly burned and lying on the floor of the quarry office, the rest hunkered down behind boulders and slabs of sandstone on the riverbank.

During the night, ashes and sand had blown into Antone Anderson's eyes, and when he awoke at dawn he found that they were swollen shut. At first he couldn't remember what had happened. He worked at his eyes and finally managed to get one open enough to see where he was—in a ditch beside the Eastern Minnesota tracks somewhere north of Hinckley.

His brother Charlie was nowhere to be seen, so Antone began to walk in the direction they had been running yesterday afternoon—north. A few dozen yards up the tracks he came across Charlie lying on the gravel, dead. The trunk of his body was badly burned, but his face was intact. Antone knelt over the body and looked at the silent, still face. Then he looked around at the alien, gray-and-black landscape surrounding him, swept clear of any sign of life. The silence was absolute and so, he realized, was his aloneness. He got up and began walking back down the tracks toward Hinckley, struggling to get his other eye open.

He'd gone perhaps a quarter of a mile when he came to the marshy meadow where he had left his mother, father, and sister Emily. The scene looked, as he would later remember it, "like the end of the world." More than a hundred bodies were huddled together in an area of about an acre. All of them were charred, none recognizable in any sense except that they had once been human beings. Many of them seemed to have clasped their hands over their mouths in their last moments of life. Wisps of smoke were still rising from some of them, and the air reeked of burned hair, flesh, and bone.

Scattered in a rough circle around the bodies were the blackened iron skeletons of wagons, buggies, steamer trunks, and baby carriages.

He wandered among the bodies looking for his mother and father, the horrific sights and smells overwhelming him, pulling at the edges of his mind, threatening to unravel it. Finally, he came across a partially burned gaiter shoe that he was sure was his mother's lying near one of the blackened lumps. Nearby was a shorter lump he thought might be his father. He couldn't find anything that resembled Emily.

Stunned, he started walking south, toward town. In places the ground was still so hot that it burned his feet through the remnants of his shoes. He stumbled down into the ravine of the Grindstone River and wet his feet in the ash-covered stream. Upstream, he saw the already bloated bodies of Ida Martinson and her four children sprawled in the mud.

When he crawled up the opposite bank and looked south, he realized for the first time that Hinckley simply wasn't there anymore. He wandered down what had been streets, among piles of bricks and burned corpses, until he came to the south end of town where the doctors were still at work in the roundhouse.

When Antone told them what he'd seen in the marsh across the Grindstone, the men stared at him and blanched, not sure whether to believe him. Then Axel Rosdahl appeared at the roundhouse. He'd been across the river as well, and he confirmed what Antone had just told them. It looked, he said, as if "the big lumberyard was picked up by the terrific gale and tossed right in among the fleeing people."

A contingent of volunteers gathered together an assortment of vehicles that had been saved in the gravel pit and went out to the marsh. Of the ninety-six bodies they loaded onto the vehicles, only four could be readily identified: Charlie Anderson, Winnie Ginder, Axel Hanson, and forty-year-old Dennis Riley, whose wife, daughter, and son had died along with him but could not be identified.

At Skunk Lake, Bill Grissinger also woke up unable to see, his eyes plastered shut with dried mud. He felt someone picking him up, pulling him up out of the ooze and carrying him toward the shore, setting him down again on the dry bank. The same someone wiped at his eyes with a damp rag, peeling back the mud until he could finally see who was tending to him—his schoolteacher, Mollie McNeil—whose own face was still covered with the black mud she had applied during the night to keep her face from blistering.

As Mollie McNeil worked on his face, Bill Grissinger looked at the people huddled in groups along the edge of the marsh. Some of them were missing eyebrows or parts of their hair. All of them were covered with mud and green slime, their clothing tattered or burned. All were in varying degrees of shock and hysteria, chattering and babbling in what he would later remember as "an incoherent tongue that seemed [to be] coming from people of a foreign land." John Powell and his men had distributed bread from their handcars, but the survivors were thirsty more than hungry, and some of them dipped their loaves in the green water alongside the tracks to slake their thirst.

Powell and his men loaded Bill Grissinger and a dozen or so other young people onto a handcar and set off toward Hinckley. But they took them only as far as the hamlet of Friesland, where a small country store had stood until yesterday. Leaving them there by the ashes of the store, the men told the young people to walk into Hinckley while they went back to Skunk Lake for more people. Bill and the others started off down the tracks toward town. Almost immediately they came to a body, the first they had seen. It looked, as Bill later described it, ". . . red and ugly lying there on the shoulder of the grade."

By the time they reached the Grindstone, they had counted twenty-two bodies, and Bill Grissinger had sunk into a kind of stupor, his mind refusing to confront what was before him. Walking through town, he saw a part of the picket fence where his house had stood, and a cluster of blackened bodies scattered just down the street from it, but he walked stonily on past without examining them.

When he came to the relief train at the south end of town and climbed aboard, a brakeman asked him where he was going, and he replied, "I'm going to Hinckley." The brakeman explained that this was Hinckley, but Bill simply cried out "No, no, no." The brakeman looked at him sadly, told him, "All right, my boy. We will take you to Hinckley," and carried him to an empty coach at the rear of the train. Bill slumped in a seat in a corner of the coach. A few minutes later Pine County's sheriff, Joe McLaughlin, swung himself up into the coach and, seeing Bill huddled in a corner, he repeated the brakeman's question: "Where are you bound for?" When Bill again said "Hinckley," the sheriff sat next to him, put his arm around the boy, and repeated the brakeman's words. "All right, my boy, we will take you to Hinckley."

And the train pulled out for Pine City.

At about 8:00 A.M., Peter Kelly and John Roper finally got their train through to Skunk Lake and found that, with the exception of the handful that Dave Williams had taken north on his handcar earlier and another forty that John Powell had taken south, all of Root's passengers were still in or near the lake. Many of them were suffering from hypothermia; all of them were cold, wet, and miserable. The morning air tasted ashy and stank of mud and foul water.

Ed and Helen Hansen had been bathing their mother's eyes with the muddy lake water since sunup, and she was finally able to see well enough to make out Kelly's train as it arrived. It was the first time she had been able to see anything reasonably well since stumbling through the burning woods toward Root's train the previous afternoon. Looking around her now, she could see that Josephine was lying on the mud nearby, white and still, staring blankly at the wreck on the tracks above her.

Marie rose from the mud, her long, wet dress clinging coldly to her thighs, and made her way up the embankment toward the men who were piling off of the relief train. As she approached them, she peered into each of their faces, and Ed, trailing behind her, realized that she was looking for his father, thinking he might be among them. When she realized that he was not, she sank to her knees on the gravel embankment, bent forward, and began to pound the gravel silently with her bare hands, her fists clenched. Ed knelt beside her in the gravel, bare-chested and shivering. During the long night his fear and grief had congealed into a cold knot in his belly. He stared at the gravel in front of him and tried to think of what he could say or do to help his mother.

John Blair helped Marie and Ed onto a coach. Helen helped Josephine out of the mud and led her to the train. When they were aboard and sitting on the wooden seats in the coach, dripping muddy water onto the floor, someone came by and put blankets around their shoulders. Someone else thrust a cold doughnut into Ed's hand. He stared at it but did not eat it. It sat there in his muddy hand—a lump of grease and dough, cold and hard like the knot in his stomach—all the way to Duluth.

As the relief train from Hinckley backed into Pine City by midmorning, Bill Grissinger saw a river and a millpond full of logs flash by outside. He leapt to the window, thinking that this must be Hinckley, but his heart sank when he saw that the buildings rolling by outside were unfamiliar. Most of the refugees got off at Pine City, but Sheriff McLaughlin told the boy to stay aboard a bit longer. The train continued on to Rush City, and there McLaughlin took Bill to his home. McLaughlin's wife washed his face, combed his hair, bandaged his burned hand, and put salve on his burned ear. She tried to give him some cold milk, but he refused it. Then Sheriff McLaughlin rented a buggy and drove him back into Pine City to see if they could find any of his relatives among the survivors.

McLaughlin and the boy drove through the streets near the railway station, among throngs of dazed refugees. McLaughlin called out the name over and over, "Grissinger, Grissinger." No one answered, but Bill Grissinger finally saw a man sitting on the edge of a wooden sidewalk, his head in his hands. Leaping over the wheel of the buggy, he ran across the street and flung himself into his father's arms. His father stared into his face incredulously, and then gushed out, "Where's your mother? Where are Callie and Mabel?" The moment he heard the question, Bill knew the answer. The cluster of bodies down the street from the picket fence came back to him, with meaning this time.

The bulk of the Skunk Lake survivors arrived at Union Station in Duluth near noon. Once again throngs of people pressed forward against police lines on the platform, calling out for missing relatives or friends. A reporter from the *Duluth News Tribune* described the scene:

> Parents were searching for children, husbands for wives and children, brothers for sisters, who had been left behind. Begrimed with dust and smoke, suffering with injuries from the fires, wound in dirty, wet blankets, and huddled together in fear and anguish, the sight they presented was more than pitiable.

When Ed Hansen stepped down onto the platform, he peered into the crowd behind the police lines. People were shrieking and gesturing and weeping as they saw, or failed to see, loved ones coming down from the train. Their faces were florid and contorted by a

hundred different emotions, and the cold knot in Ed's stomach tight-
ened as he watched them.

A doctor stepped forward and looked into Marie's face and
asked her how she was feeling, but Marie could barely make him out,
did not understand him, and responded in Norwegian, asking him
where she could go to find her husband. A porter carried Josephine
down the steps from the train in his arms. The doctor took one look
at her—pale, hollow-eyed, shaking beneath the muddy blanket in
which she was wrapped—and ordered a stretcher brought out. When
Josephine had been laid on the stretcher, the doctor told an orderly to
take them all to Saint Mary's Hospital. Ed and Helen followed the
stretcher through the crowd with their mother, who was talking to
herself now, saying something in Norwegian that Ed couldn't follow.

When they arrived at Saint Mary's, the squat three-story brick
building seemed dark and foreboding to Ed. In the waiting room,
more doctors examined them. Then nurses led Marie, Helen, and
Josephine away to the women's ward. Another orderly took Ed by
the hand and led him to the men's ward, where the sharp, mingled
smells of carron oil, antiseptic solution, urine, and vomit enveloped
him. His stomach lurched as the man led him down the middle of a
long, low room to one of the many beds stretched along each side.
The orderly helped him undress, throwing his torn, muddy clothes
into a basket at the foot of the bed. He stood naked, shivering in the
cold room as the orderly rummaged through another basket for a
long shirt for him to wear. Ed put on the shirt and climbed into the
bed, closing his eyes, trying to keep the knot in his stomach from exploding into a wave of nausea and vomit. He listened to the men and
boys in the room—some moaning, some gasping, some snoring,
some weeping—and he felt very alone.

Somewhere in Saint Mary's at about the same time, a man was rav-
ing loudly and incoherently. It was Tom Sullivan, Root's conductor,
and he was saying, over and over, that somebody must catch the little girl he'd thrown from the train.

Several press accounts written in the days after the fire reported that Sullivan had, in fact, thrown one or more children from Root's train while it was still moving through the firestorm. Others spoke more generally of Sullivan "going insane" at some point during the ordeal. *The New York Times* asserted that he had "lost his head entirely, and seemed to be raging in a perfect fit of insanity." Most eyewitnesses, though, reported that Sullivan behaved admirably during the crisis.

All in all, it's unlikely that Sullivan tossed a child from the train. He does seem, however, to have become temporarily unhinged at some point during the retreat to Skunk Lake or during his long run up the Saint Paul and Duluth tracks. What's likely is that in the hours immediately following the worst of the firestorm, Sullivan was suffering from what used to be called "shell shock" and is now called post-traumatic stress disorder (PTSD).

It wasn't until the years following World War I that anyone studied shell shock, and it wasn't until Boston's Cocoanut Grove fire that anyone systematically studied the psychological effects of fires and other disasters on civilians.

On the evening of November 28, 1942, more than a thousand people—four hundred more than the club's legal occupancy limit—crowded into the Cocoanut Grove club on Boston's Piedmont Street. The revelers, many of them servicemen on leave and their dates, danced, drank, and dined among the club's exotic displays of artificial palm trees and tropical foliage. At some point during the evening, a patron apparently removed a lightbulb from a fixture in the Melody Lounge on the basement level. When a busboy struck a match a few minutes after 10:00 P.M. in order to see well enough to replace the bulb, he inadvertently ignited something combustible. At 10:11 P.M. flames engulfed the basement level and then roared up to the main level, feasting on the artificial foliage and heavy drapery. A refrigeration unit in one corner of the club exploded, igniting the methyl chloride refrigerant and sending billows of blue flames across the ceiling of the room. The patrons pushed their way toward the front entrance en masse. But the entrance was a pair of revolving doors, with no side doors. Predictably, the crush of people trying to enter the revolving doors quickly disabled them. Another exit was hidden behind drapery. And the panic bar of a third exit had been welded shut. Most of the 492 dead were found piled four or five deep in front of the revolving doors.

In the aftermath of the fire, a Harvard-educated psychiatrist, Dr. Eric Lindemann, working with survivors at Massachusetts General Hospital, conducted the first in-depth study of how civilian disasters affect the psychiatric health of survivors and how they might best be treated. The lessons of the study would turn out to be more applicable in the twentieth and twenty-first centuries than anyone could have imagined.

A surprising 39.1 percent of modern Americans (6 to 7 percent per year) are exposed to some form of severe trauma at some point during their lives. This figure includes direct traumas, as from a physical injury, to psychological traumas, such as witnessing the unexpected death of a loved one. Most of those exposed do not develop serious psychological impairment as a result, but estimates of how many do range as high as 30 percent, and following particularly horrific disasters, the percentages may well go higher. A year after the Cocoanut Grove fire, 50 percent of the survivors still suffered from psychiatric complications. More recently, three years after the terrorist attacks on the World Trade Center on September 11, 2001, 51 percent of rescue workers who responded to the site still suffered from a variety of mental health problems, and they had four times the normal adult rate of PTSD. The startling bottom line is that an estimated 7.8 percent of Americans will suffer from PTSD during their lifetimes.

A host of other afflictions may co-occur among disaster survivors with PTSD: generalized anxiety disorder, substance abuse disorders, panic disorder, major depression, adjustment disorder, various forms of family violence, and suicide. PTSD, though, is more and more often the primary diagnosis for disaster survivors. PTSD is associated with specific neurobiological and physiological changes in the central nervous system. These seem to center around the way that the amyglia and the hippocampus process memories. The symptoms of PTSD vary widely depending on—among other things—the duration of the trauma, the subject's prior experiences, his or her psychological profile before the disaster, and, in particular, the nature and intensity of the trauma.

Generally, though, the disorder manifests itself in several categories of symptoms: *Intrusive recollections* come unbidden and cause the sufferer to re-experience the emotions felt during the initial trauma. These may take the form of nightmares, daytime fantasies, or the psychotic reenactments that we know as "flashbacks." Some survivors experience *avoidance symptoms*, which revolve around strategies, often phobic and irrational, that the sufferer employs to make certain that he or she is never again subjected to the cause of the original trauma. Others may experience *psychic numbing*, in which they find it difficult to participate in normal social relationships, or they may experience symptoms of *dissociation*, feeling temporarily separated from their own bodies. *Hyperarousal* symptoms may involve panic attacks or extreme vigilance—sometimes bordering on paranoia—as well as extreme startle reactions.

Fire disasters, it turns out, are particularly apt to cause psychiatric damage for a number of reasons. Most people rate death by fire as the most horrific demise imaginable. And among the factors that most put a person at risk for PTSD, several are particularly likely to occur in a fire: exposure to dead bodies, particularly if they are disfigured; witnessing the deaths of others; witnessing the deaths of children; disruption of one's community; ongoing pain and physical trauma, as in the case of burn injuries; and loss of basic resources like food, water, housing, and livelihood.

It's sobering to consider that while we now have a basic understanding of the workings of PTSD, and at least a small arsenal of pharmaceuticals and therapies with which to treat it, none of these were available to the survivors of the Hinckley firestorm. To the extent that they failed to pick themselves up, dust themselves off, and get on with their lives, they were likely to be deemed weak at best, crazy at worst. And, sadly, those who played the role of hero were among the most likely to suffer from psychiatric disorders. Research suggests that people who act heroically in a disaster often carry a special burden later— foisted upon them by an admiring public that holds them to a higher standard. It seems that we expect our heroes to be larger than life even after their exploits are completed. And, because we expect them to be stronger and braver than the ordinary cut of humanity, our heroes often suffer their own demons in tortured silence.

What may have produced Tom Sullivan's unhinged state of mind was a variant of PTSD that has only recently been recognized—post-traumatic stress disorder with symptoms of psychosis (PTSD-P). Psychosis frequently produces delusions, hallucinations (both visual and auditory), paranoia, and thought disorders that may result in garbled thinking and/or speech. The child Sullivan thought he had thrown from the train was probably no more, and no less, than a hallucination, or as the people who were there with him would most likely have called it, "a figment of his imagination."

At about 2:00 P.M., finally back at Union Station in Duluth, Dave Williams received another telegram. One of his work crews repairing the Saint Paul and Duluth line between Miller and Hinckley had made contact with a few settlers from near Sandstone, and they had alarming news, as the telegram related:

> There are 150 people at Sandstone without food or shelter. For God's sake, get them out of there.

This was the first that anyone had heard of Sandstone's fate. Williams had been out on the road all night, first working to get the handcars through to Root's train, and then getting the line repaired and the refugees evacuated to Duluth. Nevertheless, he rushed back into action now. He equipped another train with food, liquor, milk, coffee, ice, clothing, and medical supplies. He rounded up six doctors and four nurses from Saint Luke's Hospital, and he persuaded a prominent citizen, Major O. D. Kinney, to supervise the expedition. Then he assembled another repair crew and put together another work train to hasten the reopening of the line. At 3:30 P.M., Williams pulled out with the work train, and half an hour later the Kinney train pulled out behind him on the Saint Paul and Duluth tracks. At the same hour, a train was pulling out of Saint Paul heading north for Pine City with 4,000 dollars' worth of provisions donated by local businesses, most importantly 2,300 loaves of bread that the Horejs Brothers Bakery had baked especially for the fire victims.

The Kinney train ran into trouble almost immediately; mechanical problems with the locomotive and confusion about conditions on the road to the south delayed them for hours just south of Duluth. After switching locomotives and proceeding slowly down the line, they didn't reach the burned-out station at Miller until well after dark, at about 10:00 P.M. Here they began to search the immediate area for bodies before heading overland for Sandstone. Before long, a figure came trudging into the pool of light surrounding the train. It was a man, his clothing torn to tatters, his face streaked with black, his eyes red-rimmed and hollow. He was one of the Sandstone survivors, come from the boardinghouse at Hell's Gate in search of help. Kinney sent two men to retrace the man's steps northeast to Hell's Gate. Then he dispatched a second, larger party off to the southeast, toward Sandstone.

Even now, thirty hours after the main fire had passed through, the air here was heavy with smoke. Flames were still lapping at stumps for miles in every direction, and the sight of the flames dancing through the drifting, black smoke was eerie, unnerving many in the party. The effect was magnified when, a few minutes after they set out for Sandstone, one of the men's lanterns, swinging by his side, snagged on something.

Glancing down he saw that it was the body of a young woman lying on her back, her arms outstretched, reaching upwards as if to grab his lantern.

MONDAY | SEPTEMBER 3, 1894

Emil Anderson awoke just after midnight to find two men with lit lanterns standing over him in the boardinghouse at Hell's Gate, where he and two dozen or so other Sandstone survivors had been sheltering for the last eleven hours. The men were from the Kinney train. They wanted anyone who was able to walk to come with them and march the five miles back to the train immediately. When Anderson understood who they were, he began to rouse the other survivors, but the shouting and the flickering light of the lanterns in the middle of the night alarmed some of them. Believing that perhaps the firestorm had finally caught up with them, someone shouted, "Is there fire in the house?" People tumbled down the stairs and out through the doorway, and it took some minutes before Anderson could calm them down and explain the situation.

With only a few lanterns to share among them, they set off walking west, toward the train. If anything, the trek was harder than the one they had made when they walked here from Sandstone. Almost all of them were barefoot. Many had burns on their feet, and the burns had begun to fester, their feet to swell, so that walking any distance was now agonizing. Some of them had virtually no clothes, and in the night air they were cold almost beyond endurance, despite the coals glowing in the dark all around them. There were dozens of children with them, and before they'd gone half a mile most of the children needed to be carried.

But within a couple of hours they were on the Kinney train, where doctors began to apply linseed oil to their burns as nurses doled out cold milk, hot coffee, and bread. Only now, Emil Anderson realized as he sat on the train, did he finally believe that he was really beyond the reach of the flames.

Shortly after 1:00 A.M., the main body of the Kinney expedition made their way down the wagon road to the dark quarry at Sandstone, where more than 250 people had been stranded for thirty-two hours now. As the party entered the quarry, exhausted, ravenously hungry people; half naked, blackened people; people with much of their hair singed off and with burns on their flesh, crawled and staggered out from behind rocks to meet them. To many of them, these men coming down the bluff with their lanterns glowing seemed to be a band of angels descending suddenly out of the darkness on flickering wings of light.

The doctors made their way to the quarry office, where stretched out on the floor they found the twenty-eight people who had been lying there since they were gathered together by Peter Peterson early Sunday morning. All of these people were badly burned. Many of them were in extreme pain, shivering, moaning, and writhing on the floor. Some, mercifully, were unconscious. The doctors began to administer to the worst-off among them first, giving them brandy and applying carron oil to their burns. But it was obvious that there was no way that most of them were going to walk out of there.

Within an hour, Kinney and his men had gathered together everyone except for the twenty-eight in the quarry office. Most of the doctors and several newspapermen were to stay there with them. The rest of the rescuers and survivors set off up the wagon road, a long procession of lanterns snaking its way back up the bluff and into the darkness.

At 4:45 A.M., another relief train left Duluth southbound, this one on the Eastern Minnesota tracks, under the direction of W. C. Farrington, general manager of the Eastern Minnesota Railway. Every man on the train had been issued a shovel for the purpose of burying the dead as they found them, on the spot. The train consisted of two flatcars carrying wagons, lumber, and a rowboat; two freight cars carrying horses, food, and medical supplies; two coaches carrying fifty lumberjacks and eight doctors; and a private car. The private car belonged to James J. Hill himself, and it carried not only Farrington but also a contingent of prominent Duluth citizens. It also carried twenty-four-year-old James N. Hill, the oldest son of James J. Hill.

The elder Hill was in Helena, Montana, but during the night he had sent a telegram to Farrington saying that he wanted to know exactly what had happened on his railroad, and he wanted to provide whatever help he could to victims of the fire.

The younger Hill was there to make sure that his father's will was done.

When the sun rose over Hinckley at 5:31 A.M. Monday morning, all of the remaining refugees from the village had been evacuated south to Pine City. Passenger trains were continuing to arrive from the south, carrying reporters and work crews. Freights were also arriving with new rails, ties, and lumber for coffins. A local relief committee was formed, with Angus Hay as secretary. Far to the north, Ed Barry and Bill Best were asleep at their homes in West Superior. In Duluth, nearly 1,200 survivors were sheltered at various locations around the city—at the Armory on Michigan Street, at the Bethel rescue mission on Lake Avenue, and in dozens of churches, hotels, and private homes. To the south, in the village of Mora, Alice, Mabel, and Minnie Nelson and their parents—along with about a hundred other survivors brought in from the vicinity of Pokegama—were sleeping at the Methodist Church, which had been turned into a temporary hospital. In Pine City, Antone Anderson was asleep in a relief tent. Scores more survivors were sleeping on the floor of the skating rink. At the Knights of Pythias Hall, relief workers were setting about the enormous task of cooking breakfast for the hundreds of refugees brought into Pine City during the past twenty-four hours. Further south, in Rush City, Olive Brown was still at the key of her telegraph, where she had remained continuously for over thirty-six hours now, sending out reporters' news dispatches, passing messages from one relief party to another, relaying hundreds of frantic messages to and from refugees trying to find their loved ones up and down the line. Jim Root was asleep at his home in White Bear Lake, his neck, eyes, and hands bandaged, his wife sitting by his bed. In Saint Paul, John Blair was finally at home with his wife Emma in their house on Case Street.

At the same hour, yet another relief train was heading for Hinckley, this one from Saint Paul. As it made its way north, the crew found that at each station along the way—at White Bear, at Stacy, at North Branch—people anxious to help had piled mountains of food and goods on the platform. At each village, throngs of people stood by the tracks in the early morning chill as the train passed, many with tears in their eyes, cheering the relief workers, shouting out,

"Good luck!"

"Will you take us along?"

"Send back all the news you can."

At 7:25 A.M., the Kinney train arrived back in Duluth with 247 Sandstone survivors, including Emil Anderson. Like most of the others, Anderson was taken to the Armory. He ate a hearty meal, changed his clothes, and lay down on a cot with a blanket for a while, but he couldn't shake the thought of the injured people he'd left behind in Sandstone. He didn't know what else he could do, so he arose and walked back up Superior Street to Union Station. By 10:30 A.M., he was on another work train heading back south on the Saint Paul and Duluth line.

The Farrington party, meanwhile, after leaving their train at an impassable culvert at the remains of Partridge and walking overland, had arrived at the burned-out Kettle River High Bridge and begun to clamber down the sheer 135-foot face of the bluff. When they reached the river they hailed a survivor on the other side who, with great difficulty, poled across in a twelve-foot flat-bottom boat that had survived the fire more or less intact. Within another half-hour, the entire party had been ferried across the river and the doctors among them made their way to the quarry office, where they joined the doctors left behind by Kinney in tending to the burned people sprawled out on the pine-plank floor.

The care they were able to offer was precious little by modern standards. Burn treatment in 1894 was in many respects little better than what it had been a hundred or a thousand years before. Treating burns had always consisted principally of applying an amazing assortment of salves and ointments to the wound: black mud, cow dung, roasted dormice, raw egg and vinegar, pig fat, boiled beans, beeswax, honey, oak leaves, and powdered silver, just to name a few. To be sure, some of these, notably the last three, had at least some beneficial effect on relatively superficial, first-degree burns. Honey does, in fact, sometimes serve as a useful dressing as it contains antimicrobial agents and is hydrophilic, absorbing moisture out of the atmosphere and thus keeping the wound moist. Oak leaves contain tannic acid, an astringent that was widely used on burns during the 1920s and 1930s to seal the wounds (by effectively tanning the skin just as cowhides are tanned to make leather). And silver ions do, in fact, have powerful antiseptic properties that make silver sulfadiazine and silver nitrate among the most useful burn treatments available even today. For the most part, though, the application of these salves did little that was helpful, except perhaps to ease pain temporarily, and much that was harmful. Most notably they introduced a novel assortment of pathogens and then sealed them in the wound, creating an especially inviting environment for anaerobic bacteria like *Clostridium perfringens.*

The carbolic acid and carron oil carried in the medical satchels of most of the doctors who rushed to Sandstone were no worse, and perhaps a little better, than many of the other treatments that had been tried throughout history. Carbolic acid had a mildly antiseptic effect, cleansing the wounds of some of the many superficial contaminants that could be expected to be found in the burns. The carron oil, a mixture of lime water and linseed oil, at least soothed the pain and probably did not significantly contaminate the wounds with large infusions of new bacteria.

If they lived long enough to make it to a hospital in Duluth or Saint Paul, the Sandstone patients could expect to receive what was then the most modern treatment, likely something along the lines outlined by Dr. J. N. Plumb in a paper given before the Society of St.

Joseph and Grand Island Surgeons just six weeks before the fire. This consisted of cleansing the burns with carbolic acid and then dressing them with petroleum jelly, old linen, cotton, another layer of linen, and finally, waxed paper or oilcloth held in place by bandages.

None of this, though, would have addressed the inevitable consequences of major burns—the loss of fluid from the bloodstream, the edema and consequent swelling, the burn shock that was likely to follow, the insidious deepening and spreading of the wounds, the devastation produced by a runaway inflammatory response and a hyperbolic metabolism, the resulting self-cannibalization, and then—assuming that one was somehow still alive—the virtually certain development of massive bacterial and fungal infections under all those layers of linen and waxed paper. The burn wards of the day were notorious for their atmosphere of hopelessness and for the stench of rotting flesh.

The victims who lay on the floor of the quarry office in Sandstone had the misfortune of living and dying at a moment in history when effective treatment of burns was still just over the horizon. In the following year, 1895, Dr. William Halstead would introduce the use of silver to treat burns at Johns Hopkins. The concept of skin grafting, which had been around since the time of the ancient Egyptians, would only begin to come into widespread use for burn treatment in America at the end of the nineteenth century. Between World War I and World War II, medical researchers would make enormous strides in understanding the mechanics of fluid loss, and the use of sulfa and other emerging antibiotics would begin to produce results in the fight against infection. And in 1942, the horrific aftermath of the Cocoanut Grove fire would foster the same kind of revolution in the treatment of burns that it had fostered in the treatment of post-traumatic stress disorder. A hundred years after the Hinckley firestorm, a host of new life-saving therapies would be available, and burns that had carried near 100 percent mortality rates in 1894 would carry rates as low as 5 percent.

* * *

By mid-afternoon on Monday, Emil Anderson was back in Sand-stone, where it had begun to rain. He joined a burial detail from the Kinney party. One of the first victims that he found was August Swenson, the keeper of the town's waterworks. His body was in the rubble of the pump house where Anderson had last seen him as the fire approached the town. He was leaning over the body of his eleven-year-old boy, his hands clasped as if in prayer. At the bottom of a well nearby, the party found a woman sitting on a mattress, stooped forward a bit with her hands on her knees, staring at some-thing in front of her. She was unburned, but she did not respond to their shouts, and when they climbed down into the well they dis-covered that she was dead, apparently suffocated. Later, they would learn that her husband, finding her dead in the well, had drowned himself in a nearby creek.

On the west end of First Street, they made their grimmest find. First, they came across the half-burned trunk of Peter Englund lying in his front yard. Then, when they approached Englund's well, they were met by an overwhelming stench. Peering down into the well, they could make out the top layer of what would turn out to be a stack of eighteen bodies—Englund's wife and his seven children and nine other people, most of them neighborhood children. The bodies had been stewing in their own juices for almost forty-eight hours now. When they tried to remove them, heads and limbs separated from the torsos. No one had the stomach to deal with this now. They decided to leave the bodies for a special burial party the next day.

Stunned and sick at heart, they kept searching. On the outskirts of town, they found root cellars with whole families buried in ashes. In Frank Anderson's cellar, they found the remains of his wife and two children. Then they found Anderson himself in a shallow exca-vation at one side of the cellar. The marks of his fingers still showed in the burned soil where he had desperately tried to dig his way into the earth.

Not far away, a judge named John C. Nethaway from Stillwa-ter, leading his own small team of rescuers, was working his way west from Sandstone Junction. Seven miles northwest of Hinckley, he found a twelve-year-old boy at the bottom of a well. The boy, tired and hungry, was standing in eight inches of water as he had been since Saturday afternoon. When he was pulled out of the well, he said, "It was awful hot [down there]." Then he asked about his parents and his dog. Judge Nethaway put him on his back and carried him away from the spot where the bodies of five adults and several animals lay nearby.

By the time the searchers from the Kinney party made their way back down to the quarry late in the afternoon, several of the victims in the quarry office had died during their absence. The doctors who had remained with them made it clear that many of the rest would die soon if they couldn't be gotten to a hospital. But the mere thought of an evacuation was daunting. Even the lightest touch caused many of the patients to howl with pain, and none of them had the strength even to stand up, let alone walk. And even if the rescuers could get them across the river, they would still somehow have to get them up the 135-foot face of the bluff on the other side. Then they would have to transport them nine miles up the Eastern Minnesota line to the train waiting at Partridge.

It was the only chance these people had, though, so Farrington's men improvised a sling out of some canvas that they had brought with them. Someone found a mattress spring from which the fabric had been burned away, and they covered this with a second piece of canvas. With these two contrivances, they carried more than twenty burn patients down to the river and began the long process of ferrying them to the eastern bank on the flat-bottom boat. Eventually, all of them were on the opposite shore, at the base of the cliff. The only way to get them to the top was to carry them up by sheer brute strength.

The largest among the rescuers took the largest patients on their backs, lashing them there with ropes if the patients were too weak to hold on. The smaller among them carried burned women and children in their arms. In single file, they began inching their way up the face of the bluff, crawling more than walking, feeling with their feet for burned roots and sandstone outcroppings, anything to serve as a foothold. The patients in their arms and on their backs screamed and moaned as they were jounced and jostled up the bluff.

Finally, they were at the top, at the point where the Eastern Minnesota rails now ended abruptly at the edge of the Kettle River gorge. Waiting for them there was James N. Hill. His men had been laying new rails all afternoon between this spot and Partridge, and he personally had been traveling back and forth, bringing in supplies for a contrivance of his own invention. He had fashioned rope-and-canvas slings and suspended them between the handcars so that none of the patients would have to lie or sit on the hard boards of the cars.

When each of the victims had been laid in a sling, Hill and the others began to pump the handcars, and the last of the Sandstone survivors finally moved off into the damp, evening gloom.

By 6:00 P.M., Emil Anderson was back in Hinckley, where it had just finished raining. He'd come back to help with more burials, and to see what good he could do for the living. But the relief trains had ferried away the last of the survivors, and all that was left here now was death. The rain-soaked, bloated bodies of horses and oxen were scattered up and down the streets, their glistening legs sticking grotesquely into the air. Human remains were still piled haphazardly by the railway tracks in an ugly black heap. Some of the dead were in pine coffins bearing hasty inscriptions: "Supposed remains of Mrs. Blanchard, horribly distorted," "Girl, ten years old, no clothing." The evening air was full of the ripping sound of saws and the pounding of hammers as carpenters hurried to make more coffins before dark. Mollie McNeil, dressed in a light calico dress someone had given her after she crawled out of Skunk Lake, was wandering among the ruins, vainly searching for the trunk she'd abandoned before fleeing north on the Saint Paul and Duluth tracks.

There was little here that Anderson or McNeil could have recognized. Hinckley had become an unfamiliar place, a place of inert things rather than of people. In the deeper drifts of ashes and charred wood that marked where each house had stood, there were twisted bits of blackened leather, shards of white porcelain, chunks of fused glass, pieces of twisted iron—all mute, none revealing what it once had been. The bodies by the tracks kept their secrets too—most had no faces by which one might know them.

At 6:40 P.M., the sun began to set, sliding down behind leaden clouds on a western horizon that was level and featureless, devoid of familiar landmarks. Only the black shell of the brick schoolhouse remained, looming over the town's ash-gray streets and crumbled stone foundations. The large bronze bell that had tolled the town's doom two days before squatted amid the rubble of the town hall, immensely silent now. Crows—blown in from who knows how far away, riding on wet winds ripe with the scent of death—pecked at bits and pieces of things they found among the blackened bricks.

Black ashes blew gently down the wide-open space that had been Hinckley's main street. They swept along the heat-twisted rails of the Eastern Minnesota Railway and settled on puddles of silvery-cold steel where boxcar wheels had melted and hardened. They drifted through the burned-out shell of the brick schoolhouse. They swirled in eddies around the stone foundations of vanished houses. They crept under canvas walls and into tents where sullen men in dusty coats sat on cots under guttering kerosene lanterns, staring into tin plates of cold beans and bacon, eating little, saying less, but occasionally murmuring about what had just happened here, trying to piece it all together.

In an ashen field east of town, more men, wearing dark coats and slouch hats, stood leaning on their shovels and gazing solemnly down into a trench at their feet. In the trench before them lay the blackened and contorted remains of ninety-six men, women, and children—lately their friends, neighbors, family members, and lovers. Nearby, other men poked gingerly with the handles of their picks and shovels through a pile of charred bodies and body parts, looking for relatives. Still others stood in small clusters, holding their hats in their hands, staring at the desolate scene before them. Among the onlookers was mayor Lee Webster. Earlier in the day, thinking he might have seen his wife, Belle, among the first bodies tumbled into the trench and covered, Webster had ordered the men to unearth them. Then he had crawled into the trench himself, examined the exposed remains, and crawled back out again, shaking his head mutely. Now he stood alone, apart from the others, staring at the ashes on the ground.

Many of the men working at the trench wore handkerchiefs or bandanas over their mouths against the overwhelming stench of the methane gas escaping from the decomposing bodies, but the handkerchiefs didn't do much good. Most of the bodies had been baked, their red-and-black skin cracked and peeling off in layers, and as a result they were disintegrating quickly. Intestines were protruding from abdomens, eyes bulging out of their sockets and liquefying, foul-smelling black fluid running from gaping holes that had once been mouths. Disembodied hands, feet, and clumps of hair were scattered about the field. Near the trench, a single plaited braid of blonde hair, tied neatly with a ribbon, lay unheeded in the ashes.

In one corner of the field, Hans Paulson, searching for his wife and four children, removed some quilts that covered a pile of forty-five bodies. He examined each of them carefully, and finally picked up the blackened remains of a little girl dressed only in shreds of white cloth. He studied the clothes and what was left of her face, and then he began to sob as he carefully laid her down and resumed searching for the rest of his family.

In another corner, working alone, thirty-eight-year-old John Best was filling in the single grave he had dug for his mother, father, two sisters, and three brothers, work at which he had been laboring all afternoon, unspeaking, his jaw set. By another grave Martin Martinson, with his eleven-year-old son, John, standing beside him, stared transfixed at the bodies of his wife, Ida, and all four of his daughters lying at his feet, about to be lowered into the earth.

It was growing dark rapidly now, but all over the field men were still at work—building pine boxes, unloading more bodies from horse-drawn carts, starting a new trench for tomorrow's burials. A group of clergymen was assembling, planning to hold a brief service before the last light of day faded away. A reporter for the *Saint Cloud Daily Times* was taking notes. Another, from United Press, had just left abruptly, too sickened by the sights before him to continue working.

When the first trench was finally closed, the clergymen read from the Bible, gave short addresses, and left. Chris Best threw down his shovel and walked off into the dusk, still unspeaking. The volunteers—most of whom had been working all day and would do so again the next day, and the next, until they had dug and filled four long burial trenches—stacked their shovels and rode away on creaking wagons, wondering how they would ever manage to forget what they had seen here today.

Then all the living were gone, and dusk gave way to dark. The somber clouds of the afternoon began to break apart and drift away overhead. The bodies still piled by the trench lay on their backs, silent and still. With their charred limbs akimbo, their lipless mouths agape, their eye sockets hollow, they seemed to stare, as if aghast, into the black and star-strewn sky.

Chapter Ten

THE BROKEN SEASON

Sorrow breaks seasons and reposing hours,
Makes the night morning and the noontide night.

—Shakespeare,
Richard III

BY MID-MORNING TUESDAY, REPORTERS FROM MAJOR CITIES ALL across the Midwest and the East as well as from the national wire services began to arrive in Hinckley by the trainload. They pitched their tents amid the rubble and strung telegraph wires from one burned stump to another, making connections with Pine City and the outside world. Then they began to pump lurid headlines and sensational stories to their editors: IT WAS A HAMLET OF HORRORS, a headline in the *Duluth News Tribune* screamed. The *Minneapolis Tribune* told of flames that DANCE IN GHOULISH GLEE, LEAVING HUNDREDS OF CHARRED CORPSES IN THEIR WAKE. *The New York Times* led with THE DEAD LIE IN HEAPS AT HINCKLEY. The *London Times* announced, GREAT FOREST FIRES IN AMERICA.

With most of the bodies from the village and from the swamp across the river now accounted for, much of the reporters' attention focused on the millpond. It seemed only common sense that many people would have sought safety in the relatively deep water of the millpond. But the heat from the piles of sawdust, lumber, and logs still burning in the mill yard was so intense that no one had been able to get near enough to the pond to see how many bodies were there. Finally, by holding sheets of canvas in front of them for protection, a search party succeeded in getting within fifty feet of the millpond. When they returned, to nobody's surprise, they reported that the pond was covered with floating bodies. Angus Hay wired the story to the *Duluth News Tribune*, and papers all across the country picked it up. More than four hundred bodies had already been recovered from Hinckley, Sandstone, and the surrounding country, but the millpond added an irresistible element of suspense for the press. The *Brooklyn Eagle* called it "a pool of death." The final death toll now became the subject of grim speculation. The *News Tribune* editors, apparently taking a wild guess, declared in their next headline, IT'S UP TO 612! Relief workers made plans to dynamite the dam on the Grindstone in order to drain the pond and recover the bodies.

At about noon, a burial party from Duluth, under the direction of James Bailey, a woodsman, came across a number of safes and cash boxes that had been broken open in Sandstone. Shortly after that, they reached Peter Englund's homestead, where Emil Anderson and the Kinney expedition had discovered eighteen bodies in a single well on Monday. There they found a group of men tossing back into the well the last of a number of body parts that they had just finished robbing of their jewelry. As Bailey and his heavily armed men approached, the ghouls turned, ran, and escaped.

Governor Knute Nelson had already appointed a blue-ribbon state commission to oversee and coordinate relief efforts, naming Minnesota's most prominent businessmen to the body. Among them he appointed Mathew Norton, the timber baron from Winona, and Kenneth Clark, president of the Capital Bank in Saint Paul. No one was surprised when the commissioners chose from their own ranks the most prominent of them all—the Minneapolis flour magnate, Charles Pillsbury—to head the body. To some extent, though, appointment of the commission was a symbolic gesture. As in the case of hurricane Katrina 111 years later, it would take an excruciatingly long time for the government to organize a meaningful response. And at any rate the most important relief, the kind of help the victims really needed, had

already been pouring spontaneously out of the hearts and homes of ordinary citizens in northeast Minnesota since early Sunday morning.

Help came first from nearby places, large and small. It came in
the form of cash, useful items, and countless hours of free labor.
Money, stacks of blankets, barrels of flour, smoked hams, used clothing, carloads of lumber, crates of hardware, cartons of groceries, and
cans of milk flowed into the fire district. Material help came from
Minneapolis, from Duluth, from Two Harbors, from the nearby village of Mora, from Saint Cloud, from Stillwater, from White Bear,
from Mankato—from anyplace that a train bound for Hinckley
passed through.

Virtually every hotel, church, and school in Pine City, as well as
scores of private homes, had become temporary lodgings for the rescued. All over town people took in refugees, put them in their own
beds, fed them from their own larders, clothed them from their own
closets. Jim Hurley's impromptu relief committee distributed clothes
from the collection center at town hall and served meals at the
Knights of Pythias Hall. Dr. Barnum set up a temporary hospital in
the skating rink, paying for many of the supplies out of his own
pocket. A dozen volunteer doctors and medical aides, including Dr.
Stephan, worked at his side. By now Barnum had worked quietly and
grimly for seventy-two hours without sleep. He still hadn't heard any
news about his daughter, Kate.

At the Armory in Duluth, women from around the city had
organized another impromptu relief society. Three times a day they
cooked and served 500 meals. In the basement of the Lyceum Building, the sixty-eight members of a previously established organization—the Duluth Ladies' Relief Society—doled out the clothes that
they had been collecting since opening their doors at 6:00 on Sunday
morning. Nearly forty wagonloads of donated clothes had piled up in
various rooms, and the ladies were well on their way to distributing
what would eventually total 22,591 garments, along with 1,500 pairs
of shoes, hundreds of yards of fabric, and mountains of household
goods. Another group, the Duluth Women's Home Society, had taken

on the particularly wrenching task of gathering lost and orphaned children. At churches all around the city, chapels became dormitories and churchyards were equipped as playgrounds for the children among the survivors. At the Bethel shelter, volunteers in the kitchen pumped out 900 meals a day for the hundreds of people who were now living there on cots.

Partly as a result of this outpouring of concern and generosity, the pall of the past several days slowly began to lift for a few of the rescued. At 1:00 P.M. on Tuesday, in the Bethel meeting hall, one of the relief workers began to play the wedding march on the piano. Minnie Samuelson, with orange blossoms in her hair and wearing a veil and a pastel dress given to her by the ladies of Duluth, entered and walked up the aisle to where her groom, John Derosier, once again stood waiting for her. Duluth's chief of police stood beside him as a stand-in best man. The Reverend C. C. Salter, with wispy white hair and an equally white under-the-chin beard surrounding his face like a lion's mane, pronounced them man and wife as dozens of their fellow survivors—many of them just widowed—watched with tears coursing down their faces. Then, as the young couple sat down with their families to a small wedding feast provided again by the ladies of Duluth, a hat began to circulate among both the rescuers and the rescued, and before they left the hall, the Derosiers had a small sum with which to begin their married life. A wire service reporter, after chatting with the groom about his plans to return to his farm imme-diately and live with his bride in a boxcar while building a new house, proclaimed him "a plucky fellow, and his bride also has plenty of grit."

Among those sitting quietly watching the wedding were Marie Hansen and her children, who had just been moved here from Saint Mary's Hospital. Marie had regained her eyesight, though her eyes would ache for weeks, and Josephine was strong enough now to walk about on her own. But Marie had no money to put in the hat for the young couple when it was passed to her, and she had no idea how she would ever have any money again. When the ceremony was over, she, Ed, and Helen began to search the city for Evan, first there at the Bethel mission, then at the Armory, at Saint Luke's Hospital, at every hotel they could find up and down Superior Street. In his heart, Ed felt that his father was dead, but Marie would not hear of it, and so late into the evening, after returning the children to Bethel, she was still walking the streets of Duluth, stopping anyone who looked as if they might know where more refugees could be found.

By Wednesday, a tent city began to emerge from the ruins of Hinckley. Already, dozens of survivors had returned and begun rebuilding—with their own hands—their homes and businesses. Boxcars had been turned into temporary telegraph offices on both the Saint Paul and Duluth and the Eastern Minnesota lines. A cook shack was among the first buildings to go up. This was followed immediately by several makeshift saloons, essential if sufficient numbers of volunteers were to be recruited to rebuild the town. At the cook shack, volunteers cooked beans and salt pork in washtubs, ladled them out onto tin plates, and served them on long plank tables set out in front of the shack.

But there were still unburied human bodies stacked out at the cemetery, and hundreds of animal carcasses were scattered up and down the streets and decomposing in the fetid water of the gravel pit. The animals, especially, were becoming an almost insurmountable problem as they putrefied. No one could find enough lime to sprinkle on them, nor enough kerosene to burn them all, and as a result the stench had become all but unbearable for miles around Hinckley.

Despite this, though, by the middle of the day, the first of what would soon turn out to be dozens of trainloads of tourists arrived. They piled out of the train and fanned out over the ruins gawking at the devastation and particularly at the bodies. A *Duluth News Tribune* reporter described the scene:

> . . . there was a mad rush by passengers from the cars to see the nine bodies which lay close to the tracks. Prominent among the ones who were most persistent in the attempt to gain a view of the blackened and distorted trunks were several mere girls. They

got a close view and one of them turned deathly sick and would have fallen but for some helping hands that escorted her back to the chair car. The sight was too horrid for her, as it was for many of the men . . .

Not everyone had come just to gawk, however. Some had come for souvenirs, and they snatched whatever interested them among the ashes—gun barrels, melted coins, charred shoes, glass melted and fused into interesting shapes by the heat. Some had a more practical bent of mind and took usable items, mostly iron tools and kitchen utensils. A few had even brought shovels, and they began to dig through the ashes looking for relics the others might have missed. In the ashes of a house, one of them chanced upon a human hand overlooked by the volunteer burial crews.

The volunteers, many of whom had worked at their grisly task for three days now, were becoming hardened and perhaps numbed by their experience. A correspondent for *The New York Times* watched as they unloaded a wagon that had brought in new remains from the country outside of Hinckley:

> Late this afternoon the body of a man with intestines exposed and body black as coal was brought into town along with a child's fearfully burned body and a man's leg and shoe. All were thrown into one pine coffin and buried.

On Thursday morning, an unfamiliar young woman arrived in Pine City and quietly registered at a hotel as "Miss Cochrane of New York." But word quickly got around that Nellie Bly—as most of the world knew twenty-six-year-old Elizabeth Cochrane—was in town. There wasn't a soul in town, or in America, who didn't know of the enterprising young reporter, who four years before had traveled around the world in seventy-two days, beating the fictional record set by Jules Verne's Phileas Fogg in *Around the World in Eighty Days*. Sent to Pine County by the *New York World*, the same paper that had sent her around the world, the ever-intrepid Bly wanted to see for herself what had happened here, so she set out immediately on a fifteen-mile cross-country walking tour from Mission Creek to Skunk Lake. Along the way she took in the sweep and scope of the devastation and interviewed dozens of survivors before wiring her report to New York for Friday's edition of the *World*.

By now, every newspaper in North America and many in Western Europe had carried front-page stories about the firestorm, and largely as a result of this, a tidal wave of donations began to flow into the region from around the world.

James J. Hill's Great Northern Railway Company donated $5,000 and 5,000 acres of land for new farms. But Hill and his men had a way of making sure that money flowing out of their corporate purse provided some sort of benefit to the company. When Sam Hill, James Hill's son-in-law and president of the Eastern Minnesota, telegraphed the senior Hill to discuss the donation, he concluded with an oddly unintelligible sentence: "I think this wise in view of the question which must be met tragedy zone indelible linguist regarding thieves of lands." The telegrapher must have wondered what sort of nonsense he was keying into the machine. But the senior Hill knew how to decode the last part of the sentence, ". . . in view of the question which must be met in the legislature regarding taxation of lands." The gift was, in part, a tax dodge.

More contributions came in all kinds and sizes, from individuals and from institutions. A business associate of James J. Hill, Lord Mount Stephen, sent $5,000 from London. A class of Sunday school boys in South Woodstock, Connecticut, sent $2.00. Mary Greenleaf, sister of the poet Longfellow, sent $100 along with a telegram saying, poetically, ". . . the fires have been terrible in your midst." John D. Rockefeller wired $1,000. Jennie Babcock in Minneapolis sent a check for $8.50, and along with it she sent ten sacks of flour, one sack of potatoes, one sack of corn, one sack of beans, and an assortment of bedding and clothing. The Sultan of Turkey sent 300 Turkish pounds. The Montgomery Ward Catalog Company sent 500 pairs of shoes.

A Duluth newspaper boy, Billie Groosky, sent three cents.

* * *

By the end of the week, most people who would find their loved ones alive had already done so—the lucky gradually becoming sorted out from the unlucky. Dr. Barnum, still overseeing the medical care of survivors at Pine City, had discovered that his daughter Kate had escaped from Hinckley on Best's train and was alive and well in Duluth. Antone Anderson had been reunited with his sister Clara, but they both had learned that they were orphans, the only survivors among their family. Belle Barden had learned that her father survived by crouching in a barrel of water on the back of Al Fraser's wagon. Mayor Lee Webster, after traveling to Duluth and back and desperately digging through piles of corpses at the cemetery, had finally given up trying to find his young wife, Belle. John McNamara had learned that Annie and three of his sons had died on the Saint Paul and Duluth tracks, but that his other two sons had survived in the mud of Skunk Lake. He'd also learned, for the first time, about the $3,500 that Annie had saved for their sons' educations. Axel Rosdahl had made it to Duluth and found his mother and his missing brothers safe at the Norris House Hotel.

But Marie Hansen, like dozens of other women in Duluth and Pine City, hadn't yet learned for sure whether she was widowed or not. Like most of the others who were separated from loved ones, she had put advertisements in all the newspapers, asking for any information concerning the whereabouts of Evan. The papers were full of desperate ads placed by mothers looking for their children, fathers for their spouses, friends for their friends. At the Bethel mission and at the Duluth Armory, lists were posted each day, twice a day, of those who were known to be dead and those who were known to be alive. Each day, twice a day, Marie checked both lists. Days passed and Evan was never on either. Each day Marie slipped deeper into the abyss of depression.

When work crews finally got close to the millpond in Hinckley on Friday, they found that they could simply remove boards from the gate on the overflow and thus drain the pond gradually rather than dynamiting the dam. By the end of the day, when the last board had been removed and the searchers surveyed the black, muddy bottom of the pond, they found not the hundreds of human corpses they had expected, but just one drowned cow. And so the formal search for the victims, both alive and dead, largely came to an end.

The dead continued to make appearances in unexpected places for weeks and months to come, though. Eighteen bodies lay scattered along the bed of Mission Creek, north of what had been the village of the same name. In John Westlund's cellar south of Sandstone, searchers found the bodies of Mrs. Westlund, Mrs. Henry Lind, Sophie Wacke, and all eight of their children. Near Opstead, on the eastern shore of Mille Lacs Lake, twenty-five miles northeast of Hinckley, a hunting party found the remains of twenty-three Native Americans. The bodies—men, women, and children—were scattered along ten miles of trail, stretching from their summer camp on Shadridge Creek to the spot where the fire had finally overtaken the last of them as they had tried to outrun it. Judging their location to be too remote to bother with a burial party, and no doubt acting on the racial prejudices of the times, white relief officials callously decided to leave the bodies to the wolves and the crows.

In Pokegama, Fred Molander had been missing for over a month before someone finally found him at the bottom of his own well. The bodies of three young women—prostitutes from Emma Hammond's brothel east of Hinckley—were found and buried where they had fallen, in a field belonging to John Patrick. Patrick at first put up four posts and strung some barbed wire around the spot, but later decided he really didn't like this new feature of his property. He had the bodies removed to the cemetery, where they were interred in one of the four mass-burial trenches. Hammond herself was an enormous woman of perhaps 300 pounds. Burned over most of her body, she was expected to die, a fact that had been publicly noted on the front page of Monday's *New York Times*. When told this, she replied, "I ain't got any kick coming; most of my girls are dead and I want to die too." In fact, though, she confounded everyone (perhaps including herself) by recovering after a long convalescence paid for in part, and grudgingly, by the State Relief Commission.

The commission gradually began to take charge of the local efforts and systematize the distribution of money and goods. Representatives of the commission registered and interviewed each refugee, completing a questionnaire that detailed the victim's particular circumstances, and his or her financial needs and wants. Most people indicated that they wanted to go back and rebuild their homes and businesses, though some swore they would never go near Pine County again. The representatives evaluated each case, entering notes and affidavits concerning the worthiness of each refugee on the back of the questionnaires. In many cases, the amount and type of relief offered came down, in large part, to a question of the personal habits, reputation, and perceived moral character of the refugee in question.

Those who were lucky enough to have connections fared considerably better than those who didn't. A handwritten note scrawled across the top of Sam Hallman's questionnaire said simply: "Gov. Nelson promised." Hallman received lumber and hardware sufficient to build a three-room house, carpenters' tools, housekeeping equipment, and some cash. Many, though, had no one to vouch for them, let alone the governor. Twenty-year-old Christine McElroy asked for $100 for furniture and $75 for clothes, but on the back of her questionnaire the examiner wrote, "This young dame is a mistress for John O'Neil. She is a strumpet not worthy of consideration." She was given nothing. Seventeen-year-old Catherine Frieshan asked only for a coat and drew this response: "The father of this girl is a good-for-nothing drunken sot while the girls are rather wild and as they grow older go to the bad. This one is inclined to be gay." But she was given the coat. David Lefebre—Peter Bilado's brother-in-law and the father of seven—claimed $475 for his house, $162 for farming implements, $150 for tools, $46.50 for his hogs, $50 for hay, $200 for household furnishings, and $150 for his barn. But on the back of his questionnaire the examiner wrote, "This man overestimates his loss 75 percent. What he asks for is more than he ever possessed. He drinks at times. His wife is the better manager of the two and should be consulted if possible." The Lefebres were given transportation back to Hinckley, two tents, a team of horses, and twenty dollars in cash.

Marie Hansen could not speak English well enough to answer the examiners' detailed questions, so on September 24 Helen went with her to the interview and interpreted for her. Marie told the examiner she wanted to stay in Duluth and needed warm clothing for her children, some simple furniture for the room she hoped to rent, and enough money to get through the next few months. When asked what she needed most urgently, though, Marie said that she needed a sewing machine. With that, she could at least take in clothes for mending. The committee cut her a check for $20, just enough to buy a basic, inexpensive sewing machine, and a few days later she began to put up notices at boardinghouses around Duluth, advertising her services as a seamstress.

Then, early on the morning of October 18, more than six weeks after the fire, one of the women for whom Marie Hansen had begun mending clothes knocked on the door of her rented room, flush with excitement. The woman had just returned from Saint Paul, where a friend had told her that some displaced fire sufferers were living in a nearby boardinghouse. One of the men, she believed, was named Edward Hansen, the American name that Evan had used recently when signing important documents. The woman had the address of the boardinghouse written on a scrap of paper that she thrust into Marie's hand. Marie stared at the paper. She could not believe it, did not dare to believe it, but within ten minutes she was running down Superior Street toward Union Station. Josephine, Helen, and Ed stayed behind. All three of them had found clerking jobs at local businesses, and they didn't dare to miss work for fear of losing their jobs.

The three of them suffered through a long day at work, trying to focus on their tasks, trying not to think about what their mother was doing, wondering and worrying about what condition their father would be in when he came home. They were all back in their room waiting anxiously, trying to calm one another, when at a little after 8:00 P.M. they heard heavy footsteps on the outside stairs leading up to the room. When the door opened it was Marie's face that they saw first. It had collapsed. It was fractured with anguish and grief, a jumble of lines and fissures surrounding moist eyes that stared despairingly back at them. Behind her there was only the void of the black, frosty night air outside. Then they saw that she was wearing a new black dress, the first in a long procession of black dresses, the only kind she would wear for the rest of her life.

Chapter Eleven

DRIFTING EMBERS

There are three things that are never satisfied, yea,
four things say not, It is enough: the grave;
and the barren womb; the earth that is not filled with water;
and the fire that saith not, It is enough.

—Proverbs 30: 15–16

THOUGH IT HAS COME DOWN TO US AS THE GREAT HINCKLEY Firestorm, the catastrophe at Hinckley was only part—albeit the most horrific part by far—of a much larger complex of fires that raged that day across the Upper Midwest and all the way east to Pennsylvania and western New York. The worst of these other fires burned in northwestern Wisconsin, just across the Saint Croix River from the worst-hit areas of Minnesota.

The National Weather Service's forecast for western Wisconsin on September 1, 1894, was identical to that for eastern Minnesota— "Fair, warmer, southerly winds." Early in the afternoon of that day, the same southwest winds that were just beginning to fan the flames in Mission Creek and Quamba edged into the northwest corner of Wisconsin. When they began to blow, they awakened dozens of fires that had for weeks been smoldering in the hot, dry swamps, forests, and sawdust piles of Wisconsin. Within the period of probably no more than an hour, all these separate fires began simultaneously to race to the northeast across the state. The result was an unprecedented series of loosely related fires—the most destructive in terms of property value that Wisconsin has ever known, exceeding, in that regard, even the monstrous fire that ravaged Peshtigo and both shores of Green Bay in 1871.

The fires of 1894 burned in long strips from southwest to the northeast, moving so fast that they often left narrow strips of entirely unburned land between them. By the end of the day, the fires had ripped across 120 miles of Wisconsin, from Amery in the south to Washburn near the shores of Lake Superior in the north. Eleven counties were affected, many of them devastated.

Among the hardest hit of dozens of town affected by the fire was Barronett, a company town of perhaps five hundred people run by a Weyerhaeuser subsidiary, the Barronett Lumber Company. The town sat on the Chicago, Saint Paul, Minneapolis & Omaha Railroad, and to that fact alone would most of the townspeople owe their lives by the end of the day.

Throughout the morning, local farmers and mill workers had fought a fire that soon stretched along a front five miles long from east to west. As the winds picked up in the early afternoon, the fight quickly became untenable. At 2:00 P.M., about the same time that Jim Root was pulling out of Duluth bound for Hinckley, enormous black billows of smoke blew in over Baronett. People hastily gathered their belongings and ran for the train depot, watching for two trains that were supposed to have arrived at 2:00 P.M.—one heading south, one north. But the trains were late, and the platform was soon crowded with frightened families. A pair of haystacks on the outskirts of town took fire, and the rising wind blew the burning hay onto the roofs of houses all over town. The mill whistle shrieked an alarm. The doors of the company store were thrown open, the townspeople invited to take anything they could carry. But there were few takers—everyone was too busy scrambling for their lives.

When both trains finally pulled into town, a scene much like that which would unfold in Hinckley an hour and a half later took place in Barronett. As one roof after another burst into flames, scores of panicked villagers crowded aboard the trains, nobody bothering with the formality of tickets. Within a few minutes the crews of the two trains had loaded the entire population of Barronett aboard—all but four or five men who decided to stay behind to try to save the lumber mill—and departed, one train bound south for Cumberland, the other north for Shell Lake and Spooner.

The men who stayed behind, led by F. S. Staub, superintendent of the Barronett lumber mill, fought desperately with buckets and shovels and wet burlap bags to save the mill, but in the end there was little they could do. By a little after 2:30 P.M., flames were erupting in various places throughout the mill complex. The men ran to a nearby ditch, buried themselves in mud, and watched in dismay as Barronett erupted in flames.

When the heat finally abated and they emerged from the mud the next morning, the mill and the entire town were gone, but for one house. Among the ashes they found the body of one of their coworkers, Aleck Erickson, lying facedown in the street, a few feet from what had been his front door.

The fires rolled on, threatening, damaging, or devastating one town after another. Comstock was completely destroyed. Cable, a town of two hundred, lost thirteen houses and a railroad building. Mason, with five- to six hundred residents, was almost completely burned to the ground along with the White River Lumber Company's mill and thirty-three million board feet of lumber. On Lake Superior, Washburn lost four large lumber docks and fifteen million board feet of lumber. Parishville lost 500,000 feet of lumber along with the Kennedy Lumber Mill. Only dynamite saved the rest of the town. Iron River, a town of seven hundred, barely escaped with the loss of twenty homes and a sawmill. Granite Lake was destroyed. And on and on.

By the end of the day, fewer than a dozen people were dead, but many more towns had been severely threatened, damaged, or entirely destroyed, among them Prentice, Winchester, Fifield, Park Falls, Butternut, Glidden, Miller, High Bridge, Plummer, Hurley, Gile, Saxon, Odanah, Sanborn, Marengo, Sedgwick, Bayfield, Houghton, Ashland Junction, Moquah, Ino, Poplar, Itasca, Pratt, Agnew, Altamount, and finally—agonizingly—the small portion of Phillips that had been rebuilt since July 27.

* * *

The destruction was far from over, though. Great fires often come to us in the company of other fires, and the same pattern of catastrophic, loosely associated conflagrations that occurred in 1894 was repeated again and again in the decades after Hinckley.

In 1908 wildfires raged across the northern tier of states from the West Coast to the East Coast, destroying dozens of towns and millions of acres of timber. In Wisconsin the flames revisited Peshtigo, destroying the center of the city again, thirty-seven years after the holocaust there in 1871. In Minnesota, on September 5, they incinerated the town of Chisholm, all of whose residents escaped in fifteen boxcars on the Great Northern line.

In 1910, even greater wildfires raged across even more millions of acres of the American West and Northwest. More than a million acres burned in Minnesota alone that year according to the state's fire marshal, Christopher Columbus Andrews. In the twin towns of Baudette and Spooner on the Rainy River, the flames rained down from the sky much as they had at Hinckley, and inside of two minutes both towns were destroyed. The railroad bridge between the two towns melted.

On October 12, 1918, another series of fires raced north across cutover land in northern Minnesota. Beginning near where the Hinckley firestorm had stopped its own northward progress in 1894, they burned all the way to Duluth and beyond. The fires entered the outskirts of Duluth when four- to six hundred carloads of lumber ignited more or less simultaneously at milepost 62, resulting in an explosion of flames much like the one that had occurred in Hinckley when the Brennan lumberyards had gone up in flames. When the day was over, thirty-eight towns were destroyed or heavily damaged, most prominently Moose Lake and Cloquet. Four hundred and fifty-three people were dead, and more than a hundred more would die of burns and infections in the following weeks.

In 1925 a complex of fires in Minnesota, Wisconsin, and Michigan devastated a staggering 1.4 million acres. By the time the last flames of that final conflagration flickered out, there was little left to burn in the Upper Midwest. The tens of millions of acres of virgin pine forest that had graced the region less than one hundred years before were irretrievably gone, either logged or burned off. Much of the land that was left behind had also been burned, literally. The organic material that had accumulated in the soil over eons—in some places, as much as twelve feet thick—had been incinerated, leaving behind millions of acres of gravelly soil, sand, and rock that would never again support a white pine forest, nor any forest worthy of the name.

EPILOGUE

Chance is perhaps the pseudonym of God when
He did not want to sign.

—*Anatole France,*
Le Jardin d'Epicure

SEPTEMBER 1, 2004 | HINCKLEY, MINNESOTA
Neon lights and the usual jumble of fast-food joints and gas stations
greeted me when I pulled off of Interstate 35 at the Hinckley exit late
in the afternoon. A mile or so to the northeast, I could see the huge
portico of the Hinckley Grand Casino and Hotel, where I planned to
spend the night before continuing my research for this book in the
morning. I was anxious to see the town itself after reading, thinking,
and writing about it for the best part of the past year. So instead of
heading for the casino, I turned left on Highway 48 and crossed the
freeway on the overpass, heading west. Then it was another half-mile
to the intersection with Main Street, now Old Highway 61, at the south
end of town, not far from where the Eastern Minnesota roundhouse
used to stand. There I turned right and entered downtown Hinckley.

There wasn't much to see, at first glance, nothing we haven't all
seen dozens of times before in towns that have been bypassed by freeways and left to die slow deaths. Brick and cinder-block buildings
squatted along the main drag. Between them lay vacant lots choked
with weeds. There was a Supervalu store, a Conoco station, and a
closed-down Chevrolet dealership, the business relocated out near the
casino, where the customers were. Large satellite dishes and rusting

TV antennae perched awkwardly on some of the roofs. Railroad tracks ran behind the businesses on the west side of the street. Dumpsters, piles of gravel, and old railroad ties were scattered haphazardly between the buildings and the tracks. Rising above the whole scene was a silver water tower with faded black lettering that read, HINCKLEY.

But when I pulled the car over to the side of the street and looked hard, I could begin to see shades of what was once here. The road before me was the same wide thoroughfare that has always run along the west side of Hinckley. The railroad tracks still crossed here at the south end of town. A bit up the street, on the left, was the long, low, green Saint Paul and Duluth depot, rebuilt in the same location immediately after the fire and now the home of the Hinckley Fire Museum. With its neatly mown front lawn and fresh green paint, the museum was attractive and inviting. Before I left, I would discover that it is also lovingly maintained by dedicated volunteers, full of interesting artifacts, and marvelously informative.

I drove north a block or so and turned right on Second Street, crossing the old Eastern Minnesota railroad tracks, now the Burlington Northern Santa Fe tracks, and came to the gravel pit. It has been transformed into a lush green park, sunken below street level, the BNSF railroad embankment still cutting along its western edge. It's located in a pleasant neighborhood. Modest older homes on shady, tree-lined streets surround the park. Most of them are old enough that they must have been built shortly after the fire. I noticed the names of the streets that run through the neighborhood—Blair Avenue, Stephan Avenue, Best Avenue.

I circled the park, drove back across the tracks to Old Highway 61, turned north again, and passed the Fire Museum on my left and the downtown on my right. Looking for the site of the lumber mill, I turned left and drove west over to Dunn Avenue, crossing a remnant of the old Saint Paul and Duluth tracks, and arrived at the trailhead for the Willard Munger State Trail. The trail runs from here to

Duluth, following the old Saint Paul and Duluth route the whole way. They say it's the longest paved trail in the United States. I parked and walked north on the trail a hundred yards before coming to a footbridge over the Grindstone River. Peering down into the dark ravine, overgrown and jungle-like now, I could just make out a creek-sized stream burbling along at the bottom. The mill itself is long gone, never rebuilt after the fire. There was no forest left to cut, no logs left to saw. Now the site is just a thirty-six-acre tangle of brush and poplar trees. The millpond was spread out on my left, a lovely sheen of silver water in the soft evening light. Some boys, silhouettes against the setting sun, were fishing from a short pier.

I started walking north on the trail, thinking about Root's train, thinking maybe I'd walk along his route all the way up to Skunk Lake. But after a hundred yards or so I turned around and headed back to my rental car. There was a chill in the air and the light was failing quickly. I'd never make it to the lake and back before nightfall, and I didn't want to walk back in the dark. There were too many ghosts along the way.

In the end, somewhat more than 436 people died in Minnesota and another nine, at least, in Wisconsin. On November 24, 1894, Pine County's coroner, Dr. Wellington Cowan, submitted his official death list, naming 314 identified victims and another ninety-nine who could not be identified.

A glance at any of those last ninety-nine names on the list gives some idea of how little Cowan had to work with in making identifications:

323. Unknown—Male; age about 40; found on country road, 1 mile from Hinckley; burned beyond recognition; nothing but shoes left on his body; weight about 150.

325. Unknown—Male; found in mill yard; only bones and a few buttons left; buried in Hinckley.

326. Unknown—Male; age about 35; found near Skunk Lake; evidently a passenger from the train; nothing left on body but a pair of shoes; buried in Hinckley; reported by E. Stephan, C. Vanhoven and J. G. Howard.

327. Unknown—Male; found in lumberyard; only jackknife, watch and buttons left; not enough found to bury.

328. Unknown—Found in engine room of sawmill in Hinckley; only a few bones.

But the list did not include the twenty-three Native Americans found near Mille Lacs Lake, nor an unknown number of Native Americans, trappers, loggers, hunters, and itinerants who happened to be in the woods that day and who simply vanished with no one to mourn for them or to report them missing. Their bodies continued to be found at random times and in random circumstances for months and years after the fire.

The last fire-related burial took place in the spring of 1897 when someone brought John Currie a bag of bones he had found in the woods. Currie had been one of the first of the villagers to return to Hinckley, and he had been at the forefront of the tireless volunteers who buried the first 247 bodies in the trenches at the cemetery. He now reopened one of the trenches and buried the bones there without ceremony. No one doubted, though, that other sets of bones remained unaccounted for out in the woods or under plowed fields, as they almost certainly still do today.

John Currie remained active in Hinckley's civic life after the town was rebuilt, becoming a member of the town's board of directors and leading the effort to get funding from the legislature for a permanent fire memorial erected at the cemetery. He went into real estate, selling off parcels of burned-over land and bringing many new settlers into town. He and Amy moved to a farm east of Hinckley and had five more children, bringing their brood to eight. Amy died at the age of fifty in 1920, but John, though much her senior, lived for another twenty-eight years, dying in Hinckley in the spring of 1948.

Throughout his life he refused to talk about the fire, saying, "Nobody who had buried those people could stand to talk about it."

Dr. Stephan returned to Hinckley from Duluth on one of the first relief trains and worked tirelessly tending to burn patients. He received $200 for two months of this service, along with one mackinaw and two pairs of underwear, and he remained in Hinckley for the rest of his life. In March 1895 he ran for mayor of Hinckley but lost to the town's drayman, Joseph Tew. He remained superintendent of schools for Pine County, however, and in June 1896, he married one of his young teachers, Angus Hay's sister Clara. Over the next fifty-four years he and Clara raised a family as he practiced medicine in and around Hinckley, making house calls far out in the country, delivering babies, attending the dying, and sometimes performing surgeries on kitchen tables. He died on November 13, 1950.

Angus Hay resumed publishing the *Hinckley Enterprise* on December 18, 1894, with a headline that proclaimed, boldly, and perhaps somewhat callously, 15 YEARS WORK IN 15 MINUTES. He went on in the body of his lead story to explain: "The fire on Sept. 1 did in 15 minutes what it would have taken the husbandman 15 years to accomplish. All nature is with us; it seemingly knew our needs, and came to clear the land." No one recorded how those who lost their loved ones and their property reacted to Hay's assessment of the fire's consequences, but in September 1895, in observing the first-year anniversary of the fire, Hay remained optimistic about the town's future, despite the loss of its principal industry: "She has passed through the fever of fire. Her future is as bright as the jewels in her crown. No tarnish on the band of gold—no wrinkle on her brow."

When asked to describe what it had been like to experience the fire firsthand, though, Hay balked at the enormity of the task. It was, he felt, beyond the power of any pen to render it accurately: "Any one item in any one instance could be woven into columns of truth—startling, and, to one who was so fortunate as to have never had the experience, seemingly unreal." Within a few years, Hay decided to move to Sandstone, a town that unlike Hinckley was given a genuine reason for optimism when James J. Hill decided to rebuild the Eastern Minnesota yards there rather than in Hinckley.

Jim Root emerged from the fire a celebrity, at least for a time. Within twenty-four hours of his rescue, reporters began to interview him at his home in White Bear Lake, and within days front-page stories in every major paper in America and Western Europe extolled his heroism. The report of the Chicago *Inter Ocean* was typical: "His soul is the stuff of which heroes are made in this world—archangels in the world beyond." Poems were composed, tributes were issued; flowers, congratulations, and cash poured into his home. By early October, Root was in New York City, where a theatrical agent offered him $1,000 to star in a two-week production called *A Ride for Life*. Hesitant, but astonished by the sum, Root took the job.

He was not, apparently, a born actor. The play ran for only one week, and on October 9, *The New York Times* panned both his performance and the motives behind his appearance:

> He is not, to be sure, a particularly impressive spectacle, being exactly such a looking man as locomotive engineers always are, grimly pallid of face, heavy of build, and inexpressive of features, but no doubt he is a hero—or was. . . . One can't help wishing Mr. Root had gone into burglary or almost any of the lesser crimes instead of trading on his glory and making himself, and heroism, cheap, cheap, cheap. Mr. Root cannot act . . .

Root was mortified by the experience and by the critical reaction, and he decided never to attempt acting again, saying, "It keeps a man up too late at night, and I never did like a night run." He promptly resumed his railroad career and retired to New York on a railroad pension in 1908. He died at his home in the Bronx on December 12, 1911.

Root's conductor, Tom Sullivan, never received the kind of attention that Root did, though he was mentioned in almost every newspaper account of the ride to Skunk Lake. Sullivan eventually

regained his mental equilibrium and rejoined the Saint Paul and
Duluth. He died in Saint Paul in 1927 of a stroke, at the age of sixty-
seven. Root's fireman, John McGowan, also remained largely unher-
alded, though most of the newspaper accounts of the ride to Skunk
Lake described how he had come to Root's aid and revived him in the
cab of the locomotive. Like Root and Sullivan, he remained a railroad
man and met his end on July 5, 1903, in a spectacular train wreck in
Dellwood, Minnesota, in which his locomotive was overturned. He is
buried at St. Bridget's Cemetery in Cazenovia, Wisconsin.

John Blair received a number of accolades, mostly from within
the black community in Saint Paul, but his name was largely missing
from national press accounts of the tragedy. At a gathering in Saint
Paul during the second week of September, leading members of the
black community praised Blair and presented him with a gold badge
paid for with money raised by the community. Officials from the
Saint Paul and Duluth presented him with a gold watch, inscribed
with the words FOR GALLANT AND FAITHFUL DISCHARGE OF DUTY. Several white citizens, passengers on Root's train, did attend the event
and rose to praise Blair, among them state senator Frank Daugherty
and judge C. D. O'Brien. Following his comments, O'Brien walked
across the stage to shake Blair's hand, saying, "I am proud to be alive
to take him by the hand and thank him for his humanity." Blair himself said little that evening, but when asked earlier how he had remained so calm when others were so panicked, he had said, "I just
resolved I would not lose my head, and if I had to die, I would do it
without making a fool of myself."

By any measure, Blair's actions during the fire were extraordinarily generous and courageous. They were all the more remarkable
when one considers the racial climate of the day. Though no one in
the room the night Blair received his accolades likely knew it, none
of them would have been terribly surprised to learn what had happened 1,000 miles to the south at about the same hour on the same
day that Blair was saving so many white lives. As Blair was leading

panicked passengers through smoke and flames to the safety of Skunk Lake in Minnesota, a crowd of white men in Millington, Missouri, were pumping round after round of shotgun fire into five manacled African-American men who, accused of arson but never tried, had been chained together in the back of a wagon.

In their official reports to the Eastern Minnesota's holding company, James J. Hill's Great Northern Railway, as well as in accounts they wrote for publication, Bill Best and Ed Barry gave conflicting versions of what happened as their combined train sat in Hinckley and the fire closed in around them. Conductor Harry Powers and many other witnesses corroborated Best's account—that he had held the train for many long minutes to allow more passengers to board while Barry had tried frantically to back it out of town. Best said, "It was the hardest place I ever stood in." Immediately after the fire, he went out of his way to praise Barry's conductor, W. D. Campbell, calling him, "as plucky and brave [a] fellow as ever passed a milestone," but he had little to say about Barry's performance. Barry, in his accounts, avoided any mention of his aborted efforts to leave, saying simply, "I knew if we stayed there any longer we would all be burned."

He may have had a point. It's easy enough, in retrospect, to condemn Barry for trying to pull the combination train out of town before Best would release the brakes, but not many mortal men or women would have had the raw courage that Best demonstrated in the face of the tidal wave of fire that was about to wash over and obliterate the train. Then, too, it is worth considering that from his vantage point on the north end of the train, Barry may not even have been able to see many of the stragglers that were running through the smoke toward Best's end, perhaps sixty or seventy yards closer to the heart of town.

Shortly after the fire, the passengers on the Best-Barry train collected money and tried to give it to Best and George Ford in gratitude, but the two promptly turned it over to the relief effort. Neither Best nor Barry, though, received the kind of public attention nor the official accolades that Root did, a fact that grated on both of them as they watched Root's fame grow. In some quarters, in fact, they were criticized for having brought their trains into Hinckley at all, given the conditions there. In December, Best responded by quoting actor Frank Chanfrau's epitaph—"I've did the best I could and I ain't got nothing to take back." Barry was a good deal less circumspect: "If it hadn't bin [sic] for me they all would have bin [sic] lost. . . . I think I am deserving of the credit instead of Best."

Barry returned to work within three days and continued to work for the Great Northern Company for a number of years. He died of heart disease in Saint Paul on July 26, 1904, at the age of forty-six. Best also resumed working for the Great Northern, but in 1903 he returned to his native Manitoba where he went to work as an engineer for the Canadian Northern Railway. In 1914, he was elected general chairman of his union, the Brotherhood of Locomotive Engineers, a position he maintained until he retired in the late 1920s. He died at his home in Coaticook, Manitoba, on February 18, 1934, at the age of seventy-eight. Few people in Coaticook—other than close friends and family—had any idea of what he had done in Hinckley.

Family friends took care of Alice, Mabel, and Minnie Nelson in the nearby village of Mora until their father recovered from pneumonia contracted after he ran two miles through the burning and smoke-filled woods to reach his family at the millpond in Pokegama. Minnie never recovered her shoes. Antone and Clara Anderson were reunited in Duluth and sent to live with an uncle and aunt in Moorhead, Minnesota, where Antone had a long, slow, and painful recovery from the burns on his chest and legs. Clara eventually married and moved to Portland, Oregon. Antone also married, but remained in Minnesota. Their cousin Mary returned with her family to Hinckley on October 7, Mary's eighteenth birthday, moving into one of the standard sixteen-by-twenty-four-foot relief houses built by the State Relief Commission. Mary married, taught school, and lived with her husband, John Kofoed, on a farm outside of Hinckley for forty years before moving back into town. Mary died on November 10, 1977, at the age of 101. Bill Grissinger remained in Hinckley and was still living there, alert and independent at the age of eighty-three, seventy-five years after the fire.

Ed Hansen, my grandfather, worked his way up from a clerk's position in a Duluth hardware store to an executive position at Crown-Zellerbach. He lived to witness more national tragedies—World War I, the Great Depression, World War II, President Kennedy's murder, and the beginnings of the war in Vietnam. But he also lived to watch color television, fly on a jetliner, and drive an air-conditioned car on the freeways of Southern California, where he retired after a long career at Crown-Zellerbach. He married, had two daughters, divorced, and remarried. Somewhere along the line, he lost track of Josephine and Helen. He died in Sun City, California, in 1966.

Marie Hansen never stopped grieving for Evan. As Ed grew up, she moved with him wherever his growing career took him, a permanent part of his household until he married, and even after that, never far from him. By the time my mother was old enough to take note of her, Marie had become a small, dark figure—always hunched over, always dressed in black, always muttering ominous-sounding things in Norwegian. She died with Ed at her side in Berkeley, California, in 1923, a long way from Oslo, where thirty-five years before she had first taken a chance and stepped off the quay on her voyage to a new life in America.

Hinckley itself survived, but never again thrived. The tent city that emerged in the days immediately following the fire gave way over the following months to a more permanent settlement of shops and simple wood-frame relief houses paid for by the State Relief Commission. Real commerce first resumed when a barbershop was built, then several permanent saloons, followed by a blacksmith shop and a hotel. By early October, 150 relief homes were under construction and another hundred were planned. A temporary school was cobbled together, though it proved to be cold and drafty in the hard Minnesota winter that followed. By the following May, a new town hall had been built. The dedication ceremony for the hall, presided over by Governor Nelson and a party of dignitaries from the State Commission, prompted Angus Hay to boast in the *Enterprise* several days later, "Our town will stand though a thousand destructions come upon us . . . God made the world, but we built Hinckley."

Hay's boosterism and his optimistic belief that the fire had opened the way for a prosperous era of farming were characteristic of the age. They echoed, in fact, what a *Detroit Post* writer had written in 1881, following the catastrophic Michigan fires of that year. The *Post* writer had asserted, with strained logic, that: "There are other great advantages, also. The insects and forest pests of the farmer are nearly all extinct. There will be no potato bugs, no weevils, or army worms, no curculio, very few birds or squirrels for several years to come on these lands. Fences will be little needed, because the cattle, sheep, and hogs have been largely destroyed."

Despite Hay's buoyant optimism, though, Hinckley's real reason for being was gone forever. The great forests that had nourished her had not just been damaged, they had been obliterated, and much of the burned-over land left in the fire's wake turned out to be sandy and gravelly, not well suited for agriculture beyond growing potatoes or providing pastureland.

The final blow for Hinckley came not from the fire but from the hand of the Empire Builder himself. Immediately after the fire, and unbeknownst to the people of either town, James J. Hill began to ponder a plan to move the Eastern Minnesota's terminal facilities and rail yards from Hinckley to Sandstone. There—rather than in the more obvious Hinckley area—he planned to buy up burned-over land at bargain prices and build a stone roundhouse and as many as thirty sidetracks with the capacity to hold up to 2,800 railroad cars. When the scheme became public before he desired, thwarting his plan to buy the land on the cheap, Hill angrily said, "This place shall flourish and prosper accordingly as I shall command." The new facility was built, and Hinckley was left with little choice but to watch the Eastern Minnesota trains pass by on their way to and from Sandstone.

As Hill had commanded, Sandstone did flourish—for a time. By the following July, the town boasted more than 1,054 residents as compared to Hinckley's 589. In another ten years, in 1905, it would be home to 1,589 people, as large as Hinckley had been before the fire, and almost four times Hinckley's 1905 population. But early in the twentieth century the demand for monumental stone buildings began gradually to subside as newer, more economical building materials were brought into use, and Sandstone, like Hinckley, began to lose jobs and people. When the quarry closed in 1919, Sandstone—as Hinckley had in 1894—lost its principal reason for being.

If the Hinckley firestorm left us any kind of positive legacy, it may be that it began the slow, creeping process of ushering in an era of better forest management across the country. To be sure, a few prophets had called for better management of the northern forests since at least 1867, when Increase A. Lapham—one of the pioneers of both weather science and fire science—had published a study titled *Report of the Disastrous Effects of the Destruction of Forest Trees Now Going on So Rapidly in the State of Wisconsin*. But Lapham's voice and others like it, among them Minnesota's own Christopher Columbus Andrews, had been quickly and efficiently silenced by the lumber interests and the enormous influence they wielded in the states' legislatures. Even after the catastrophe at Peshtigo in 1871, the lumber companies in all the forested states continued to lay waste to vast areas of timber, leaving behind mountains of slash, vast accumulations of dense brush, scores of silted-up streams, and hundreds of dry, gully-washed hillsides.

The Hinckley firestorm, though, seemed to get people's attention in a way that the Peshtigo disaster had not, despite the even greater magnitude of the horror at Peshtigo. The difference may simply have been that the Peshtigo disaster unfolded on the same day as the Great Chicago Fire and therefore got relatively little attention from the national press. Or it may have been that by 1894 people were finally growing weary of watching the same kinds of tragedies occurring year after year. Whatever the reason, it was hard to ignore the human suffering and the vast destruction of natural resources that this particular fire brought to Minnesota. Editorial pages around the state and the nation screamed for some kind of action. In 1895, largely over the objections of the lumber interests, the Minnesota legislature passed a limited set of forest-use laws, and the state auditor named Christopher Columbus Andrews as Minnesota's first chief fire warden. The legislature, however, allowed Andrews an annual budget of only $6,000 and neglected to give him a staff.

Andrews jumped on the job with gusto nonetheless, appointing local fire wardens for the seven hundred townships around the state. He deluged them with requests for information and urged them to be vigilant and take swift action against offenders. But the wardens were paid for only one or two days of work per year. They were hardworking men; they had their own jobs and lands to attend to, and they didn't much like the idea of prosecuting neighbors whose help they might need getting through a tough winter or raising a new barn.

In the end, little changed in what remained of the north woods of Minnesota and Wisconsin, until the relentless toll levied by the wide-ranging and devastating fires of 1908, 1910, 1918, and 1925 gradually led the state legislatures and the lumber interests to grudgingly embrace meaningful conservation and fire-protection measures. By then the nation had finally had enough, and even the lumber concerns understood that the old methods of logging were against their own interests.

It was far too late for places like Hinckley—too late not only for those who had died and suffered in the firestorm of 1894, but for those who had tried to make a living there afterwards. Droves of new settlers—drawn by the advertising pamphlets of the railroad companies and enthusiastic (and often deceitful) land developers—had long since discovered that grubbing out burned stumps and plowing the gravel-and-sand soil of Pine County was unlikely to yield them a living, let alone a fortune.

* * *

In September of 1954, on the sixtieth anniversary of the firestorm, the town of Hinckley held a commemorative pageant and memorial service, attended by dozens of survivors, all them now gray and many of them stooped with age. Bill Grissinger, Antone Anderson, Clara Anderson McDermott, and Belle Barden Raymond—at whose house Clara had danced the night before the fire—were all there. Horace Gorton and Axel Rosdahl attended and wrote memoirs of their fire experiences for the occasion, as did Alice Nelson Wilcox. Another reunion was held on September 1, 1964, to celebrate the seventieth anniversary. Ninety-one survivors were known to still be alive, but by now only thirty-four were able to attend. By 1969, only nineteen survivors were able to celebrate the seventy-fifth anniversary at a small gathering in Hinckley. The oldest survivor, Sigrud Westrud Stromgren—seven years old the year of the fire—died in 1994 at the age of 107. And the last known Hinckley survivor, Ann Anderson Darling, died at the age of 102 in 1996.

SEPTEMBER 3, 2004 | 6:30 P.M.

Red, white, and blue plastic flags fluttered in front of the Hinckley Flea Market next to the cemetery as I pulled off of Fire Monument Road and into the gravel parking lot. I parked my rental car, gathered up a bouquet of flowers, walked around to the front of the cemetery, and entered through a squeaky wrought-iron gate. With my research completed for now, I'd come to pay my respects before starting back to Saint Paul, the airport, and home the next day. As I closed the gate behind me, I remembered reading somewhere that it was John Currie who had built this fence and gate, sometime after he buried the last bag of bones. I stood and studied the tall obelisk that dominated the cemetery. It was erected in 1900, dedicated on September 1 of that year. Made of alternating blocks of rough-hewn and polished Saint Cloud granite, in silhouette against the evening sky it looked to my twenty-first-century eyes oddly like a missile poised for launch against some unseen enemy. I worked my way around the monument, reading the inscriptions on each of the four sides. The one on the north face told me what I already knew all too well—what lay in the trenches behind me.

I turned around and looked at the four long, green mounds that stretched out silently before me. A low, single strand of chain was strung from one concrete post to the next all around the plot. I could easily have stepped over it and walked up and down the lengths of the mounds, but of course I didn't. There were whole families in there, dozens of them, in fact—all five of the Ginders, all five of the Rodgers, all eight of the Costigans, all seven of the Wolds, all six of the Reynolds, thirteen Strombergs, twelve Shermans.

My great-grandfather Evan Hansen was in there somewhere, too. As far as I knew, this was the first time anyone from my family had been back to Hinckley since my grandfather and great-grandmother escaped on Root's train the day of the fire. I figured Evan would be interested in the fact that someone had come back after all these years. I stood silently and tried to think of him as if he were there before me. I tried to let him know that somebody still cared about what had happened to him here. I wanted him to know that somebody still thought about how unfair it was, how unlucky he was to lose everything just when he had realized his dream, how horrific it must have been dying in that marsh, not knowing whether his wife and children were also dying somewhere out there in the smoke, flame, and confusion.

Like almost everyone else that day, he hadn't seen what was coming at him out of the smoke and murk until it was too late. But, I wondered, who ever does? Who among us can see the drunk driver coming our way, careening out of control just around the next bend in the road? Who can see the cluster of cells silently careening out of control deep within some vital organ? Who knows how the dice we cast upon a green felt tabletop will finally come to rest?

After a while I laid the bouquet of flowers on one of the mounds and stepped back to take a final look. The cemetery before me was lush with trees. The grassy mounds were a soft but vibrant green, luxurious, almost inviting in the dim light. The air smelled sweet and grassy. The plastic flags next door rustled a little in the light breeze. Car tires hissed by on the pavement behind me. Farther away, the interstate murmured of people coming and going.

I lingered a little longer. The tug of kinship held me there, bound me to the place and to a man I had never known, but without whom I would never have been. I conjured up his image one more time, and then laid it back to rest. The late summer darkness drifted down from the sky like a warm mist, enveloping me and the graves before me, uniting us in its soft embrace. The world spun eastward beneath me, and the darkness deepened and spread over Hinckley, over Minnesota, over the American countryside, covering all of us in the same black shroud, tenants in common, tenants of time.

To the northeast, the bright lights of the casino illuminated the sky. I turned and walked back out through the gate, swung it closed behind me, climbed into the car, and pulled out onto the dark highway, following the cones of light from my headlights, letting them lead me back down the dark road to the casino, to take my chances.

CHAPTER NOTES

MORE THAN TWO THOUSAND PEOPLE EXPERIENCED THE Hinckley firestorm firsthand, and every one of them who survived it had a story to tell. Most of those stories never made it into print, and we will likely never hear them. However, because there were hundreds of survivors, scores of stories were eventually told either in newspaper accounts or in the several books that were published during the life span of the survivors. In seeking to discover what happened in Hinckley on the day of the firestorm and in the following days, I have read and pondered all of these accounts. Ultimately, in order to present the larger tale in a coherent fashion, I have necessarily had to focus on a sampling of those stories. That is not to say, however, that I have disregarded the thousands of details revealed in the stories I have not retold. I have isolated and correlated those details—located them in time and place—and then built as many of them as possible into an overarching, minute-by-minute narrative of what happened.

Several nineteenth-century books are essential starting points for anyone interested in delving more deeply into the Hinckley firestorm. The first—the bedrock in many ways—is the Reverend William Wilkinson's *Memorials of the Minnesota Forest Fires*, published by Norman Wilkinson in Minneapolis in 1895. Unfortunately, the book (hereafter referred to as Wilkinson) has little that can be recognized as a principle of organization, even after one finally discovers the table of contents on page 409. The book is invaluable, though, in that it contains dozens of firsthand accounts of the disaster compiled at a time when memories were still fresh. It also contains vital factual resources, including Dr. Cowan's complete "Death List," detailed records from the State Relief Commission's report, transcripts of telegrams sent among the various rescue parties, and many compelling photographs.

Much easier to navigate is another book published in Minnesota in 1895, Elton T. Brown's *A History of the Great Minnesota Forest Fires* (Brown). Like Wilkinson, it contains many firsthand accounts, as well as a scattering of photographs taken shortly after the firestorm.

The only other book to come out of the immediate aftermath of the firestorm is *Eld-Cyklonen eller Hinckley-branden* (Akermark). Written in Swedish by Gudmund Emanuel Akermark and published anonymously in 1894, it was later translated into English by William Johnson and published as *The Hinckley Fire* by the American Publishing Company of Askov, Minnesota, in 1976, and reprinted as *Eld-Cyklonen or Hinckley Fire* by the Hinckley Fire Museum in 1978. Despite some typically florid Victorian prose and some seeming exaggerations, it is, like Wilkinson and Brown, valuable for the contemporaneous, eyewitness accounts it contains.

Several more modern books are also available. The most comprehensive and valuable of these is a 1979 book, *From the Ashes: The Story of the Hinckley Fire of 1894* by Grace Stageberg Swenson (Swenson). The book is clear and thorough, replete with dozens of historical photos and much useful detailed information, such as the timetables for the various trains involved in the disaster. Swenson's accounts of the relief efforts following the firestorm, as well as her accounts of the subsequent lives of some of the survivors, are particularly interesting.

Also very helpful is *The Hinckley Fire: Stories from the Hinckley Fire Survivors*, by Antone A. Anderson and Clara Anderson McDermott (A. Anderson), published in 1954 and reprinted in 1993. As the title suggests, this is largely a compilation of firsthand survivor accounts, and even though some of them were set down as much as sixty years after the fire, they provide a good deal of detail and context for the events surrounding the firestorm.

Finally, there is the one scholarly study of the fire ever published, *Wall of Flames: The Minnesota Forest Fire of 1894* by Lawrence H. Larsen (L. Larsen). This book, published in 1984, is most valuable for understanding the movements of the various trains involved in the tragedy and the subsequent relief effort.

In piecing together the story of the firestorm, I have also drawn information from a number of other book-length publications on subjects related indirectly to the fire, contemporary newspaper accounts, interviews, occasional Web sites, personal papers, correspondence, maps, and even in one case, the message on the back of a serendipitous postcard that I bought at an online auction site. All of these are cited where appropriate in the following chapter notes and included in the list of sources that follows the notes.

PREFACE

The epigram, "The experience of one . . ." is taken from Angus Hay's comments in Brown, page 199. Hay was just one of a number of survivors who asserted that no one could adequately describe the firestorm in words. My own efforts here notwithstanding, I suspect he was ultimately correct. You probably had to be there to fully comprehend it.

PROLOGUE

The epigram, "If a man look sharply . . ." is from Francis Bacon's essay, "Of Nature in Men."

Moose Kenyon's report on the Phillips fire, "Flames shot a full thousand feet . . ." is quoted in Stewart Holbrook's *Burning an Empire: The Story of American Forest Fires*, page 80.

CHAPTER I | NIGHT MUSIC

The epigram, "On a starred night . . ." is from George Meredith's "Lucifer in Starlight" in *The New Oxford Book of English Verse*, page 722.

Details of Bill Grissinger's story, here and elsewhere, are derived primarily from an unpublished typescript by Harold L. Fisher housed in the archives of the Minnesota Historical Society (Fisher). Entitled "The Hinckley-Sandstone Fire," it presents Grissinger's recollections of the fire as told to Rose Larson and later transcribed by Fisher. Belle Barden Raymond describes the party at her house the night before the fire in A. Anderson, pages 45–47. I have based my description of the party on her account and also on other contemporaneous descriptions of similar house parties. That Clara Anderson was present for the party is an assumption on my part, based on Belle's comments that her "school chums" were all there and her subsequent mention of Clara as one of her school chums. Details of Emil Anderson's late-night train trip from Hinckley to Sandstone, as well as his later experiences during the fire, are based on his own account in Wilkinson, pages 86–97.

My reference to the time of sunrise on September 1, 1894, as well as many other similar references throughout the book to the movements of the sun and moon, are drawn from the U.S. Naval Observatory's Web site (www.usno.navy.mil), which allows a researcher to determine precise times for such celestial events as sunrise and moonset for any given historical date. The description of the Hansen homestead and its location are based partly on my own family's lore, but also on a description of its location that Ed Hansen provided in a letter published in the *Hinckley News* on March 17, 1960. By locating and studying the inventory of household possessions that Marie Hansen submitted to the State Relief Commission following the firestorm, I was able to fill out my understanding of the house and its contents. Hers is just one of hundreds of such inventories housed in the archives of the Minnesota Historical Society. The description of the countryside between the homestead and Hinckley, as well as the description of the Brennan lumber mill, is based on contemporaneous photographs and, to a lesser extent, on my own experience walking the route early one morning in 2004.

CHAPTER 2 | MORNING

The epigram from *Julius Caesar*, "Oh that a man might know . . ." is Brutus, on the plains of Philippi, where he will shortly throw himself upon his sword. Act V, scene i, lines 122–123.

Information on the history of white pine lumbering and the role it played in Hinckley's development is drawn principally from a wonderfully informative and detailed treatment of the subject, Agnes Larson's *History of the White Pine Industry in Minnesota* (A. Larson). Also fascinating on the subject of the eastern white pine, *Pinus strobus Linnaeus*, is Donald Culross Peattie's *A Natural History of Trees of Eastern and Central North America* (Peattie) pages 3–14. Among other things, Peattie tells us that during one twenty-four-year period in Michigan, Wisconsin, and Minnesota, eighty-three billion shingles were riven from the wood of this tree. Only the bottom few feet of a prime tree were used; the rest of the tree (as much as $^{14}/_{15}$) was often left to rot or burn on the forest floor. Today there are no remaining virgin stands of eastern white pine anywhere in America.

The issue of the *Hinckley Enterprise* quoted, "Hinckley is a city . . ." was the last issue printed before the firestorm, on August 29, 1894. Many details about the daily life of Hinckley before the firestorm were gleaned from microfiche copies of the *Hinckley Enterprise* at the Minnesota Historical Society. I carefully studied every advertisement, every news story, every bit of gossip or social intelligence that Angus Hay published from early July through August of 1894 to understand the life of the town. Also useful, of course, were innumerable passing comments and references to local businesses and residences in all the different survivor stories that I consulted in Wilkinson, A. Anderson, Akermark, Brown, Swenson, and L. Larsen. Maps provided in Brown and Swenson also helped provide a basic sense of the geography of the pre-firestorm town.

My understanding of the relationships between Dr. Stephan, Dr. Cowan, and John Currie and their respective business and personal connections was greatly expanded by Carol Currie Eddleman who shared with me many treasures, including items saved by her aunt Margaret Currie Sanford in a scrapbook of fire mementos. Many of these pertained to the Currie and Stephan families in particular. One of these items, an undated letter from Dennis Dunn—son of one of Hinckley's original pioneers—to Mae and Ross Newman also provided many useful details of daily life in the lumber camps and in Hinckley. John Currie's daughter, Ethel Currie, a child at the time of the fire, also left an account that is printed in A. Anderson.

My brief discussion of the state of weather science in 1894—and the weather proverbs I cite—are derived in part from information available on a helpful Web site maintained by the National Oceanic and Atmospheric Administration (NOAA) at www.history.noaa.gov. The specific facts and figures about the temperatures and relative humidity in areas surrounding Hinckley come from Wilkinson, pages 17–18, and from a U.S. Forest Service publication authored by Donald A. Haines and Rodney W. Sando, "Climatic Conditions Preceding Historically Great Fires in the North Central Region" (Haines and Sando) in 1969. Sando, who grew up just thirty miles from Hinckley, has taken a lifelong scientific interest in the fire. I am particularly indebted to him for additional information and interpretation that he provided me in a phone interview at the beginning of this project, at a time when he was more than a little busy serving as the director of the Department of Fish and Game for the state of Idaho. The quote from Christopher Columbus Andrews, "For the American people thus . . ." comes from his address to the American Forestry Association on August 24, 1894. My assertion that the two separate fires that ultimately merged to form the firestorm were born at Quamba and at Beroun respectively derives from my own analysis of firsthand accounts along with a close study of maps of the area and, more importantly, the scientific research reported by Haines and Sando in the paper and the interview cited above.

A typescript account, "The Hinckley Fire," written by Mrs. G. C. Wilcox (Alice Nelson) in 1954 and archived at the Minnesota Historical Society, provided me with much information about the experiences of the Hans Nelson family. Other parts of the Nelsons' story, here and in subsequent chapters, are from firsthand accounts in Wilkinson.

CHAPTER 3 | HOME

The epigram, "Home is a notion . . ." is from Wallace Stegner's novel, *Angle of Repose*, page 159.

The details of the Hansens' emigration from Norway to the United States are drawn from genealogical research conducted by various members of my family over many years. My description of the life Evan Hansen encountered in the logging camps outside of Hinckley is based on several very useful sources: *Early Loggers in Minnesota* (Vol. 3) by J. C. Ryan; A. Larson's *History of the White Pine Industry in Minnesota*; Stewart Holbrook's *Holy Old Mackinaw*; and the letter from Dennis Dunn to May and Ross Newman, cited above. Also useful for general background information, and fascinating reads in their own rights, were a series of oral histories collected by the Forest History Foundation of Saint Paul, Minnesota, detailing the late-nineteenth-century logging-camp experiences of the following individuals:

W. E. Dexter (August and October 1953), Wirt Mineau (September 1955), Mrs. Maggie Orr O'Neill (October 1955), and Hans Larson (August 1953).

In their 1969 study of the Hinckley firestorm and other great fires of the Great Lakes region, Haines and Sando point out the role low-pressure systems played in spawning the 1871 Peshtigo disaster as well as the Cloquet-Moose Lake fires of 1918. They do not directly address the question of synoptic patterns in the case of the Hinckley fire, though in my phone interview with him, Rod Sando did speculate that a low-pressure system must have been involved. When I later checked the daily bulletins put out by the National Weather Service, and printed in *The New York Times* for the week leading up to the Hinckley firestorm, it was clear that in fact a large low-pressure system had been working its way across the northern tier of states and, by the morning of September 1, 1894, was located exactly where it would cause the kind of southwesterly winds that began to fan the flames toward Hinckley. That is not to say, however, that the ferocious winds that tore through the forests around Hinckley at the height of the firestorm—winds that probably topped 100 miles per hour—were caused by synoptic conditions. Winds like that could only have been produced by the tremendous forces at work within the firestorm itself.

CHAPTER 4 | SOMETHING WICKED

The epigram, "Nature works out its complexities . . ." is from Annie Dillard's *For the Time Being*, page 169.

Helpful in understanding the interplay of temperature, weather, relative humidity, and different classes of fuel were Margaret Fuller's *Forest Fires: An Introduction to Wildland Fire Behavior, Management, Firefighting, and Prevention* (Fuller) and another Forest Service publication, Mark J. Schroder and Charles C. Buck's "Fire Weather: A Guide for Application of Meteorological Information to Forest Fire Control Applications" (Buck). Most valuable of all, though, was Stephen J. Pyne's monumental work, *Fire in America: A Cultural History of Wildland and Rural Fire* (Pyne), particularly the chapter on fire behavior, pages 20–33. Pyne's is a book that should be kept permanently at the bedside of anyone seriously interested in the subject of wildfire.

For anyone interested in learning more about the massive and horrific Peshtigo fire of 1871, many fine books are available. The most important of these is the firsthand account of the Reverend Peter Pernin, *The Great Peshtigo*

Fire: An Eyewitness Account (Pernin). I also consulted *Firestorm at Peshtigo* by Denise Gess and William Lutz (Gess and Lutz). Pyne (pages 202–205) also contributed to my understanding of Peshtigo and to the similarity between the conditions there and at Hinckley twenty-three years later.

The quotes from Angus Hay regarding the fire precautions at the Brennan lumberyard, ". . . the most thorough system . . ." and "The fire king would most surely . . ." are both from the July 25 edition of the *Hinckley Enterprise.*

Erik and Richard Thompson of the Iron Horse Central Railroad Museum in Chisago City, Minnesota, kindly provided numerous details about the construction and history of Jim Root's locomotive, extending even to a copy of the original blueprints for its construction. Following the fire, the locomotive was equipped with a new cab and a rebuilt tender and brought back into service on the Saint Paul and Duluth line. It served later on the Northern Pacific where, after being renumbered several times (as #1109, #1135, and finally, #640) it was still working secondary lines as late as 1908. It was finally scrapped in 1912.

Biographical details about James Root here and in the epilogue come from a number of sources including Wilkinson, Brown, and an obituary published in *The New York Times* on December 14, 1911. What little we know about John Blair comes from the many admiring comments recorded in Wilkinson and Brown and also from Blair's personal papers, which are archived at the Minnesota Historical Society. Blair's actions on the day of the fire are truly inspirational and have recently been chronicled in a fine children's book, *John Blair and the Great Hinckley Fire,* by Josephine Nobisso. Biographical details about William Best come from an obituary in the *Coaticook Observer,* May 31, 1934, and from a January 2003 article by Richard Evans, "William Best, Minnesota Hero" published in the *Quebec Heritage News.*

William Vogel's harrowing ride south into the heart of the fire, and the destruction of Pokegama and Mission Creek, are all documented by a number of firsthand accounts included in Wilkinson and Brown. The quote from Jay Braman—"you go; I can make a place of safety"—is from Wilkinson, page 32. I garnered additional information about the Braman family from an article in the *Brooklyn Eagle,* September 3, 1894, "A Wave of Flame."

The dramatic events that unfolded as the fire began to enter Hinckley are recounted in detail in numerous survivor stories published in Wilkinson,

Brown, A. Anderson, and Akermark. The quote from Father Lawler, "Leave all you have . . . " is from Wilkinson, page 52. The quote from John Craig, "We can't save the town . . ." is taken from Angus Hay's account printed in Brown, page 200. The longer quote from Angus Hay, "Teams hauling water were dashing along the street . . ." is from the same page in Brown. Hay's accounts were particularly valuable to me because he was a journalist and tended to note the kinds of details that bring a scene to life. The accounts of William Best and Ed Barry were also particularly valuable, not only because of the controversy that later arose over their actions that day, but also because they had a unique perspective on the unfolding drama from the vantage point of their respective cabs on the northeastern side of town.

CHAPTER 5 | THE CAULDRON

The epigram, "From here on . . ." is from Norman Maclean's wonderfully moving and informative account of the Mann Gulch fire of 1949, *Young Men and Fire,* page 269.

Facts pertaining to the Sundance Fire are drawn largely from a 1968 U.S. Forest Service publication: "Sundance Fire: An Analysis of Fire Phenomena" by Hal E. Anderson. The fire, which raced forward sixteen miles in just nine hours on a front four miles wide, was unusual not only in its ferocity but also in the fact that it was one of the first mass fires to be studied scientifically and in detail. The results are interesting in their own right, but even more so for what they imply about the magnitude and staggering ferocity of the much larger Hinckley firestorm.

My discussion of the physical characteristics of large fires also owes much to Pyne. One of the most interesting and unusual of these characteristics, attested to both by Pyne and by numerous Hinckley survivors, is the phenomenon of fireballs floating through the air. Again and again, survivors talked in awed terms about flaming balls—ranging in size from bushel baskets to railroad cars—falling from the sky. Mary Parsons, for instance, running out of her home in Hinckley ". . . saw one ball hit the Morrison Hotel across from the depot, another hit the Northern Pacific [Eastern Minnesota] depot, and both went down like ten pins" (A. Anderson, page 63). And over and over, survivors also talked about another phenomenon noted at the Sundance Fire and discussed by Pyne—the sudden ignition of everything combustible, even the air itself: ". . . suddenly there was a report, and the whole mass of smoke burst into a living sheet of flame with a roar of everything inflammable of all descriptions . . ." (Brown, page 19).

The quote "My God, we'll die," uttered by an unnamed passerby, is from Mary Anderson Kofoed's account in A. Anderson, page 19. The quote from Bill Grissinger's mother, "It seems to be getting worse . . ." is from Grissinger's own account in Fisher. The quotes "The depot roof is on fire," "But I haven't any money," and "Oh to dickens with the money" are all from Mary Anderson's account in A. Anderson, pages 18–19.

Exactly where Evan Hansen was at any given moment during the early stages of the firestorm is at least partly a matter of conjecture on my part. We know that he was among the mill workers sent to the south end of town to battle the fire; we know that he knew his family had planned to be in town for the day; we know he could not have found them there because they were in fact at home; and we know that he ultimately died in the swamp north of town. So when the fire line broke, it's a near certainty that he looked for Marie and the children in town first before joining the panicked crowd that surged desperately across the Grindstone and toward the swamp. My description of what he must have seen and felt during these moments is based on the accounts of survivors who were there in the crowd with him at the time.

We do know precisely what Bill Best did, said, and even thought as he watched refugees streaming out of the burning town toward his train. Best left several detailed accounts, and many of his passengers and fellow crew members later wrote about his heroic actions. The quote from W. D. Campbell, "Barry will cut off his engine and pull out," and Best's reply "I guess not," are both from fireman George Ford's account in Wilkinson, page 175, as is the following quote from panicked passengers: "Back up. Back up . . ." and Best's reply, "Boys, don't get excited . . ." The quote from O. L. Beach, "Barry says to let the brakes loose . . ." is from Best's own account in Wilkinson, page 169, as is his rhetorical query, "Good God, George! Will I sacrifice the train at last?" The quote from the Reverend Knudsen, "No, others are left in the village . . ." is from A. Anderson, page 146.

My determination of who was where as the fire closed in on the desperate victims running north of the Grindstone and toward the swamp is based largely on Dr. D. W. Cowan's "Death List" in Wilkinson, pages

103–125. Cowan's list provides names, ages, and often the locations of the bodies of those who could be identified. Although no one in the death swamp survived, the survivors on Jake Barden's wagon were close enough to hear and to some extent see what happened in those final few minutes. My description of those last moments in the swamp is based on their accounts, as well as descriptions that Antone Anderson and others provided of the scene they found there the next morning.

CHAPTER 6 | RAGNAROK

The epigram quotes Lysander in Act I, scene i, lines 144–148, of *A Midsummer Night's Dream*.

Contemplating the specific mechanisms by which fire kills human beings is far from pleasant, but I felt I needed a detailed understanding of those mechanisms in order to describe what my great-grandfather and the four hundred some-odd other victims of the firestorm went through. It was surprisingly difficult to find a single, comprehensive source for the subject, but I was able to piece together the picture by drawing from the following sources: Barbara Ravage's *Burn Unit* (Ravage), Nicholas Faith's *Blaze: The Forensics of Fire* (Faith), and a number of useful Web sites—the U.S. Department of Health and Human Services Center for Disease Control and Prevention (www.cdc.gov), the Signal Hill Fire Department's "Fire Basics" (www.shfd.net and click on "fire prevention"), the U.S. Fire Administration (www.usfa.fema.gov), and the U.S. National Library of Medicine (www.nlm.nih.gov).

The Mary McNeil quote, "With heartbreaking screams . . ." is from Akermark, pages 41–42. The following three quotes, "Jack, there is something wrong," "For God's sake, will you . . .," and "Jim, everything is burned up . . ." are all from Root's own account printed in Wilkinson, page 129, as is the exchange between Root and Sullivan beginning, "Look after the end of the train. . . ." The intervening comment by Sullivan, "Jim, we can't stay here long . . ." is from Sullivan's account, found on page 147 of Wilkinson.

The information presented in my discussion of the Pullman strikes is drawn primarily from three excellent online resources: "The Pullman Virtual Museum," found at www.eliillinois.org, an article entitled "Carnivals of Revenge" on PBS's American Experience site at www.pbs.org/wgbh/amex/carnegie/revenge.html, and an article entitled "The Pullman Era" on the Chicago Historical Society's Web site at www.chicagohs.org/history/pullman.html. The quote beginning "There are nearly six thousand people . . ." is from a letter to George Pullman from Illinois Governor John P. Altgeld, dated August 21, 1894, and available on a site maintained by the American Social History Project and the Center for History and New Media at George Mason University, www. historymatters.gmu.edu.

The quote, "Can you do anything for my hand . . ." is from Sullivan's account in Wilkinson, page 149. Root's exclamation, "My God! Give me some more . . ." is from his own account on page 131 of Wilkinson, as is his next remark, "My hands are all burnt. . . ."

A number of passengers on Root's train later gave statements of what transpired in the coaches, and many of these are printed in Wilkinson and Brown. Taken collectively they paint a vivid picture of the conditions the passengers endured, and I have drawn many facts and details from them. Otto Daugherty's query, "Have we got to die, Papa?" and an anonymous passenger's panicked outburst, "We are all going to heaven . . ." are from Frank Daugherty's account in Wilkinson, page 137.

The exchange between Root and McGowan beginning with, "Leave me alone and go . . ." is from Root's account in Wilkinson, page 131. The pleas of a desperate passenger, "Help me! Help me! I am burning," are from C. A. Vandaveer's account in *The New York Times*, "Hundreds Perish in Forest Fires," September 3, 1894. Details of Albert Speyer's rescue of a child from the flaming wreckage of Root's train, and the quoted exchange beginning, "Did you hear a child crying?" are from Akermark, pages 53–54.

CHAPTER 7 | UNDER THE STONE
The biblical epigram, "Every man's work . . ." is from the First Letter of Paul to the Corinthians, verse 3.

Bill Best's comment to his fireman as their train sat temporarily immobile in the burning woods south of Sandstone, "George, the jig is up," is from Best's own account in Wilkinson, page 170. The grateful words of Mary Anderson's parents on being reunited with her on the Best-Barry train, "What a great blessing—we are all saved!" are from Mary Anderson Kofoed's account in A. Anderson, page 20.

Information I garnered from e-mail interviews with Terry Boerboom, geologist with the Minnesota Geological Survey, greatly aided my understanding of the processes behind the development of the sandstone formations that gave Sandstone its name, as well as the subsequent evolution of the Kettle River Gorge. Also helpful was an article by Mark Jirsa, "Minnesota Geology in Cross Section," on www.geo.umn.edu, as well as two articles by Raymond R. Anderson, "The Mid-continent Rift, Iowa's Almost Ocean," and "Mid-continent Rift System in Iowa," both on www.igsb.uiowa.edu. A few details about Sandstone's early history came from an undated booklet compiled by Richard VanDerWerf, *Sandstone in By-Gone Days*.

The exchange between Best and Barry upon their arrival, beginning with "The conductors are going to stop here . . ." is recorded in Best's account on page 176 of Wilkinson. The final, apparently grudging, comment in the exchange, addressed by conductor Powers to Barry, "All right, go ahead. You are running the engine . . ." is from Barry's account in Wilkinson, page 182.

My discussion of the role that scripted behavior often plays in victims' initial response to disasters (or more to the point, their *lack* of response), as well as some of the examples cited, derive in part from Nicholas Faith's *Blaze: The Forensics of Fire*, particularly chapters 11 and 12 of that book. The more contemporary example of the phenomenon, though—during the 2003 fire at the Station nightclub in West Warwick, Rhode Island—is my own. It's also important to note that the kind of scripted, role-playing behavior discussed here is only one of several ways that people threatened by imminent disaster may react. Another, of course, is panic. We know that panic also played a major role in the Hinckley firestorm, particularly among many of the passengers on Root's train, a number of whom tried to fling themselves through windows. It was evident as well in the mad rush over the Grindstone River toward what was about to become the "death swamp." For an interesting example of how both reactions can play out almost simultaneously, see the *Toronto Globe and Mail*'s August 3, 2005, and August 4, 2005, coverage of the crash landing of Air France flight 358 on August 2 of that year. Even after the plane belly-flopped into a ravine following a long, lurching, screeching slide off of the runway, some passengers—despite overwhelming evidence to the contrary—assumed that they had landed where they were supposed to and calmly went about gathering their bags. Others, particularly those who could see the smoke and flames already consuming the left wing and rear of plane, panicked immediately and began pushing and clawing their way toward the exits without regard for anyone else.

The quote from the bridge watchman, Wallace Damuth, "For God's sake, go on . . ." is from Brown, page 38. The exchange between Peter Bilado and his daughter Emma, beginning, "We can't stay here . . ." is from Peter Bilado's own account on page 75 of Wilkinson. The tragically similar exchange between Louise Bilado and her daughter Flora, beginning, "Are we going to die?" is from Louise Bilado's account on page 77 of Wilkinson. The cry of one of the wedding guests at Minnie Samuelson's wedding, "The root cellar can save us!" is from Akermark, page 69.

The comment of an unnamed resident of Partridge, "It [the train] stopped briefly . . ." is quoted from Akermark, page 75. Abraham Lincoln Thompson's frantic and aborted telegram, beginning "The country is all burning up . . ." is reprinted in Wilkinson, page 235. Tom Sullivan's remark on encountering Robert Bell on the tracks, "Oh, Mr. Bell, all the passengers are burned," is from Bell's own account in Wilkinson, page 132.

Although Sullivan, Bell, and most of the party from Root's train who had made it to Miller Station continued running north as the fire approached, several section hands apparently stayed behind. Led by Saint Paul and Duluth section foreman Sievert Haglin, they set about saving the section house that held all their possessions. They threw water on the flames and beat at them with wet burlap bags. Then they hastily dug a hole in the Saint Paul and Duluth embankment, crawled in, and put the wet burlap bags over their heads. According to Haglin's daughter Helen, who recounted the story to Richard Thompson in 1982, they all survived, as did the section house, which stood until 1940.

The hymn sung by Emil Anderson and other survivors huddled on the large rock in the Kettle River, "Rock of Ages, give, oh give me . . ." appears in Wilkinson on page 91, where it is titled "The Mighty Fortress." It is not the better known hymn, "Rock of Ages." Wilkinson tells us that the verses have been translated from Swedish by K. E. Larsen. It's not clear whether the survivors sang the hymn in Swedish or English.

CHAPTER 8 | INTO THE RING

The epigram, "There is an electric fire . . ." is from John Keats's letter to George and Georgiana Keats, composed from Sunday, February 14, through Monday, May 3, 1819.

The description of the scene in Duluth on the evening of the fire, ". . . as the sun went down, the great whirlwinds of flame . . ." is from Wilkinson, page 233. The excerpt from Dave Williams's first telegram in search of a relief train, "Hurry, for God's sake . . ." appears in Wilkinson, page 235. A slightly different version appears in Brown, page 115.

I learned only by accident that it was Amy Currie's cow that provided the milk Mrs. Knudsen gave the refugees in the gravel pit, when I bought a 1952 postcard on an online auction site. From the message on the card, I also learned that John Currie made the ironwork fence that still surrounds the Hinckley Fire Monument.

Ravage's *Burn Unit: Saving Lives After the Flames* provided much of the information on the pathology of burn wounds. The quote beginning ". . . a burn is an evolving wound . . ." is from page xii of Ravage's book. Additional information came from "Pathophysiology of burn shock and burn edema" by George C. Kramer, Tjolstove Lund, and David N. Herndon in *Total Burn Care*, 2nd edition (Herndon) and from "Burn Wound Infections" by Karl Schwarz, MD, and Scott Dulchavsky, MD, PhD, on www.emedicine.com. Still more useful information (and some very gruesome photographs) can be found on www.burnsurgery.org, a site maintained by Burn Surgery.Org, a nonprofit organization dedicated to educating health-care professionals about burns.

Angus Hay's description of his fellow survivors at the gravel pit, "the worst used-up crowd I have ever seen," is from Hay's own account in Brown, page 202. Tom Sullivan's cry upon coming across Kelly and Roper at Finlayson, "John, is that you?" is from Sullivan's account on page 150 of Wilkinson, as is his next remark, "I'm afraid you cannot do it." Bell's comment when asked by Williams what the conditions were at Skunk Lake, "Everything is burned, everyone dead," is also from Wilkinson, page 236.

The series of increasingly dire telegrams that John Stone sent from Pine City to the *Saint Paul Pioneer Press,* beginning with, "There is no communication with Hinckley . . ." can be found on pages 192 and 193 of Wilkinson. The telegram received by Olive Brown in Rush City, "Hinckley, Mission Creek and No. 4 train are all burned up . . ." is reprinted in Wilkinson, on page 211. Robert Bell's query to Dr. Magie, "Can it be that they are all dead?" is from Bell's own account in Wilkinson, page 135. Jim Root's comment, "I'm chilling to death," is from Root's account in Brown, page 144.

CHAPTER 9 | OUT OF THE ASHES

The epigram, "Each new morn . . ." is Macduff, bewailing the state of Scotland's affairs, in Act IV, scene iii, lines 4–6 of *Macbeth*.

It is difficult today to conceive of just how completely devastated the landscape of northeastern Minnesota was on the morning following the firestorm. For many miles in every direction there was simply nothing to see but burned stumps. For decades following the firestorm, farmers routinely pulled the stumps from their fields and dragged them to their property lines, laying them on their sides in long rows so the roots could serve as field fences. Even today, Hinckleyites say, if you dig down into the soil anywhere in the fire area you will find, about a foot down, a line of black cinders four or five inches thick.

The exchange between John Powell and Root, beginning "Hello, Jim! How do you feel?" is from Powell's own account recorded on page 216 of Wilkinson, as is the anonymous remark, "A doctor is no good now."

The brief news article datelined, "Pine City, Minn., Sept. 2—1 A.M." is from *The New York Times*. This was the first account in the New York papers of a story that within a few hours would make headlines on the paper's front pages. Antone Anderson's comment that the death swamp looked "like the end of the world" is from his own account on page 7 of A. Anderson. Many of the other details of the scene are also from Anderson's account.

Axel Rosdahl's observation that the death swamp looked as if "the big lumberyard was picked up by the terrific gale and tossed right in among the fleeing people" is from his account in A. Anderson, page 39. It seems to support the idea that a particularly violent, explosive event occurred when the firestorm hit the Brennan lumberyard, and that this was what blew the windows out of the cab of Jim Root's locomotive. Although the exact location of the death swamp is no longer known with certainty, it's clear from survivors' accounts that it was north of the Grindstone River, and most accounts suggest that it was well east of the lumberyard—perhaps as much as three-quarters of a mile east—not far from the Eastern Minnesota tracks.

Bill Grissinger's description of the sounds made by his companions in Skunk Lake, "an incoherent tongue . . ." are from his account as given in the Fisher typescript, as is Grissinger's description of the bodies he found lying alongside the tracks, ". . . red and ugly lying there. . . ." The exchange between Grissinger, an unnamed brakeman, and Sheriff Joe McLaughlin, beginning

"I'm going to Hinckley," is also from Fisher, as is the exchange between Bill Grissinger and his father, beginning, "Where's your mother?"

The quoted description of the scene at Duluth's Union Station, "Parents were searching for children . . ." is from the *Duluth News Tribune*, September 5, 1894. *The New York Times*'s assertion that Tom Sullivan had "lost his head entirely . . ." appears in the paper's September 3, 1894, edition.

In studying the causes and effects of post-traumatic stress disorder, I have relied heavily on online sources simply because so much has changed so quickly in our understanding of PTSD. The many medical Web sites available on this topic have the most up-to-date information and the most recent research. The most comprehensive single source I have consulted is the Web site of the National Center for PTSD (www.ncptsd.org) where I found "Psychotic Symptoms in Post-Traumatic Stress Disorder," by Steven E. Lindley, Eve Carlson, and Javaid Sheikh to be of particular interest. Also very useful were "Two Years Later: The Prolonged Traumatic Impact of a Fire Disaster," by Viola Mecke at www.aaets.org and "Psychiatric Dimensions of Disaster: Patient Care, Community Consultation, and Preventive Medicine," by Robert J. Ursano, MD, Carol S. Fullerton, PhD, and Ann E. Norwood, MD at www.uic.edu.

The telegram Dave Williams received concerning the fate of Sandstone, beginning "There are 150 people at Sandstone . . ." was reprinted in the *Saint Paul Pioneer Press* on September 5, 1894. The cry that went up at the boardinghouse at Hell's Gate when rescuers entered with lanterns, "Is there fire in the house?" appears in Emil Anderson's account, on page 93 of Wilkinson. The encouraging remarks shouted by villagers watching the relief train head north from Saint Paul, "Good luck!" are reported in Wilkinson, who was himself aboard the train, on page 336.

My discussion of the history of burn treatment, and the state of burn treatment in 1894, draws again from Herndon's *Total Burn Care* and Ravage's *Burn Unit*. Dr. J. N. Plumb's method of treatment, presented in an address to the Society of St. Joseph and Grand Island Surgeons in July of 1894, is outlined in an article entitled "The Treatment of Burns," in the October 1894 edition of the *International Journal of Surgery*.

The comment of the unnamed boy Judge Nethaway pulled out of a well, "it was awful hot" is recorded under the headline STILL THE CALAMITY GROWS, in *The New York Times*, September 5, 1894. The inscriptions on the

coffins in Hinckley, beginning with SUPPOSED REMAINS OF MRS. BLANCHARD
. . . are found in "The Dead Lie in Heaps at Hinckley," *The New York Times*,
September 4, 1894.

My description of the scene at the cemetery draws heavily from news
accounts given in the *Saint Paul Pioneer Press* (September 5, 1894), the *Duluth News Tribune* (September 8, 1894), and *The New York Times* (September
4, 1895). Some additional details also come from Wilkinson, pages 48–49.

CHAPTER 10 | THE BROKEN SEASON
The epigram, "Sorrow breaks seasons . . ." is from Act I, scene iv, lines 74–75,
of *Richard III.*

The quoted headlines, beginning with IT WAS A HAMLET OF HORRORS,
are from the September 5, 1894, edition of the *Duluth News Tribune* and from
the September 4, 1894, editions of the *Minneapolis Tribune*, *The New York
Times*, and the London *Times*. The *Brooklyn Eagle*'s description of the Brennan millpond as "a pool of death" is from the September 3, 1894, edition of
that paper. The *Duluth News Tribune* headline, IT'S UP TO 612! is from the
September 4, 1894, edition. The description of John Derosier, "a plucky fellow . . ." is from the September 3, 1894, edition of the *Brooklyn Eagle*. The
quoted description of the scene that unfolded when tourists piled off of a
train to gawk at the ruins on Wednesday, ". . . there was a mad rush by passengers . . ." is from the *Duluth News Tribune*, September 6, 1894. The quote
from *The New York Times*, "Late this afternoon the body of a man . . ." is from
the September 5, 1894 edition.

The discussion of Sam Hill's coded telegram to James J. Hill is based
on information in Swenson, pages 127–129. Swenson also provides splendid
copies of the original telegram with the decoded words written in a different hand above the coded words. She does not explain who did the decoding, but the telegram can be found in file 2679 of the *Great Northern Railway
Co. President Subject Files* at the Minnesota Historical Society.

The original accounts of Native American casualties scattered along
a trail near Mille Lacs Lake appeared in the *Duluth Evening Herald* on
September 7. The story asserted that the dead were members of the Ojibwa
tribe and that their leader was a chief named Wacouta. Jeanne Coffey of the
Hinckley Fire Museum, however, has interviewed elders of the Mille Lacs
Band of the Ojibwa, and they report that there is nothing in Ojibwa tradition

to support this, and that Wacouta is, in fact, a Sioux name at any rate. Since the Sioux had been forced out of the Mille Lacs area long before 1894, it is unclear who these Native American victims were.

That the madam of a brothel near Hinckley, Emma Hammond, was expected to die was first reported in *The New York Times* on September 3, 1894. The *Duluth Evening Herald* reached a similar conclusion, saying in their September 5 edition, "Emma Hammond, who will die, is a large fleshy woman who kept a house of ill fame at Hinckley." Hammond's quoted reaction to the news of her impending death, "I ain't got any kick coming . . ." is from the September 9 edition of the *Duluth Evening Herald*.

The various quotes from the State Relief Commission examiners, beginning with the comment on Sam Hallman's questionnaire, "Gov. Nelson promised," and also the items and amounts awarded, are all from information on the original questionnaires, now housed in boxes 2 and 3 of the *Governor's Files: Minnesota Commission for Relief of Sufferers, 1894–95* at the Minnesota Historical Society. One cannot help but be struck, looking through the questionnaires, by how often the examiners based their recommendations for aid on what they perceived to be the applicant's moral character. Most of the comments regarding character are written on the backs of the questionnaires, as if to shield them from the eyes of the applicants.

CHAPTER II | DRIFTING EMBERS

The epigram, "There are three things . . ." is from Proverbs 30, lines 15–16, of the King James Bible.

The weather forecast for Wisconsin, "Fair, warmer, southerly winds . . ." is from the National Weather Service and appears in *The New York Times*, September 1, 1894.

Stewart Holbrook's *Burning an Empire: The Story of American Forest Fires* provides a useful overview of major American forest fires from Hinckley through the Bandon, Oregon, fire of 1936. Stephen J. Pyne documents the history of wildfire in the Lake States in chapter 4, "The Great Barbecue," in *Fire in America*, and I have found this chapter particularly useful in understanding the massive scope of the fires of 1908–1924. Pyne is also the author of a highly informative book, *Year of the Fires*, on the 1910 fires. For more on the 1871 Peshtigo fire, see Gess and Lutz, *Firestorm at Peshtigo*. *The Fires of Autumn: The Cloquet-Moose Lake Disaster of 1918*, by Francis M. Carroll and

Franklin R. Raiter (Carroll and Raiter), documents the fires of that year. Chapter 1 of Carroll and Raiter, pages 3–19, also offers a particularly helpful discussion of how small fires blow up to become killers like the Cloquet-Moose Lake disaster.

EPILOGUE

The epigram, "Chance is perhaps . . ." is from Anatole France's "Le Jardin d'Epicure."

The opening of the Grand Casino on the east side of Hinckley in May of 1992 has been a mixed blessing for the town. According to Richard Meryhew, in a May 14, 2002, article in the *Minneapolis Star Tribune*, "Casino Brings Jobs, Development to Hinckley—At a Price," the $26 million casino complex has upped the population, increased employment, and added amenities like a golf course and a four-screen movie theater. But it's also raised taxes, created congestion, and diverted the flow of traffic and business from downtown to the casino complex east of the I-35 freeway. The latter, especially, grieves many longtime residents who have watched one family business after another die off in the old downtown area. And, ironically, even as more and more people have flocked to Hinckley because of the casino, fewer and fewer people have any awareness of what happened there in 1894. Jeanne Coffey, executive director of the Hinckley Fire Museum, noted in Meryhew's article that the museum now gets "only half the visitors it did a decade ago." It deserves to get many more.

Dr. Cowan's official death list, including the excerpt I've used as an example, can be found on pages 103–125 of Wilkinson. It is grim reading indeed, but enormously helpful for anyone wanting to comprehend the enormity of the disaster. John Currie's observation that "nobody who had buried those people could stand to talk about it" appears in a fact sheet provided by Carol Currie Eddleman. The *Hinckley Enterprise* headline, 15 YEARS' WORK IN 15 MINUTES, as well as the copy that follows, "The fire on Sept. 1 . . ." and "She has passed through . . ." are from the first edition to appear after the firestorm, on December 19, 1894. Hay's later remark about the impossibility of accurately portraying the fire in words, "Any one item in any one instance . . ." appears in Brown, page 205.

The Chicago *Inter Ocean*'s praise of Jim Root, "His soul is the stuff of which heroes are made . . ." appears in Swenson, page 170, and also in the

Duluth News Tribune, September 9, 1894. The savage review of Jim Root's theatrical performance, "He is not, to be sure, a . . ." is from A RIDE FOR LIFE in *The New York Times*'s October 9, 1894 edition. In the lines that may have been most hurtful to Root, the review goes on to say, "Of course, there is no legal or even logical objection to driving an engine through a blazing forest fire and saving a lot of lives one day, and then earning money by posing as a freak the next." Whatever his acting skills, Root deserved better. His repudiation of acting, "It keeps a man up too late at night . . ." appears in Swenson, page 172, quoting from Root's hometown paper, the *White Bear Lake Breeze*, November 17, 1894.

The complete inscription on the gold watch awarded to John Blair, FOR GALLANT AND FAITHFUL DISCHARGE OF DUTY . . ., can be found in Wilkinson, page 163. Judge C. D. O'Brien's comment about Blair, "I am proud to be alive to take him by the hand . . ." appears on page 162 of Wilkinson. Blair's own comment, "I just resolved I would not lose my head . . ." was reported on the front page of the *Duluth Evening Herald*, September 7, 1894.

I came across the account of the murder of five manacled African-American men in Millington, Missouri, by chance as I was browsing the *Saint Paul Daily Globe*'s September 2, 1894, coverage of the firestorm. I was shocked when I realized that the murders must have taken place at about the same time that John Blair was acting so heroically to save the lives of so many of his white countrymen.

Bill Best largely held his peace for some time after the fire. But much second-guessing and various criticisms circulated in the newspapers. When, on December 22, he did finally give the account recorded in Wilkinson, pages 166–173, he did so only "in justice to myself and others," and because "a great many people, I'm sorry to say, have carped about the conduct of the trainmen . . ." Best's comment that sitting in his cab, holding the train in Hinckley was "the hardest place I ever stood in" is from a statement made to railroad officials, and is found in Swenson, page 178, reprinted from file 94 of the *Samuel Hill Subject Files*, the Great Northern Railway Company, Eastern Railway Company of Minnesota, housed at the Minnesota Historical Society. Best's praise of W. D. Campbell, calling him, "as plucky and brave [a] fellow as ever passed a milestone," is recorded in BRAVE DEED PROMPTLY DONE, in *The New York Times*, September 5, 1894. Ed Barry's seemingly defensive comment, "I knew if we stayed there we would all be burned," is from his account in Wilkinson, page 181. Best's final comment on the matter—"I've did [sic] the best I could . . ."—is recorded in Wilkinson, page 173. Barry's final comment, "If it hadn't bin [sic] for me they all would have bin [sic] lost . . ." is from his report to company officials and can be found in the *Samuel Hill Subject Files*, quoted in Swenson, page 181.

The unsinkable Angus Hay published his optimistic opinion of the town's future, "Our town will stand though a thousand destructions . . ." in the May 8, 1895, edition of the *Hinckley Enterprise*. The similarly optimistic comments following the disastrous Michigan fires of 1881, "There are other great advantages . . ." are quoted in Pyne, page 211, from the *Detroit Post*, September 13, 1881. James J. Hill's regal proclamation that "This place shall flourish and prosper accordingly as I shall command" is quoted in Swenson, page 156.

The names, ages, and dates of demise of the last two Hinckley survivors—Sigrud Westrud Stromgren and Ann Anderson Darling—were provided by Jeanne Coffey of the Hinckley Fire Museum.

SOURCES

Akermark, Gudmund Emanuel. *Eld-Cyklonen Eller Hinckley-branden*, 1894. Translated and reprinted as *Eld-Cyklonen or Hinckley Fire*. Askov, Minnesota: American Publishing Company, 1976.

Altgeld, Governor John P. Letter to George Pullman, August 21, 1894. "Broken Spirits: Letters on the Pullman Strike." *American Social History Project*, www.historymatters.gmu.edu.

Anderson, Antone A. and Clara Anderson McDermott. *The Hinckley Fire: Stories from the Hinckley Fire Survivors*. New York: Comet Press Books, 1954. Reprinted by Hinckley Fire Centennial Committee, 1993.

Anderson, Hal E. "Sundance Fire: An Analysis of Fire Phenomena." Intermountain Forest and Range Experiment Station, U.S. Department of Agriculture. Research Paper INT-56, 1968.

Anderson, Raymond R. "The Mid-continent Rift, Iowa's Almost Ocean." www.igsb.uiowa.edu/browse/rift97/rift97new.htm.

_____. "Mid-continent Rift System in Iowa." www.igsb.uiowa.edu/browse/rift/mrsnew.htm.

"Andrew Carnegie: Carnivals of Revenge." *The American Experience*. The Public Broadcasting Service. www.pbs.org/wgbh/amex/carnegie/revenge.html.

Bacon, Francis. "Of Nature in Men."

Boerboom, Terry. E-mail interview, July 10, 2001.

Brooklyn Eagle. September 3, 1894.

_____. September 5, 1894.

Brown, Elton T. *A History of the Great Minnesota Forest Fires.* Saint Paul: Brown Bros. Publishers, 1894.

Buck, Charles C. *see* Schroder, Mark J.

Burn Surgery.Org. www.burnsurgery.org.

Carroll, Francis M. and Franklin R. Raiter. *The Fires of Autumn: The Cloquet-Moose Lake Disaster of 1918.* Saint Paul: The Minnesota Historical Society, 1990.

Coaticook Observer. May 31, 1934.

DeLaittre, Calvin. Interview with Elwood R. Maunder. Forest History Foundation, Inc., May 29, 1967.

Dexter, W. E. Interview with John Larson. Forest History Foundation Inc., August 1953 and October 1953.

Dillard, Annie. *For the Time Being.* New York: Vintage Books, 1999.

Duluth Evening Herald. September 5, 1894.

_____. September 7, 1894.

_____. September 9, 1894.

Duluth News Tribune. September 1, 1894.

_____. September 2, 1894.

_____. September 3, 1894.

_____. September 4, 1894.

_____. September 5, 1894.

_____. September 6, 1894.

_____. September 7, 1894.

_____. September 8, 1894.

_____. September 9, 1894.

Evans, Richard. "William Best, Minnesota Hero," *Quebec Heritage News,* January 2003.

Faith, Nicholas. *Blaze: The Forensics of Fire.* London: Channel 4 Books, 1999.

"Fire Basics." Signal Hill Fire Department, www.shfd.net and click on "fire prevention."

Fisher, Harold L. "The Hinckley-Sandstone Fire." Unpublished typescript, 1968. Minnesota Historical Society Collection 00-43453518.

France, Anatole. "Le Jardin d'Epicure." 1894.

Fuller, Margaret. *Forest Fires: An Introduction to Wildland Fire Behavior, Management, and Prevention.* New York: Wiley Nature Editions, 1991.

Gess, Denise and William Lutz. *Firestorm at Peshtigo: A Town, Its People, and the Deadliest Fire in American History.* New York: Henry Holt and Company, 2002.

Haines, Donald A. and Rodney W. Sando. "Climatic Conditions Preceding Historically Great Fires in the North Central Region." U.S. Department of Agriculture. Research Paper NC-34, 1969.

———. "Fire Weather and Behavior of the Little Sioux Fire." North Central Forest Experiment Station, Forest Service, U.S. Department of Agriculture, 1972.

Hansen, Marie. Relief application. Minnesota Historical Society Collection: *Governor's Files, Minnesota Commission for Relief of Sufferers,* boxes 2 and 3.

Herndon, Dr. David N., ed. *Total Burn Care,* 2nd edition. Philadelphia: W. B. Saunders, 2002.

Hinckley Enterprise. July 4, 1894.

———. July 18, 1894.

———. July 25, 1894.

———. August 1, 1894.

———. August 22, 1894.

———. August 29, 1894.

———. December 19, 1894.

———. May 8, 1895.

Hinckley News. May 13, 1948.

———. September 2, 1951.

———. March 17, 1960.

———. September 10, 1964.

Holbrook, Stewart H. *Burning an Empire: The Story of American Forest Fires.* New York: The Macmillan Company, 1945.

———. *Holy Old Mackinaw: A Natural History of the American Lumberjack.* New York: The Macmillan Company, 1954.

Jirsa, Mark. "Minnesota Geology in Cross Section." www.geo.umn.edu/mgs/xsections/sect.html.

John W. Blair. Papers. Minnesota Historical Society Collection 09-00000467.

Keats, John. "To George and Georgiana Keats." Ed. George W. Meyer. *Major British Writers, Enlarged Edition*, Vol. II. New York: Harcourt, Brace & World, 1959.

Larsen, Lawrence H. *Wall of Flames: The Minnesota Forest Fire of 1894*. Fargo: The North Dakota Institute for Regional Studies, North Dakota State University, 1984.

Larson, Agnes M. *History of the White Pine Industry in Minnesota*. North Stratford, New Hampshire: Ayer Company Publishers, Inc., 1988.

Larson, Hans. Interview with John Larson. Forest History Foundation, Inc., August 17, 1953.

Lindley, Steven E., Eve Carlson, and Javaid Sheikh. "Psychotic Symptoms in Post-Traumatic Stress Disorder." National Center for PTSD, www.ncptsd.org.

London *Times*, September 4, 1894.

Maclean, Norman. *Young Men and Fire*. Chicago: University of Chicago Press, 1992.

Mecke, Viola. "Two Years Later: The Prolonged Traumatic Impact of a Fire Disaster," www.aaets.org

Meredith, George. "Lucifer in Starlight." Ed. Helen Gardner. *The New Oxford Book of English Verse*. New York: Oxford University Press, 1972.

Mineau, Wirt. Interview with Helen McCann White. Forest History Foundation, Inc., September 30, 1955.

Minneapolis Star Tribune. May 14, 2002.

Minneapolis Tribune. September 4, 1894.

National Oceanic and Atmospheric Administration, www.history.noaa.gov.

New York Times, The. August 27, 1894.

_____. August 31, 1894.

_____. September 1, 1894.

_____. September 3, 1894.

_____. September 4, 1894.

_____. September 5, 1894.

_____. September 6, 1894.

_____. September 8, 1894.

_____. October 9, 1894.

Nobisso, Josephine. *John Blair and the Great Hinckley Fire*. Boston: Houghton Mifflin Company, 2000.

O'Neill, Maggie Orr. Interview with Helen McCann White. Forest History Foundation, Inc., October 1, 1955.

Peattie, Donald Culross. *A Natural History of Trees of Eastern and Central North America*. Boston: Houghton Mifflin, 1966.

Pernin, Peter. *The Great Peshtigo Fire: An Eyewitness Account*, 2nd Edition. Madison, Wisconsin: The State Historical Society of Wisconsin, 1999.

"The Pullman Era." The Chicago Historical Society. www.chicagohs.org/history/pullman.html.

"The Pullman Virtual Muscum," www.eliillinois.org.

Pyne, Stephen J. *Fire in America: A Cultural History of Wildland and Rural Fire*. Seattle: University of Washington Press, 1997.

_____. *Year of the Fires: The Story of the Great Fires of 1910*. New York: Penguin Books, 2002.

Ravage, Barbara. *Burn Unit: Saving Lives After the Flames*. Cambridge, Massachusetts: Da Capo Press, 2004.

Robbins, William J. *Lumberjacks and Legislators: Political Economy of the U.S. Lumber Industry, 1890–1941*. College Station: Texas A&M University Press, 1982.

Ryan, J. C. *Early Loggers in Minnesota*, Vol. 3. Duluth: Minnesota Timber Producers Association, 1980.

Saint Paul Daily Globe. September 1, 1894.

_____. September 2, 1894.

Saint Paul Pioneer Press. September 5, 1894.

Samuel Hill Subject Files, the Great Northern Railway Company, Eastern Railway Company of Minnesota, file 94, Minnesota Historical Society Collections.

Sando, Rodney W. Phone interview. March 10, 2001.

Schroder, Mark J. and Charles C. Buck. "Fire Weather: A Guide for Application of Meteorological Information to Forest Fire Control Operations." *Agricultural Handbook 360*, U.S. Department of Agriculture, 1970.

Schwarz, Karl and Scott Dulchavsky. "Burn Wound Infections." January 25, 2005. www.emedicine.com/med/topic258.htm#section-introduction.

Shakespeare, William. *The Complete Signet Classic Shakespeare*. Ed. Sylvan Barnet. New York: Harcourt Brace Jovanovich, Inc., 1972.

Stegner, Wallace. *Angle of Repose*. New York: Doubleday, 1971.

Swenson, Grace Stageberg. *From the Ashes: The Story of the Hinckley Fire of 1894*. Stillwater, Minnesota: The Croixside Press, 1979.

Thompson, Richard E. Letter, April 14, 2002.

Toronto Globe and Mail. August 3, 2005.

_____. August 4, 2005.

"Treatment of Burns, The." *International Journal of Surgery*, Vol. 3, October 1894.

Ursano, Robert J., Carol S. Fullerton, PhD, and Ann E. Norwood, MD. "Psychiatric Dimensions of Disaster: Patient Care, Community Consultation, and Preventive Medicine," www.uic.edu.

U.S. Department of Health and Human Services, Center for Disease Control and Prevention, www.cdc.gov.

U.S. Fire Administration, www.usfa.fema.gov.

U.S. National Library of Medicine, www.nlm.nih.gov.

U.S. Naval Observatory. "Data Services," Astronomical Applications Department, www.usno.navy.mil.

VanDerWerf, Richard. *Sandstone in By-Gone Days*. Self-published, no date.

Wilcox, Alice Nelson. "The Hinckley Fire." Unpublished typescript, ca. 1954. Minnesota Historical Society Collection 09-00322201.

Wilkinson, Rev. William. *Memorials of the Minnesota Forest Fires in the Year 1894*. Minneapolis: Norman E. Wilkinson, 1895.

ACKNOWLEDGMENTS

I HAVE HAD THE GOOD FORTUNE TO RECEIVE HELP AND GUIDANCE from a number of people who have given generously of their time and energy to make this a better book than it would otherwise have been.

First, I want to thank Jeanne Coffey, executive director of the Hinckley Fire Museum, who has been a wellspring of helpful information and support—reading the manuscript, gathering photographs, sketching maps, and generally sharing with me her deep understanding of the Hinckley tragedy. I appreciate her generosity more than she can possibly know. I am also grateful to Sandy Hines at the museum who probably does not remember me but, who first introduced me to the many treasures housed there, and helpfully drew a map on a napkin directing me to the approximate location of the "death swamp" north of town. The museum is a delight and a treasure that visitors to northeastern Minnesota would do well to patronize at every available opportunity.

I am grateful also to Carol Currie Eddleman and her late aunt, Margaret Currie Sanford, for making available to me a large number of documents relating to the Currie family's experience of the firestorm. Richard and Erik Thompson, of the Iron Horse Central Railroad Museum in Chisago City, Minnesota, provided me with extremely helpful information about the locomotives involved in the firestorm and about steam locomotives in general. Terry Boerboom, geologist at the Minnesota Geological Survey, answered my e-mail inquiries with much useful information about the geological prehistory of the Sandstone area. Rodney Sando, then the director of the Department of Fish and Wildlife for the state of Idaho, enthusiastically shared his considerable expertise about the science behind the Hinckley firestorm. At the magnificent Minnesota Historical Society in Saint Paul, Ruth Anderson cheerfully pointed me in the right direction to find the information I was looking for.

I also want to thank fellow writers Dave Edelman and Ol' Bill Burnette for reading and commenting on early drafts of the manuscript. Your comments saved me from many missteps. My agent, Agnes Birnbaum, believed immediately in the project, made many insightful suggestions for improvements, offered valuable mini-lessons in "Publishing 101," and paid careful attention to detail as the proposal turned into a publishing contract. What more could one want? And I want to thank a newfound ally, my editor at The Lyons Press, Jay McCullough, who asks hard questions in a soft voice—fine qualities in an editor.

Finally, I want to thank the three bright-shining stars who light up my life: my daughters, Emi and Bobi—for being the fascinating and magical young women they have become—and my lovely wife Sharon—for being my best reader, my best friend, my everything.

INDEX